Curriculum and Instructional Designing

Curriculum and Instructional Designing

Prof. H. S. Srivastava
Former Dean
National Council of Educational Research and Training
New Delhi

SHIPRA

(First Published in India in 2017)

Rs. 1495; US$ 50

ISBN: 978-93-86262-31-8

2025 Impression, PoD

Published by:
SHIPRA PUBLICATIONS
LG 18-19, Pankaj Central Market
I.P. Ext., Patparganj, Delhi 110092, India
91 11 47322068; 9650028065, 9810522367
info@shiprapublication.com
www.shiprapublication.com

Preface

The study of the subject of curriculum implies the study of educational objectives; course content; instructional methodology; support material and aids to instruction; and educational evaluation.

This book travels through the concept and manifestations of curriculum at the macro-level, basically focussing on Curriculum Transaction. In this process, it attempts to translate the theoretical principles and precepts into their practical applications, in both conventional and unconventional settings of teaching and learning.

The suggestive and not prescriptive educational dynamics presented, offers ample freedom and flexibility to the teachers to pick and choose what s/he considers most suitable for a particular situation.

The book also in addition endeavours to introduce the teachers to some sparingly used approaches which s/he could explore and use for being more successful in enabling learners to digest and internalise learning as an attrition-free life time treasure.

It is my hope and confidence that the contents of the book will be found to be of practical use by both teachers and students, as also by teacher educators and student teachers. Those conducting and attending in-service courses in the corporate sector will also find the book as a ready reference.

Prof. H.S. Srivastava

15.07.2017
The Humanity House
143, Dayanand Vihar
Delhi – 110092, India
M: 9953532995

Contents

Section III
SOME CONVENTIONAL INSTRUCTIONAL METHODOLOGIES

Section IV
SOME UNCONVENTIONAL INSTRUCTIONAL METHODOLOGIES

Section V
ICT IN INSTRUCTIONAL DESIGNING

Section VI
SOME ANCILLARY TEACHING-LEARNING FACETS/ SITUATIONS

Section VII
INSTRUCTIONAL AIDS AND SUPPORT MATERIAL

Section VIII
EVALUATING LEARNING OUTCOMES

Section IX
CURRICULUM EVALUATION

SECTION I
Foundations of Instructional Designing

1

Education in the 21st Century— Learning the Treasure Within

(Report of UNESCO's International Commission on Education)

1.1 Introduction

The Report of the International Commission on Education for the Twenty first Century entitled "Learning – The Treasure Within" is the most exquisite document that presents the diverse facets of education in the perspective of the emerging global needs of the present century. The Commission had 15 members from different countries and was chaired by Mr. Jacques Delros. Dr. Karan Singh was the Indian representative on the Commission. The report was published by the UNESCO (to which it was submitted) in 1996.

No discussion on education in the present century can in fact be complete without a reference to this report, which *not only contains a robust philosophy of education but almost charts-out a road map of what education should be.*

It is not really passable to summarise the report as such. Therefore, what is proposed to be done here, is to quote some statements, adapted or as such from the report containing different ideas which are likely to be of interest and use to the Indian educationists.

1.2 Education: The Necessary Utopia

Humankind sees in education an indispensable asset in its attempts to attain the ideals of peace, freedom and social justice and as an instrument for reducing poverty, exclusion, ignorance and oppression.

The ideals on which UNESCO has been founded is the hope for a world that is a better place to live in, where people will have learned to respect the rights of women and men, to show mutual understanding and to use advances in knowledge to foster human development rather than to create further distinctions between people.

1.2.1 Looking Ahead

All out economic growth can no longer be viewed as the ideal way of reconciling material progress with equity, respect for human conditions and respect for natural assets, that we have a duty to hand on in good condition to future generations.

1.2.2 Tensions to Overcome

Confronting and overcoming the following tensions is likely to be the central problem in the 21st century:

- Global and local
- Universal and individual
- Tradition and modernity
- Long-term and short-term considerations
- The need for competition and the concern for equality of opportunity
- Reconciling three forces:
  - ➢ competition which provides incentives
  - ➢ cooperation which gives strength and
  - ➢ solidarity which unites people
- Expansion of knowledge and capacity to assimilate it
- Spiritual and material dimensions of existence

1.2.3 Designing and Building Our Common Future

There is every reason to place renewed emphasis on the moral and cultural dimensions of education.

Valid responses have to be made for meeting problems of mismatch between supply and demand in the labour market, through a more flexible system that allows greater curricular diversity and builds bridges between different types of education or between working life and further training.

- To create tomorrow's society, imagination will have to keep ahead of technological progress,
- Education should impart both the desire for and the pleasure in learning, the ability to learn how to learn and intellectual curiosity.
- There is no substitute for the teacher pupil relationship..... It is the responsibility of the teacher to impart to the pupil the knowledge that human kind has acquired about itself.

1.2.4 Learning Throughout Life: The Four Pillars of Education

People need to return to education in order to deal with the new situation.

Each industrial nation has to learn how to learn and.... to acquire a better understanding of other people and the world.

- *Learning to live together* by developing an understanding of the history, traditions and culture of others, appreciating the growing interdependence of nations and the common sharing of risks and challenges.

- *Learning to know.* A broad general education with the possibility for in-depth work on a selected number of subjects. This lays the foundations for learning throughout life.
- *Learning to do.* Dealing with a variety of situations often unforeseeable and working in teams including work experience and social work.
- *Learning to be.* Exercise of greater independence and judgment, a greater sense of personal responsibility for the attainment of personal goals, lapping of hidden talents which often remain untapped like, memory, reasoning power, imagination, physical ability, aesthetic sense, communication etc.

Educational policies have also to achieve the twin aims of high educational standards and equity.

1.2.5 The Stages and Bridges of Learning

The vital need for basic education, urging a review of the role of Secondary Education and to examine the issues raised by developments in Higher Education constituted the basic premises of the recommendations of the Commission. Some of the ideas addressed to in this regard by the Commission are:

- Learning throughout life makes it possible to organise the various stages of education, to provide a passage from one stage to another and to diversify the paths through the system while enhancing the value of each. This is attempted for avoiding the invidious choice between selection by ability and education for all.
- A grounding in three Rs (Reading, Writing and Arithmetic) — with the combination of *in-and-out-of school learning* would enable children to experience the three dimensions of education:
    - the ethical and cultural
    - the scientific and technological
    - the economic and social

In secondary schools there is a rapid increase in enrolment, overcrowded curricula, school learners feel disturbed at the dearth of opportunities and mass unemployment.

The only way out is to provide a very broad diversification of the types of study available.

In regard to Higher Education stringent selection for easing pressure is unacceptable. Universities ought to contribute by diversifying what they offer

- as scientific establishments
- offering occupational qualifications

- opening their doors
- as leading partners in international cooperation
- by resolving the conflict between the logic of public service and the logic of the job market

1.2.6. Getting the Reform Straight Right

- there is need for a long term approach if the reforms are required to succeed.
- the social, cultural and material status of education should be considered as a matter of priority.
- the dialogue with the teachers be carried out to put an end to the teacher's feelings of isolation and frustration to make change acceptable.
- the policy makers cannot leave it to the market forces or to some kind of self-regulation to put things right, when they go wrong.
- Education is an effort for public good and that it should be available to all.
- At a time when young people are struggling with the problems of adolescence, when they feel in a sense mature, but are still in fact immature, when instead of being carefree they are worried about their future, the important thing is to provide them with places where they can learn and discover, to give them the wherewithal to think about their future and prepare for it, and to offer them a choice of pathways suited to their abilities.

1.2.7 Broadening Economic Cooperation

- The international institutions offering funds for education ought to give them as partnership ventures rather than aid and reform their rules for becoming more effective.
- While developed countries can assist developed countries, they also stand to gain and learn in the process.

The commission has specifically recommended:

- encouragement for the education of girls
- allocation of a minimum percentage of development aid for funding education.
- policies for reducing internal and external deficits upon public spending on education.
- Introduction of new technologies in all countries to prevent the increase of the gap between rich and poor countries.
- tapping the potential of non-govt. agencies.
- external assistance in this regard should be seen in the context of partnership rather than aid.

1.3 Directions to Move Towards

1.3.1 From the Local Community to a World Society

Worldwide economic, scientific, cultural and political development dictated by the need for opening up, under pressure of free-trade theories of economic and financial frontiers.

Crime is also getting globalised.

The free flow of images and words world-wide which is one of the accelerators of globalisation surely has its negative side as well.

A handful of countries enjoy a virtual monopoly of the cultural industries. This is becoming a powerful factor for the erosion of cultural distinctiveness of societies.

Inequalities in levels of development have in some cases got worse.

Education, therefore, has the special responsibility to exercise in the building of a more mutually supportive world.

The sense of *shared values and a common destiny* is, in fact, the basis on which any scheme for international cooperation must be founded.

Pointers and Recommendations

- Worldwide interdependence and globalisation are major forces in contemporary life. They are already at work and will leave a deep imprint on the twenty-first century.
- The major danger is that of a guff opening up between a minority of people who are capable of finding their way successfully about this new world that is coming into being and the majority who feel that they are at the mercy of events and have no say in the future of society, with the dangers that entail a setback to democracy and widespread revolt.
- We must be guided by the Utopian aim of steering the world towards greater mutual understanding, a greater sense of responsibility and greater solidarity, through acceptance of our spiritual and cultural differences.

1.3.2 From Social Cohesion to Democratic Participation

The cohesion of any society is predicted not only on shared activities and purposes but also on shared values which represent different aspects of the desire to live together. These material and spiritual links enhance in course of time and take the form of cultural heritages.

The concept of democracy too is being criticised for widening the gap between those who govern and those who are governed.

The democratic ideal too needs to be reinvented or at the least re-vitalised.

Values only have meaning when they are freely chosen by the individual.

The full potential of new information and communication technologies should be harnessed to serve education and training.

Pointers and Recommendations

- Education policy must be sufficiently diversified and must be so designed as not to become another contributory cause of social exclusion.
- The socialisation of individuals must not conflict with personal development.
- Education cannot, on its own, solve the problems raised by the severance (when this happens) of social ties.
- Schools cannot succeed in this task unless they make their own contribution to the advancement and integration of minority groups.
- Democracy appears to be progressing, taking forms and passing through stages that fit the situation in each country. Its vitality is nevertheless constantly threatened. *Education for conscious and active citizenship must begin at school.*
- Democratic participation is, so to say, a matter of good citizenship, but it can be encouraged or stimulated by instruction and practices adapted to a media and information society.
- It is the role of education to provide children and adults with the cultural background that will enable them, as far as possible, to make sense of the changes taking place.

1.3.3 From Economic Growth to Human Development

Under pressure of technological progress and modernisation, the demand for education for economic purposes has been constantly on the rise.

International comparisons have for some time highlighted the importance for increased productivity of human resources and hence of investment in education.

Education can no longer be expected to train a labour force for stable industrial jobs, it must instead train individuals to be innovative, capable of evolving and adapting to a rapidly changing world and assimilating change.

Education and training have become one of the prime movers of development.

Seen in that light, investment in research and education is a necessity.

A very clear correlation has been established between the educational level of women and the overall improvement in the population's health and sanitation and the drop in fertility rates.

Illiterate mothers, bringing-up illiterate daughters who are married off too early easily fall into yet another cycle of poverty, illiteracy, high fertility and early mortality.

Women can greatly contribute to the progress of the society.

Education has other purposes than only to provide a skilled workforce for the economy.

Pointers and Recommendations

- A future-oriented study of the place of work in society, taking into account the effects of technical progress and change in both private and community life.
- The establishment of new links between educational policy and development policy, with view to strengthening the bases of knowledge and skills in the countries concerned : encouragement of initiative, teamwork, realistic synergies taking local resources into account, self-employment and the spirit of enterprise.
- The necessary improvement and general availability of basic education.

1.3.4 The Cornerstone of Education

This type of learning is less a matter of acquiring itemised codified information than of mastering the instruments of knowledge themselves and it can be regarded as both a means and an end in life.

Understanding the various aspects of environment better arouses intellectual curiosity, stimulates the critical faculty and enables people to make sense of reality by acquiring independence of judgment.

Regarding memory it would be dangerous to imagine that it has now become unnecessary. It has to be cultivated and cannot be reduced to automatic functioning.

Learning to know and learning to do are to a great extent indissociable. Learning to do, however, is more closely linked to vocational training.

The future of industrial economics depends on their ability to transform advances in knowledge into innovations that generate new business and new jobs.

Learning can no longer be regarded as the simple transmission of more or less routine practice/s.

Higher skills at all levels will be called for because employers are seeking competence which is a mix of abilities.

- individual professional skills
- aptitude for team work
- initiative
- readiness to take risks

Highly subjective qualities (innate or acquired) often termed as "life skills" combined with knowledge and know-how, make up the competence required.

The relationship with the material and the technological is secondary to the inter-personal relationships.

Contemporary world is too often a world of violence. The media and the general public is becoming an impotent observer, even the hostage of those who create or maintain conflicts.

If one is to understand others one must know himself.

The teaching of the history of religions and customs can thus serve as a useful benchmark for future behaviours.

The Commission firmly restated the fundamental principles that education must contribute to the all-round development of each individual's—

- mind
- body
- intelligence
- sensitivity
- aesthetic sense
- personal responsibility
- spiritual values

All human beings must be enabled to develop independent critical thinking and form their own judgment in order to determine for themselves, what they believe they should do, in different circumstances of life.

More than ever, education's essential role seems to be to give people the freedom of thought, judgment, feeling and imagination they need for developing their talents and *remain as much as possible in control of their lives.*

Education should also provide children and young people with every possible opportunity for discovery and experimentation in aesthetic, artistic, sporting, scientific, cultural and social spheres.

Art and poetry which are too often taught in a manner that has become more utilitarian than cultural should be given more importance and directed to the development of imagination and creativity.

Pointers and Recommendations

- Education throughout life is based on four pillars; learning to know, learning to do, learning to live together and learning to be.
  - *Learning to know*, by combining a sufficiently broad general knowledge with the opportunity to work in depth on a small number of subjects. This also means learning to learn, so as to benefit from the opportunities education provides throughout life.
  - *Learning to do*, in order to acquire not only on occupational skill but also, more broadly, the competence to deal with many situations and to work in teams.
  - *Learning to live together*, by developing an understanding of other people and an appreciation of interdependence in a spirit of respect for the values of pluralism, mutual understanding and peace.

- *Learning to be*, so as to better develop one's personality and be able to act with ever greater autonomy, judgement and personal responsibility. In that connection, education must not disregard any aspect of a person's potential: memory, reasoning, aesthetic sense, physical capacities and communication skills.

1.3.5. Lifelong Education

Education throughout fife is essential for people to retain mastery of their own destinies.

Knowledge, know-how, knowing how to live with other people and "life skills" constitute four intimately linked aspects of the same reality.

Learning throughout life is a day-to-day experience punctuated by periods of intense effort to understand complex data and facts and is a product of a multi-dimensional dialectic, non-formal and formal learning.

All education begins at home and the family and this provides the link between the emotions and the intellect and passes on values and standards.

The school does not merge with the community but while retaining its specific character, it must avoid cutting itself off in any way from the social environment.

The education of women and girls is the pre-condition for the genuine equal participation of women in community life.

Education thus concerns all citizens who should all be active participants in and not just passive consumers of education.

Pointers and Recommendations

- The concept of learning throughout life is the key that gives access to the twenty-first century.
- In its new guise, continuing education is seen as going far beyond what is already practised, particularly in the developed countries, i.e. upgrading, with refresher training, retraining and conversion or promotion courses for adults. It should open up opportunities for learning for all, for many different purposes - offering them a second or third chance, satisfying their desire for knowledge and beauty or their desire to surpass themselves, or making it possible to broaden and deepen strictly vocational forms of training, including practical training.
- In short, 'learning throughout life' must take advantage of all the opportunities offered by society.

1.3.6. From Basic Education to University

The idea of learning throughout life has not misled the Commission into overlooking the importance of formal, non-formal or informal education.

Secondary Education must be seen as a crucial point in the life of individuals where they decide their own future and acquire abilities that will make for a fully successful adult life.

Pupils should be offered a choice of educational pathways so as to cater to the diversity of their talents and there should be greater emphasis on guidance with remedial teaching or changes in direction.

Education should at the same time be both universal and specific. It must provide the common factors uniting all human kind, while at the same time, it must deal with the specific challenges of very different worlds.

In order to escape the educational segregation that today divides the world, it is necessary to see how to make good the "knowledge deficit" that is so closely linked with under development.

By defining cognitive and affective competencies it ought to be ensured that all children of all countries attain *minimum levels of competence* in the main areas of cognitive skills.

Secondary education should prepare young people for adulthood - not only for higher education but also for the world of work.

Enough attention is also not paid to the acquisition of attitudes and values.

The requirements of the labour market create a pressure owing to which years of schooling tend to increase.

Taken world-wide, in terms of enrolment ratios secondary education, is the fastest expanding sector of formal education:

Secondary Education can thus be linked in the context of life long education to three major principles:

- diversity of courses
- increased emphasis on alternating study and work
- attempts to improve quality

Diversifying the course structure and paying greater attention to preparation for life should be among the aims of any reform.

Combining work, and study at the secondary level can only be of interest if it makes it possible to return to continuing education.

Learning about Science and Technology must be an integral part of education for everyone, as it can bridge the gulf between industrialised and non-industrialised countries.

Quality of the training of teachers and the quality of teaching in higher education institutions takes on, ever greater importance.

Higher Education institutions have a key responsibility in training teachers and teacher educators.

Each University should become an "open" university offering possibilities for distance learning and learning at various points of time.

Higher education should provide a "judicious mix" of

- media correspondence courses
- computer communication technology and
- personal contact

This can broaden the options at a comparatively low cost.

Greater use should be made of specialists other than faculty members.

Opportunities for switching back and forth between business or industry are conducive to better integration in a working environment.

Pointers and Recommendations

- A requirement valid for all countries, albeit in various forms and with different types of various forms and with different types of content — the strengthening of basic education : hence the emphasis on primary education and its traditional basic programmes - reading, writing, arithmetic — but also on the ability to express oneself in a language that lends itself to dialogue and understanding. The need, which will be still greater tomorrow, for receptivity to science and the world of science, which opens the door to the twenty-first century and its scientific and technological upheavals.
- The pressing needs of literacy work and basic education for adults are to be kept in mind.
- *Secondary education must be rethought in this general context of learning throughout life.*
- Universities should be central to the higher level of the system, even if as is the case in many countries, there are other, non-university establishments of higher education.
- Universities would have vested in them four key functions :
  - ➢ To prepare learners for research and teaching.
  - ➢ To provide highly specialised training courses adapted to the needs of economic and social life.
  - ➢ To be open to all, so as to cater for the many aspects of lifelong education in the widest sense.
  - ➢ International cooperation.
- The universities should also be able to speak out on ethical and social problems as entirely independent.
- The diversity of secondary schooling and the possibilities afforded by universities should provide a valid answer to the challenges of mass education by dispelling the obsession with a one-and-only educational 'king's highway'.

1.3.7 Teachers in Search of New Perspectives

The importance of the role of the teacher as an agent of change, promoting understanding and tolerance has always been there. It will become even more critical in the twenty first century. This need puts enormous responsibilities on the teacher as the change is envisaged

- from narrow nationalism to universalism
- from ethnic and cultural prejudice to tolerance, understanding and pluralism
- from autocracy to democracy in its various manifestations
- from a technologically divided world to a technologically united one

The stakes are high and the moral values formed in childhood and throughout life become of particular importance.

Improving the quality of education depends on first improving the recruitment, training, social status and conditions of work of the teachers. For meeting the expectations teachers need

- appropriate knowledge and skills
- personal characteristics
- professional prospects and
- motivation

Teachers must adapt their relationships with learners

- switching roles from 'soloist' to "accompanist"
- shifting the emphasis from dispensing information to helping learners, seek, organise and manage information
- guiding them rather than moulding them

On the other hand they need to display great firmness in relation to fundamental values that should guide each individual's life.

Teacher's great strength lies in the example they set of

- curiosity
- open-mindedness
- willingness to put their assumptions to test
- acknowledging mistakes and
- love for learning

Regular opportunities should be offered for practising teachers to learn through group sessions and through in service courses. Such reinforcements offered in a flexible form can contribute to

- enhancing their skiffs
- offering motivation and
- improving their status

Teachers should also spend some time outside school for getting closer to the world of work for which they are preparing learners.

Pointers and Recommendations

- While the psychological and material situation of teachers differs greatly from country to country, an upgrading of their status is essential.

- The concept of learning throughout life leads straight on to that of a *learning society*, a society that offers many and varied opportunities of learning, both at school and in economic, social and cultural life, which need more collaboration and partnerships with families, industry and business, voluntary associations, people in active cultural life, etc.
- Teachers are also concerned about the imperative requirement to update knowledge and skills.
- Even though teaching is essentially a solitary activity, teamwork is essential, particularly at the secondary level, in order to improve the quality of education and adapt it more closely to the special characteristics of classes or groups of pupils.
- The Commission stresses the importance of exchanges of teachers and partnerships between institutions in different countries.
- All these lines of emphasis should be the subject of a dialogue, over and above their aims of defending the moral and material interests of their members, teacher's organisations have built up a fund of experience which they are willing to make available to policy-makers.

1.3.8. Choices for Education : The Political Factor

An impartial public evaluation system of educational projects is also called for.

One of the main aims of educational reform is to involve the stake holder.

Education is a collective asset that cannot be left only to the market forces. The state must assume some responsibilities.

In the field of education it is important to rise above short-term responses or reforms. Long term planning based on in-depth analysis of realities is called for.

It is not only justifiable but also desirable to raise money from private sources in order to ease the pressure on national budgets.

Technological developments can create a cultural and educational environment capable of diversifying the sources of knowledge and learning. They are also capable of individualising learning.

The growing convergence between distance learning and other kinds of remote activity like "*tele-working*" are also likely to bring education and work closer.

Computers and multi-media systems help design individual learning paths, *enabling a learner to move at his own pace and making it easier for the teachers to organise learning material for mixed ability classes.*

Compact disc technology capable of handling huge amounts of information complete with sound, picture and text, is capable of taking the process of learning still further.

Using new technologies is also a way of combating underachievement.

A crucial point worth recalling and recording in this regard is that the *development of the new technologies does not at all diminish the role of the Teachers.*

In the age of new technologies teachers do not remain the sole repositors of knowledge but partners, in a collective fund of knowledge.

Both pre-service and in-service courses should give them a real command of these new tools.

It will no longer be exclusively a matter for teachers about teaching pupils to learn but also of teaching them how to seek, link-up and appraise facts and information.

Pointers and Recommendations

- Choosing a type of education means choosing a type of society. In all countries, such choices call for extensive public debate, based on an accurate evaluation of education systems in order to reach a democratic consensus, this being the best route to success for educational reform strategies.
- The Commission advocates the implementation of measures for involving the different persons and institutions active in society in educational decision-making : administrative decentralisation and the autonomy of educational establishments are conducive in most cases, it believes, to the development and generalisation of innovation.
- In view of the foregoing, the Commission reaffirms the role of the political authority, which has the duty clearly to define options and ensure overall regulation, making the required adjustments in education which is a community asset and cannot be regulated by market forces alone.
- The progress of the new information and communication technologies should give rise to a general deliberation on access to knowledge in the world of tomorrow. The Commission recommends :
  - ➢ the diversification and improvement of distance education through the use of the new technologies;
  - ➢ greater use of those technologies in adult education and especially in the in-service training of teachers;
  - ➢ the strengthening of developing countries' infrastructures and capabilities in this field and the dissemination of such technologies throughout society; these are in any case prerequisites to their use in formal education systems; and
  - ➢ the launching of programmes for the dissemination of the new technologies under auspices of UNSECO.

1.3.9 International Cooperation in the Global Village

Globalisation, henceforth irreversible calls for global responses : building a better or less-bad world has become (as never before) everyone's business.

Education is without any doubt one and perhaps the most fundamental of these responses.

Cooperation in education should thus be viewed in the broader context of what the international community must do.

The denial of equality with men to which the women are still subject....., by its extent and gravity is, a violation of the right of the individual.

It is the duty of the international community to make every effort to do away with these inequalities.

Whether the purpose be to improve family health, the schooling of children or community life in general, the best chance societies have of succeeding, lies in educating mothers and raising the status of women.

Pointers and Recommendations

- The need for international cooperation is felt also in the field of education.
- At the level of international cooperation, a policy of strong encouragement for the education of girls and women should be promoted.
- So-called aid policy should be made to evolve towards partnership by fostering, among other things, co-operation and exchanges within regional groupings.
- A quarter of development aid should be devoted to the funding of education.
- National education systems should be helped to gain strength by encouraging alliances and cooperation between ministries at regional level and between countries facing similar problems.
- Countries should be helped to stress the international dimension of the education provided (curricula, use of information technologies and international cooperation).
- New partnerships between international institutions dealing with education should be encouraged.
- The gathering, at international level, of data on national investment in education should be encouraged, in particular by the establishment of suitable indicators : total amount of private funds, investment by industry, spending on non-formal education, etc.
- A set of indicators should be developed for revealing the most serious dysfunctions of education systems, by cross-relating various quantitative and qualitative data, such as : level of spending on education, drop-out rates, disparities in access, inefficiency of different parts of the system, poor-quality teaching, teachers' etc.

- With an eye to the future, a UNESCO observatory should be set up to look into the new information technologies, their evolution and their foreseeable impact on not only education systems but also on modern societies.
- Intellectual cooperation in the field of education should be encouraged through the intermediary of UNESCO : UNESCO professorships. Associated Schools, equitable sharing of knowledge between countries, dissemination of information technologies, and learner, teacher and researcher exchanges.
- UNESCO's normative action on behalf of Member States, for instance in relation to the harmonisation of national legislation with international instruments, should be intensified.

What has preceded is a vision of the Delors Commission about the depth and dimensions of education as also its content and process for the Twenty First Century, which far from being overlooked cannot even be underestimated for making education a process of enablement and empowerment

2

Our Changing Environment and Ethos

2.1 The Over-riding Concept of Change

Change is the key-word today, but somehow when we think of change our thinking stops at the boundaries of science and technology. In this context, we fail to realise that even History has changed. The recent excavations in Haryana and Jamnagar and in Mexico have pre-dated History. Even Geography has changed with so many new countries, which never existed before, having come into existence. Politics too has changed with so many erstwhile monarchies and dictatorships having become democracies.

In this age, which has come to be designated as the "knowledge age" and knowledge society, its core element of "knowledge" too is growing very fast and at the same time becoming redundant faster. Knowledge has therefore remained only a temporary and an undependable asset to possess making it obligatory for all of us to continuously keep on updating our knowledge, not just for remaining relevant but for sheer survival.

2.2 Life-long Education

Thus one-time education has remained completely inadequate for life-time employability. This in turn has led to the emergence of the concept of life-long-education starting with berth and coming to a close only at death. Education, therefore, has to get geared for offering educational possibilities and opportunities for all stages of life.

- The innocent infancy
- The charming childhood
- The turbulent teen-age
- The try-out twenties
- The thorough thirties
- The flaming forties
- The flourishing fifties
- The serene sixties

- The saintly seventies
- The undependable eighties
- The nice-nice nineties
- The celebrating centuries

It is in this context that the *life-cycle of individuals* too has undergone a marked change. It used to be "Education – Work – Retirement" but has now got transformed into "Education – Work, Education – Work, Education – Work, Education – Work and no retirement" proving thereby that education has only "commas" and no full-stops".

Thus, if we do not update our knowledge and our ability of using it on a continuous basis, we will fall into the dark and deep well of ignorance because the illiteracy of the 20th century was the illiteracy of the illiterates while that of the 21st century will be that of literates. It can thus be concluded that learned are those who keep on learning.

2.3 Knowledge v/s Competence

Our schools and colleges, however, are still continuing to provide only knowledge to learners. This may have been alright when in the past we used to be preparing our learners for a by-and-large 'known' future, but future now has not only become *unknown* but more so *unpredictable*. It is, therefore, that we should conceive such a content and process of our education which continuously undergoes the process of review and revision as a matter of routine and which, helps and aims at developing "competencies" which would be permanent and multiuse. Such education will need to shift focus from being "content-based" to becoming "process-based" with learnability, educability, employability as its watch-words.

2.4 Holistic Development

All this will imply an educational structure starting with holistic educational experiences, verified and conformed by holistic evaluation and leading to holistic development. This education would thus become *enabling, empowering and enriching* not just flogging a process of moulding learners but one of guiding them for attaining their optimum level of development. It *will not just aim at educating learners but at improving their educability* and thereby becoming a powerful instrument for not just preparing them for "earning a living" but for 'living" a fulfilling, profitable and a socially worthwhile life.

In this context we will neither have to be remain content with romancing with the past nor with selling ourselves to the so-called modernity but by pursuing a middle path, dictated by reason and foresight.

We will also have to constantly remain conscious of the fact that all that is western is not essentially modern, resolving on our part, that we shall not be doing *tomorrow* only what the west has done *yesterday*. Our education will also have to consciously and deliberately strive for what we have all along been professing – the balanced all-round development of personality catering to the development of the three domains of growth viz. the intellectual, (cognitive – head), attitudinal (affective – heart) and actional (psychomotor – hands). It will not therefore remain confined to the boundary walls of the institutions but fan out to the extended environment with continuously readjusted forward – marching goals and beckoned by with new horizons and challenging our inquisitiveness and motivation.

2.5 Distance Education

It will be "Education for All" in letter and spirit *dismissing the traditional notion that the elite work with the head and the lowly with the hands*. The educational facilities now catering to the few will need to open up and get extended. The realisation that the channels of formal education have left large gaps to be filled-in by the non-formal routes of open and distance education without compromising on quality. We have to be doubly sure to remove the stigma from distance education as being second rate education. The quest for "quantity (numbers)" should not be allowed to overshadow that of "quality". We will have to be at our innovative best in this regard, to overcome the alleged shortfalls. As we know the curriculum prepared by the open learning agencies (both at the school and university levels) compares very favourably with those of formal education in-vogue, the self-learning material too is in many ways of outstanding quality, but the *examination procedures and standards and certification norms do need improvement*.

We have but to find ways and means of constructively overcoming the shortcomings resulting from the absence of *regular contact between the teachers and the taught* with full cognisance of the reality of the handicaps of the inability of the learners of distance education from pursuing formal education, because of either lack of access or their current professional pre-occupations, their age brackets etc. We should thus endeavour to satisfy in all respects, the slogan of "*Reaching the Unreached*" so that the pass-outs only carry these certificates with quality assurance and hence with a sense of pride and confidence in the job market, dismantling all the traditional public perceptions. The efforts being made in this direction are praiseworthy and generate great hopes.

2.6 Demystifying Technology

It is in this background, that technology has to play a big role and it will be able to play that role if it is demystified and used as an enabler and not just a subject of study. This idea is fast catching up but there is still a long way to go. Technology infact possesses the potential of transforming the conventional group education into individual and self-learning, video lessons and e-learning should thus in a large measure replace the print material in course of time making learning easy and more effective. This is also likely to yield another incidental gain of off-setting low achievement among those who are capable of achieving higher.

2.7 Comprehensive Evaluation of Educational Gains

Evaluation on the other hand too has to change. Instead of being targeted at the assessment of the attained level of advancement, it should be directed towards further improving the level of attainment, through diagnosis and remedial/enrichment educational measures, heralding the idea of *assessment for learning rather than of learning.* This will have to be done not just by identifying gaps in learning but by addressing them. It should not by the farthest stretch of imagination, project a situation of examination oriented education but establish an era of *education oriented examination.*

2.8 Vision About Learners

With learners as our single minded focus we do envisage some radical transformations in regard to them as well. In the aforesaid new contexts, learners will move from being—

- *objects* of education to becoming *subjects* of education
- *passive* recipients of dispensed knowledge to becoming *active* explorers, adventures and discoverers of knowledge
- *creatures* of circumstances to becoming *creators* of circumstances
- *consumers* of knowledge to becoming *producers* of knowledge
- *means* of development to becoming *justifications* for development
- *human beings to becoming human resources*
- persons to becoming personalities with an identity

With—

Inquisitiveness *to know more*
Motivation *to learn more* and
Capacity *to do more*

A word of caution however appears necessary at this point. Mistakes in education are all unpardonable and all punishable. We should never forget this. Furthermore, the sufferings resulting from the *mistakes of moments are suffered by centuries.*

3

An Overview of a Futuristic Perspectives of Education

3.1 The Changed Purpose of Education

Education for education sake, is no more an acceptable proposition. It has to be purposeful and demonstrate usefulness not just to the individual and the community, but to the nation and the world at large. In the context of the present situation it has to be:

- a *literacy enhancement programme* for attaining cent per cent literacy in course of time with particular reference to girls.
- a *poverty eradication programme* through the imparting vocational skills for making a living.
- an *employment creation programme* by opening up professional possibilities in unexplored fields and avenues particularly for self-employment.
- a *wealth generation programme* which will be a natural off-shoot of the above ventures, through economic elevation of individuals and communities in both rural and urban areas.
- a *health promotion programme* through awareness about keeping healthy and thus improving efficiency in both quantitative and qualitative terms. Reduction in child and female mortality and increasing functional longevity of all.
- a *social regeneration programme* through participative and cooperative initiatives.
- a *cultural enrichment programme* for taking advantage of our ancient wisdom and heritage.
- a *religious enlightenment programme* incorporating and advocating the concept of religion as a flowing stream and not a stagnant pool incorporating values of peaceful co-existence through tolerance and non-violence preached by all of them.

- a *human emancipation programme* heralding freedom from conservatism rigidity, and dispelling blind-faith, superstition and narrow-mindedness.
- a *visionary futuristic programme* offering opportunities for inculcation of abilities and proficiencies for meeting the challenges of the future with confidence and success. Entrepreneurship will be an essential component in this regard.

Education must aim at training individuals to be innovative, capable of evolving, adapting to the rapidly changing world and assimilating change.

Education for the future too deserves a more elaborate analysis. Future as we perceive it, is no more just *unknown* but has become *unpredictable. Yesterday's education has no more remained relevant today and today's education will become even more irrelevant tomorrow.* With reference to this phenomenon *one time education has thus remained completely inadequate for life-time employability.* Continuous upgradation of skills has therefore become imperative, further reinforcing the concept of '*life-long-education*'.

In the words of Dr. R.H. Dave, "*Education in the life-long perspective, is a process of human transformation, human enlightenment and human empowerment for the attainment of a better and a higher quality of life.*"

Objectives, aims and goals have also to be conceived, stated and defined comprehensively yet specifically in all the three domains of development. Cognitive (thinking), Affective (feeling) and Psycho-motor (doing). Focus of attention here, has to be not just on acquisition knowledge but application of knowledge in life situations. In addition, aesthetic sense, values and reflection about what is acquired, have also to be incorporated in the programmes of education, which would need to cover the development of total personality of the learners in both scholastic and non-co-scholastic aspects.

3.2 New Directions in the Content of Education

A shift of focus in regard to the content of education is also be called for and this will have to imply change in spirit and not just in name like the overnight change of name of Primary Schools into Basic Education Schools, just by the change of the sign boards.

Collaboration with business and industry in the development and transaction of educational content than just lip-serviced *consultation* too is needed. This will be necessary for developing industry and business related proficiencies and thus strengthening the relationship of education with the clients/consumers of our products (the educated work-force).

A shift from the concept of *Syllabus* to that of *Curriculum,* will also be called for, by moving beyond course content to the enunciation of objectives, of course content, of methodology of teaching and learning, of aids to instruction and of evaluation.

Change in the enunciation of content with a *disciplinary* approach to an *integrated* one, will also have to be a part of this process.

From discipline-based *fundamentals to applications* of the basic elements of content will also be needed. Thus from the teaching of say the history of Physics (Newton did this Einstine did this) to Applications of Physics, will need to be focussed upon.

A shift from only vertical treatment of subjects (Like Babar, Humayun, Akbar, Jahangir.....) to both vertical and horizontal treatment of content (like who ruled France when Shajahan ruled India) will be called for. Japan it may be mentioned has introduced a new subject '*Contemporary Society*' in its new curriculum in this context.

A move from *abstract to concrete* entities and examples of realities will also be necessary for consolidating the elements of content in the minds of learners.

In addition to the *immediate* use of the contents in life, to their *long range implications*, will also be needed to be incorporated in the courses of study for inculcating in learners not just insight but also foresight in their decision-making abilities.

Besides facts, generalisations in terms of *basic understandings* would also need to be incorporated as part of content. This would imply moving beyond the statements like Aryan civilisation flourished on the banks of the rivers of the Indo gangetic plain. Persian Civilisation on the banks of Euphrates and Tigris, Egyptian civilisation of the banks of the Nile. *Basic understanding based on these facts would be "Early civilisations grew in river beds."*

The fast growing changes in content would also need to be taken care of through the incorporation of the concepts of *Frontline Curriculum*, where the major part of the prescribed contents (say 90%) may be changed after four or five years, but a 10% segment of it, listing new developments called the Frontline Curriculum may change say every two years.

There has to be yet another change in content. Instead of defining parameters of content an attempt should be made to explain them so as to bring them within the effortless comprehension of the learners. Pictorial or diagrammatic or graphical representations prove to be valuable instruments in such a consolidation of content. This not just leads to self-growth but influences the *total overall perceptions and growth* as such.

3.3 Curriculum Transaction

With different institutions following the same prescribed courses, the marked differences in the quality of education imparted by them occur mainly because of methodology of teaching and learning they advocate and practice. Transaction of curriculum thus becomes one of the key foundations of education chiefly responsible for the degree of realisation of the goals set.

The first thing that needs to be mentioned in this regard is the need for an immediate shift form the traditional *tongue and ear method* to a variety of unconventional approaches of teaching and learning. (An independent chapter is being devoted to these methods in the book.)

With the enormous advances in the different subjects of study the prescribed content too has swelled up. Thus an individual learner finds it difficult to cover it. *Group and participatory learning practices* have, therefore to be encouraged and adopted. Apart from this, group and participatory learning becomes more illuminative, leading to better internalisation. It also generates team spirit which turns out to be a great asset in the live realities of professional situations.

Learning only from the *print media to internet surfacing,* CD-ROMs etc. have also to be fully explored for enrichment of learning. Approaches to effective utilisation of these sources has also to be imparted to the learners.

This will also make the teacher conversant with the new techniques and enable him to assume his real role of being a *guide rather than just a dispenser of information.* With knowledge growing fast the teacher too will need to become a *co-learner with the learners* particularly so in regard to the content of the Frontline Curriculum.

Learners will thus *not only learn but learn-how-to-learn* and finally voluntarily assume the responsibility of moving ahead in their crusade through *self-directed learning* and subsequently to other innovative initiatives in this regard.

The locale of teaching and learning will, in this situation, move *beyond the classroom* to laboratories, environmental observations, different life and work settings etc. With these situations emerging as the new locations of learning there will naturally be another great educational transformation. The learners would thus be better prepared to meet and tackle live *natural challenges and instead of testing imaginary concocted hypothesis (and these too) in simulated situations.* Such experimental learning will pave the way for immediate assimilation uprooting the need for memorisation.

Field Surveys and library research will also, in this context, become everyday pursuits of learning, when things like *Engel's Law of Consumption* will not need to be memorised for reproduction at examination time, but a self-deduced conclusion on the basis of interviews of people of different economic levels which would be impossible to forget.

These new approaches will, quite naturally and not just incidentally improve the *pace* of learning, and the *quality* of learning beside enhancing the *quantum of learning.*

Interactions of different kinds, with the teachers, with peers and with ones own self, will also then take place with increased levels of motivation and concentration as one moves from one stage to another.

The *marriage of technology and pedagogy* will also enable transversing longer distances and digging deeper into the treasures of knowledge through all possible delivery modes, be they instructor led, or of distance learning or of on-line learning or learning through CD-ROMs or other devices and modes.

Curriculum Transaction will also need to acquire and demonstrate flexibility for being adaptable to the needs of different times, different content, different individuals and become relevant and accountable to the particular settings. The *bright children* will only need to be introduced to the learning material and learning processes and they would then move on, on their own. The *mediocre children* with initial exposure will also need reinforcement. The *weaker learners* would need repeated teaching and repeated reinforcement for consolidation and internalisation of learning.

3.4 Learning Materials and Aids

The emergent realities will as mentioned earlier expect and require the learning materials to *move beyond the print media to technological aids* (the CD-ROMs the internet etc.). These could be used both for *teacher-directed learning as also self-learning*. Both teachers and learners would, therefore, need to acquire the needed proficiencies for effectively and profitably using them. In this context *they would all, not just need to be computer literate but computer savvy.*

3.5 Evaluation of Learner Growth

With education as a process of human enablement, human empowerment and human enlightenment, growth among learners, will also be recorded in different facets of personality. Thus evaluation would need to:

- be a process spread over the total span of education.
- consist of exercises related to the collection of evidences about the kind and degree of growth occurring among the learners in the context of the inputs provided.
- be designed to cover all the three domains of development Cognitive, Affective and Psycho-motor—and related growth in both scholastic and co-scholastic areas.
- press into service a variety of conventional and unconventional techniques and tools of evaluation.
- capable of providing in both qualitative and quantitative terms.
- not just assess growth but help to improve its pace of development and its quantum.
- enable meaningful declaration of results and become useful in taking a variety of decisions about individuals and/or groups evaluated.

The above descriptive definition of evaluation assumes greater importance particularly because customarily *we only teach what we test and not so much test what we teach.*

With shortcomings in our external/public examinations and with institution-based evaluation too becoming their replica, only academic aspects by-and-large come under the purview of our testing programmes with almost complete neglect of the non-academic (co-scholastic) areas, which are in fact to be more important for success in life.

The exigencies and emergencies, the inherent defects and operational shortfalls go to greatly erode the sanctity and credibility of our external examinations. Furthermore the irreversibility of the results of such unfair examinations, do call for the emancipation of our helpless learners from them.

Selective teaching and selective learning too have become common features, because of the short-falls in our traditional question papers which had few questions to be attempted out of those given and provided options.

In these traditional external/public examinations the inter-examiner variability, variations in the ranges of scores and patterns of their distribution from subject to subject, year to year and examination to examination led to the non-equivalence of a particular score in different subjects. *The use of sacrosanct cut-off scores (33%, 45%, 60% and 75%) for classifying the levels of achievement of learners in all subjects in all examinations and in all years thus became atrociously unscientific propositions.* It has been to overcome these shortcomings that the National Policy on Education 1986/92 has suggested the use of *grades in place of marks.* When grades are used, the cut-off scores for grades are *determined and declared subject-wise for each examination* and in *relative grading* on the basis of the obtained scores of the learners and not on the basis of adhoc and arbitrary determination of the boundary scores of grades in advance of the examination for being used perpetually. The concept of Pass and Fail is also alien and not admissible when grades are awarded. The aggregation of these non-equivalent entities (marks) for obtaining an overall indicator of performance in terms of divisions and distinctions is *like adding temperature (in celcius), humidity (in percentage) and rainfall (in centimetres) for obtaining an index of weather.*

The prescription of year long courses in different subjects, and with all subjects required to be cleared simultaneously in a single attempt for obtaining a certificate of qualification, are provisions which have all along been the cause of undue pressure and stress on the learners. It has been to eliminate this that the NPE has also recommended a change over to the *semester system,* where credits could be earned and accumulated by clearing examinations in parts, finally encashing them into certificates of qualification when the requisite number of credits have been earned.

The traditional examinations also mainly attempted to test *memorisation* and not so much other higher abilities. *Certificates of qualification* for having cleared the examination did not also effectively assess and testify to the possession of specific competencies by the learners. *They were, therefore, wallets without any money in them.*

Yet another thing which needs a special mention is that with a perpetually used 33% score in all the prescribed subjects as the qualifying level, the all India pass percentage of class X examinations is around 65% and declaration of candidates as failure is disqualification for entering a course of higher education or a job for which these are eligibility qualification. Does it therefore mean that this rather high proportion of the total number of candidates who are declared as failures are good for nothing. Even otherwise the faith in the results of external examination is continuously on the ebb with employers and institution of higher education instituting their own selection tests. The institution of external examination by itself displays a mistrust of the teacher who teaches. What is really required is the effective introduction of Continuous and Comprehensive School-based Evaluation with an independent certificate issued by the school covering both scholastic and non co-scholastic aspects of pupil growth *as a supplement to the certificate of external* examinations which could become the bases of selecting learners for several Jobs.

Meaningful certification of abilities, proficiencies, achievements, skills etc. is another important aspect to be realised. Thus instead of being a certificate of having crossed the minimum required level of attainment, the examinations should certify the possession of specific competencies by the concerned learners.

3.6 Globalisation of Indian Education

The educational ventures of our country in their aspiration of reaching out to the skies should not get their feet uprooted from the soil. We must also appreciate that *everything that is western is not essentially modern.* Our conceptual starting point in India is *idealistic* whereas that of the west is *materialistic* from beginning to the end. We conceive things idealistically and practice realistically. The west aims mainly at *physical fulfilment. Spiritual fulfilment* too is one of the main targets of Indian Education beside other things. We cannot and should not become islands in the ocean and try to compete with other nations in material progress as well.

Indians unlike the west do not discard and reject the past, they assimilate it. If the west explores life, the orientalists celebrate it.

These are things, which our education should also take into consideration for enabling us to *live our lives nationally and think globally.*

It is with the above in mind that we should *proceed towards globalisation* appreciating and releasing that :

- There is no escape from globalisation now.
- Globalisation has to be perceived as a holistic concept and not just a truncated one focussing on economic issues alone.
- Globalisation ventures have so far touched only macro-economics and not so much other facets of life and that the road map for its percolation on to the micro-level has yet to be charted.

- Globalisation has to be perceived as a reciprocative, concept involving give and take and should not be taken only as a one way traffic under any condition.
- Globalisation of Indian education presents both prospects and dangers. The pros and cons of the issues and their implications, therefore, need to be critically examined for evolving an Indian point of view.
- India should not succumb to pressures and firmily guard against onslaughts on the soul of Indian culture, in the name of liberalisation and globalisation.

3.7 Let Us Continue To Be Givers

Althrough the history of civilisations, India has all along been contributing to growth and progress of the world we live in. We have given to the world.

- the concept of *zero* which has revolutionised mathematics.
- the concept of *decimals* which has helped in re-inventing calculation.
- the concept of the *wheel* which became the basis of Industrial Revolution in Europe.
- the *numerals* which are the basic foundations of life and living.

Let us continue this process by further expanding such an export, presently in areas like information technology and aspire to become world leaders in as many fields as possible, for which we have an inherent capacity and potential.

Our strengths and export oriented initiatives are not just ancient relics but a modern reality. We are indisputably accepted as the second largest supplier of technical manpower in the world and are also exporting it. The expertise we possess is largely an outcome of our indigenous education.

However we have not been good salesmen because of not being adequately outgoing. Let us now realise that *modesty is no doubt a great virtue but the introvert behaviour which often generates, invariably proves to self-defeating, as it invariably inhibits even due publicity to our ligitimate strengths and achievements.*

In this context while educational philosophies and ideologies which originated in other countries, have been extensively researched upon and documented (through modern methods) those that evolved in our own country have comparatively remained less noticed by the world community.

Let us come out of this shell with sturdier determination, even though important breakthroughs in this regard have already occurred.

Some safeguards too are necessary. We cannot afford to glorify the accomplishments made in the past and even the present, without a futuristic perspective for making further advances by empowering ourselves for successfully competing with other advanced nations in all fields, through an assimilation of international developments. This, however, should not be done without critically analysing these for their compatibility with our culture and needs.

In this context, it will also be necessary to first establish a balanced alignment between our national goals and educational aims which is being attempted hereunder in a broad manner.

3.8 National Goals

In regard to India the National Goals derived mainly from our constitution and the cultural heritage could be listed broadly as under:

- Promotion of the principles of democracy.
- Respect for the individual.
- Equality of opportunity for all, regardless of race, sex, language and religion and in all other aspects.
- Respect for the Constitution and the law.
- National integrity, unity and security.
- Social and economic justice, and development.
- Preservation and promotion of the diverse cultures of the country and the world.
- International co-operation and peace on the basis of tolerance, reciprocity, mutual respect and trust.
- Support to UN and other international bodies and contribution to their activities for international understanding and peace.

3.9 Aims of Education

In the context of the above National Goals, the Aims of Indian Education could be spelt out as under :

- To develop a human person with desirable abilities, proficiencies, attitudes, values and qualities of self-confidence and creativity.
- To develop culturally conscious individuals with pride in the country and a desire to contribute to its development as good citizens of the country and the world.
- To kindle a desire for preserving and promoting democracy, secularism, unity, social justice and ethics with accountability in pursuing life situations.
- To prepare the young generation for entering the world of work easily and effectively through the development of appropriate, flexible, adaptable and multi- use competencies and a requisite mind set (This aim is best actualised through the development and transaction of courses of study not just in consultation but with the active involvement of business, industry and the larger job market).
- To develop sound physical health and fitness among learners for undertaking physical activities, demanding dexterity, diligence and hardwork.
- To develop the innate abilities, talents and potentials to the optimum level and to further enrich the same through appropriate inputs.

- To acquire the ability of critical thinking, problem-solving, decision making and of squarely facing unforeseen situations, while pursuing education or at the work places.
- To develop abilities for meeting the social, cultural, economic, technological needs and aspirations of the country through an appropriate design of the curriculum and its transaction as also evaluation procedures, practices and instruments.
- To develop attitudes and values aimed at not just realising a better quality of life but a higher quality of life.
- To develop a sense of international brotherhood, through an understanding of contemporary society in different parts of the world and mutual gestures of goodwill.

4

Curriculum

The Anvil of Instructional Designs

4.1 Introduction

A Curriculum is:

- an adaptable road-map for realising educational targets
- an instrument for optimum physical, intellectual, social and spiritual growth of the educands.
- a hope capsule for realising individual and collective aspirations.

Methods of Teaching also acquire a meaning only in the contextual framework of the curriculum, which the teachers attempt to transact. It is, therefore, desirable that the concept of curriculum, its diverse facets, the process of its development, its transaction, its review and renewal along with learner evaluation are deliberated upon.

Though, it will be incorrect to say, that the modern concepts and principles of curriculum are not well understood in India, we should have no hesitation in admitting that they have not found appropriate applications in the country. In actual application situations they have often been brushed aside as, expensive, time consuming and even sometimes dubbed as being not practicable.

There have no doubt been attempts at the scientific construction of curriculum in certain places like NCERT but they are just a counted few. Despite these curriculum development based on technically sound principles and procedures does continue to be a neglected area in Indian education.

What are sometimes referred to as 'curricula' for certain courses, designed by the various agencies particularly the Universities, are just the enumeration of the topics of study. They are commonly known as *syllabi* and are nothing more than that. Even the topics of study in most cases do not stand adequately defined in terms of desired parameters. It is then left to the textbook or the teacher to provide an operational explanation of a particular syllabus. In some cases now copying the NCERT the educational agencies have started giving subject-wise instructional objectives in the beginning of the syllabi for the various courses. But, this is more ornamental than functional, because the objectives in most of such situations are superimposed on the already existing syllabi really reversing the sequence of the process. Above all even this innovation does not make them curricula.

It is no exaggeration to mention that even in teacher education courses where 'Curriculum' is the core concept, the courses of study stand enunciated in terms '*Papers*' and the topics covered by them. No curriculum as such, based on fundamental principles of curriculum construction is developed and prescribed.

The main purpose of this chapter is to present a functional structure and strategy for curriculum development which the educational agencies prescribing courses could consider adopting or adapting.

In this process, it will be attempted to spell out the concept of curriculum development as could be feasibly applicable in actual settings in practical rather than theoretical terms.

4.2 Basic Considerations

There are mainly three basic paradigms in curriculum construction. These are:

4.2.1 *The Individual* : Learners, their probable age group, level of mental growth, background (family & social) as well as level of knowledge possessed, aspirations etc.

4.2.2 *The Society* : This will include the social order, national economic policies, political system, cultural heritage philosophy of life of the nation etc.

4.2.3 *The Human Knowledge* : The existing store of human knowledge in various areas, which is fast growing and exerting an influence on our life-styles.

The above three considerations will provide the foundations of the curriculum and also be the most important of the sources of educational objectives.

4.3 Derivation and Statement of Objectives

The above basic considerations when spelt out for specific areas and subject domains are a pointer to the educational objectives. These overall objectives become the basis of deriving the objectives for different stages of education (primary, secondary, university). And finally the stage-wise objectives of education become the basis for developing instructional objectives of various subject areas and courses.

These instructional objectives will determine the *real operational framework of the curricula* for various courses. They will need to be conceived in all the three domains of pupil growth viz. the cognitive, affective and psychomotor.

4.4 Curriculum Development a Collaborative Venture

After the identification of the various courses of study and their respective objectives the next step is to develop a curriculum for each of these. While developing curriculum it has to be kept in mind that *curriculum is not a one man's job and certainly not the monopoly of the subject specialists as has been the case in the past*, in several places. Curriculum Development is a process requiring inputs from several areas of specialisation. These are mainly eight specialised inputs required as is shown through the Diagram 4.1.

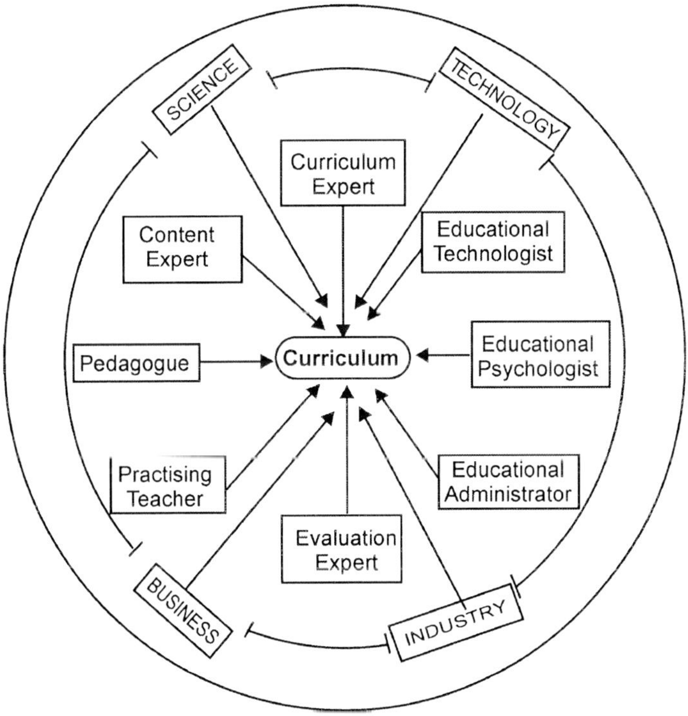

Diagram 4.1: Curriculum Development a Collaborative Effort

Each one of these eight has to play a distinct role. To state briefly the *curriculum specialist* will look after the general framework of the entire endeavour. He will help establish and ensure a feasible coordination between the different experts. The *subject matter expert,* who could be an individual drawn from higher education or University, will ensure that the content matter included is accurate and updated and that its organisation does not distort the facts. The *educational technologist* will see to it that the methodologies of instruction and modern aids to teaching (including technological ones) proposed are the most appropriate for the situations for which they are suggested. He will also be instrumental in establishing a relationship between the objectives, content and in instructional techniques. He should be an educational technologist rather than a technologist without any educational background. The *educational psychologist* will scrutinise the potential of the proposed content and methodology for achieving the targets in respect of the expected outcomes. He will look to their appropriateness from the point of view of the mental level of the learner-group and the likely adequacy of their mental preparedness for the proposed intakes. The *educational practitioner* will indeed be the practising teacher, whose job will be to see that the objectives, content and methodology are all suitable for the learners, that the objectives are neither pitched too high nor too low, that the content is graded and in line with the likely background of previous knowledge and competencies of the group and that the methodologies proposed can be employed either through the existing resources or those that can be easily manipulated or procured. He will also have to judge the implementability of the curriculum in respect of the time-budget. Above all he will also be required to do a little introspection for finding out whether the average existing teacher can manage to impart instruction as contemplated through the proposed curriculum. The *pedague* will critically examine the reliability of the instructional methodologies proposed. *The evaluators* job will be to identify and select the techniques of evaluation for assessing the quantum of growth in all the three domains (cognitive, affective and psycho-motor). He will also be required, in most cases, to develop tools of evaluation of different types and forms for assessing the degree of achievement of the predetermined objectives the mastery of content on the part of the learners. He will as well be entrusted with the task of devising formats and procedures for the recording and reporting of evaluation data and for suggesting the various uses of the results of evaluation in different situations.

The inputs from Business and Industry as also from scientific and technological developments will enable the curriculum to remains updated. They will also take of the employability facet of education.

It may be mentioned here that the main presumption of the present thesis is that curriculum will be developed centrally and will be meant for a large number of institutions. At present each university prepares the curriculum for different subjects at different levels for all the departments and institutions that send learners for its examinations. At the school stage in India, a National Curriculum Framework is developed by the National Council of Educational Research and Training (NCERT), New Delhi. This is adopted or adopted by different state level education agencies—the State Boards of School Education; and of the State Departments of Education (for elementary, secondary and senior secondary stages). Since no structural changes are proposed through the proposals of this chapter, it may not be difficult to implement the suggestions contained in it by any agency involved in the process of preparing curriculum. It will, however, be necessary for these agencies to create conditions and provide the necessary infrastructure and facilities including specialised manpower for the development of curricula which may satisfy the felt needs and help remove the imbalances that are commonly known to exist in them. They have also to realise that *returns in the field of education, are not as quick as they could be in business or industry.* The benefits of what we invest now, will be reaped only by the next generation and *our interest in the future generations will be estimated with the investments in terms of time energy we make for them.*

4.5 The Types of Educational Curricula

The educational targets of the aforesaid contexts, will be comprehensive – cognitive, affective and psychomotor. The growth in these three domains of development will be an outcome of the teaching-learning activities, designed and pressed into service as a part of the defined and undefined curricula.

Instructional Curricula, however gets unavoidably supplemented by:

- Curriculum of the Home
- Curriculum of the Immediate Environment
- Curriculum of the Peer Group
- Curriculum of the Courses
- Curriculum of the Television
- Curriculum of the Internet and the WWW.

Curriculum of the Home

The curriculum of the *home* imparts to an individual the *dynamics of living together* with a status and responsibilities of our own, the personal, social, cultural *values*, the language patterns, pronunciation, life styles consisting of habits, customs and manners, interests, attitudes and obligations, etc. etc.

Curriculum of the Immediate Environment

The curriculum of the *immediate environment* helps imbibe the appreciation of nature with its helpful and harmful potentials for the human race, the animal kingdom and the plant life, etc etc.

Curriculum of the Peer Group

The curriculum of the *peer group* is often a gap fulfilling curriculum, for example what we normally know about sex, in fact and unauthentic education we have received from the peers who are a little younger and older than ourselves.

Curriculum of the Institutions

The curriculum of the prescribed courses is somehow the only curriculum we take to be curriculum. The following distinct though inter-related parts:

- Instructional objectives in the three domains of development
    - Cognitive Domain
    - Affective Domain
    - Psycho-motor Domain
- Course Content
    - Theoretical
    - Practical
- Instructional materials
    - For teachers use
    - For learners use
    - For use by both learners and teachers
- Instructional methodology
- Scheme of evaluation
    - Continuous and comprehensive institution-based evaluation for improvement
    - External evaluation for measurement of attained levels of achievement

This is prescribed by the educational authority holding the reins of education, in the particular case. Somehow, it is more often than not confused with '*syllabus*' which is just a list of topics in different subjects of study (course content) which is just one part of the curriculum as we can see from the above listed components of the curriculum.

It is curriculum which, in fact, lies as the bottom of the vision of current book as a fundamental foundation.

The different aspects of curriculum are therefore proposed to be treated in detail in the subsequent chapters of the book.

Curriculum of the Television

Somehow it has become a very powerful instrument of education for all individuals of all ages.

As the television, in a substantial part of its programmes, depicts enlarged images of negative aspects of life it brain-washes children to believe that they have a right to be wrong. The TV also has effortlessly brought street culture the homes.

The propagation of the ideas of consumerism, which has in many cases proved detrimental to a host of traditional personal values, have had a mixed social reaction.

The Curriculum of the Internet and the www

This is an enrichment curriculum signified by motivation for self-gain, with a view to adding to ones' knowledge for further enrichment or for filling in the knowledge gaps. The physical availability of the hardware only proves to be a handicap in enabling individuals to take advantage this curriculum in its becoming an instrument of education for all.

4.6 Developing Curriculum Content and Materials

Textbooks were probably the only item in this category used in a traditional set-up. Till recently they were developed solely by private individuals and the educational agencies simply selected a few out of the many submitted to them for a particular course. These were called 'approved' or 'recommended' textbooks and were used by learners preparing for the courses concerned. However, at the school level many of them are now being developed by official agencies.

At the school stage, Teachers' Guides and Learners' Workbooks entered the educational scheme in India only in the sixties. No deliberate effort was made to develop them earlier. Those that were available had been developed in foreign countries and were unrelated to the curriculum in use in India. Furthermore being imported they were expensive. This somehow created the wrong impression that even if they are developed in India, they would essentially be costly and out of the reach of the purchasing power of the users. This fear was a constant discouragement for initiating any project for their development. Ultimately in the sixtees the *National Council of Educational Research and Training* (N.C.E.R.T.), New Delhi, developed comprehensive curriculum projects. This was thus the first official agency in the country that planned and developed a wide variety of instructional materials. Besides textbooks, teachers guides, learners workbooks, handwriting books and a reading readiness kit were developed. In Social Studies, teachers guides and instructional charts were developed to go with the textbooks. In Science, teachers' guides, kits of improvised and inexpensive apparatus (for demonstration and experimentation purposes) and laboratory manuals were developed to supplement the textbooks.

The above description gives some of the main kinds of instructional materials, the development of which now needs to be explored further by the various educational agencies responsible for the different stages of education. The plea again is that the development of instructional materials of different kinds may be taken up as an integral part of the programme of curriculum development. It is not necessary for these educational agencies to create an elaborate, top-heavy machinery for doing this task but a core team will no doubt be necessary.

This will mean a deviation from the existing practice where the members of Boards of Studies in different subjects decide on the syllabus for courses in their respective subjects. Each Board of Studies or Committee of Courses, as it is sometimes called, works independently of the other. The situation often causes lack of coordination and often the binding thread between the various courses is found missing particularly at the school stage where integrative approach is advocated. At the university stage however subjects are treated as independent entities/disciplines. What is attempted to be made out here, is that curriculum construction is a highly specialised job which can best be done by an educational agency, through a centrally operated ongoing programme of curriculum development review and renewal. This could be entrusted to what may be called the Academic/Curriculum Unit set-up within the organisation. It may consist of specialists in Curriculum, Evaluation, Instructional Materials, Educational Technology besides educational psychologists and subject matter experts etc. This core body may coopt. specialists from other areas, as and when necessary, for accomplishing specialised jobs. At the present time it has become more necessary than ever before, to collaborate with *business and industry. This may not just be limited to consultation but their active involvement in the development of courses and their transaction for incorporating elements relevant to the needs of the job market.* But the sole responsibility for constructing the curriculum and having curriculum and evaluation materials prepared should rest with it. It will be only then that a coordinated curriculum development will be possible. In such a set-up the Committees of Courses or the Boards of Studies, will take the form of the curriculum development committees for various courses at the school stage for example (adapting or adopting from the National Curriculum Framework in the Indian context). With the broadening of the concept of the curriculum, the services of persons represented on these committees will need to be utilised not only for the development of instructional and evaluation materials of various types but also for a variety of other related academic endeavours. The proposal envisages that there may be two distinct divisions within the infrastructure of the educational agencies one for the development of course content methodology of transaction and supporting aids and the other for matters related to evaluation and certification. One of these may be incharge of curriculum specialist and the other under the charge of an evaluation expert. Both the wings will of course, need supporting staff which will have to be provided. Academic work will thus acquire a status that it deserves. As could be seen the academic work has very wide dimensions and hence it does deserve better attention and position than what has so far been given to it, particularly by the examining agencies which by and large remain more than pre-occupied with the fire-fighting operations related to the conduct of examinations.

Steps of Developing Curriculum Content

- Listing of expected learning competencies in the three domains of development.
- Examining the implications of identified learning competencies in terms of the themes of content
- Identification of themes and sub-themes of content (subject matter) which can be pressed into service for realising the objectives
- Deciding about the graded complexity of the themes in the context of
  - The subject discipline in question
  - The age group of the learners
  - The preceding and the following learning
  - The environmental setting and the ethos
- Ensuring
  - Continuity
  - Gradation
  - Integration
  - Life application

4.7 Developing Evaluation Procedures and Materials

Work on the development of evaluation procedures and materials has to go on simultaneously with that of the development of instructional methodology and materials. While the purpose and function of the latter, is to help the learners realise the instructional objectives, that of the former is to assess the level of achievement of the same on the part of the learners in the context of the inputs offered.

An evaluation programme to be so developed, will need to embody the following characteristics.

1. *Objective based*—It should provide for the evaluation of all the related instructional objectives of the cognitive, affective and the psychomotor domains, in a valid and a reliable manner. It should thus help gauge the strengths and shortfalls in pupil growth in a precise manner, not just for assessing and certifying the attained level of competencies but for further improving them through remedial measures.
2. *Continuous*—It should provide for a continued process of assessment built into the total teaching-learning process as an integral part instead of the usual periodical examinations which tend to test achievement only in one or two strokes. This will also help provide regular feedback to both learners and teachers for improving the level and quality of their performance.
3. *Comprehensive*—It should cover both the academic and the non/ co-academic aspects of pupil growth and thereby provide a

compelling motivation to the institutions in offering adequate and appropriate opportunities of the desired type, for developing the various competencies among learners some of which could otherwise have been overlooked.

4. *Use of a variety of techniques and tools*—As the evaluation programme will be designed for covering both the scholastic and co-scholastic aspects of pupil growth, it will need to exploit various types of testing situations. They may for example also need to focus on observation as an important technique of evaluation and necessitate the use of variety of unconventional tools of evaluation like check-lists, inventories, rating scales, observation schedules etc.

4.8 Curriculum Transaction Implementation

This is a crucial step. It is here that the use of the vast inputs in curriculum construction is made. This is mainly the teacher's jurisdiction where he is the master of the situation in manipulating or providing learning experiences to the learners as envisaged by the curriculum. This is the stage of interaction between the curriculum on the one hand and the teacher and the learners on the other. The phenomenon could be diagrammatically represented through the Diagram 4.2 below :

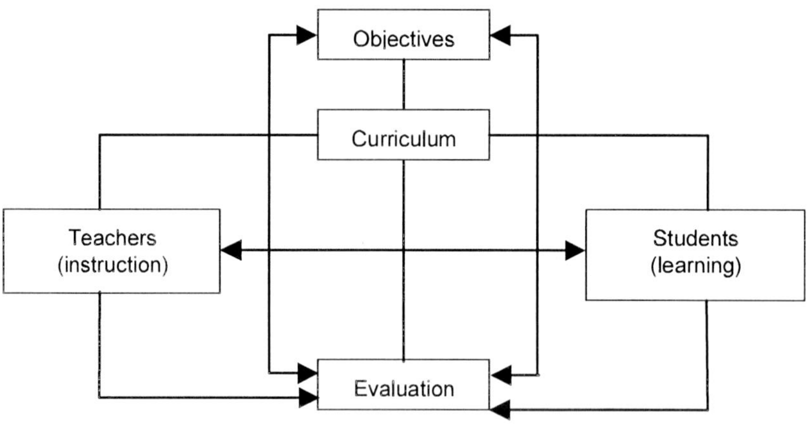

Diagram 4.2

Objectives are the anchor of the curriculum which in turn are the basis of the work of teachers and learners. Teachers and learners both work for the realisation of the objectives through the curriculum transaction which are ultimately evaluated through a well defined procedure of evaluation. The operation of this strategy could be called curriculum implementation and its process consist of objective-based instruction and learning.

It may be mentioned here that several forces, both internal and external, influence the aforesaid process of instruction. *From the teachers point of view* they are his personal academic background and training, availability of resources and aids to instruction, his interest in and commitment for the job and the satisfaction he derives from its execution, etc. etc. *From the learners' point of view* they are his interest in and attitude towards study, his level of achievement and growth, his previous preparation for assimilating the course, his future plans and his motivation etc. *From the point of view of both the teacher and the learner*, it may be the ethos and the atmosphere of the school and the encouragement and motivation it provides, besides the availability of instructional materials and their use etc.

Approach to instruction is yet another factor deserving attention in this regard. Normally while we educationalists view a teaching-learning situation, we are often guided in our thinking by the concept of the symmetrical normal curve and the *stanine scale* (this is being discussed in greater detail in the chapter on grading). We think that in a population only about 4% will get the top grade and another 4% will get the last one. As a nine point scale this notion has overtaken our thinking so much that we often refuse to view the situation from another angle.

In fact a normal distribution of scores presumes chances and accidents. Indeed the distribution should not be normal if some carefully manipulated inputs are not introduced in the process of instruction. It should then take a negatively skewed form. Thus we have reason to argue that *the closer a distribution is to the normal one, the more ineffective has our instruction been*. This logic advocated by Dr. B.S. Bloom of the University of Chicago is bound to be of great interest to the teacher and has the potential of adding to their confidence in picking up their instructional challenges. We should, therefore, have faith in enabling even the weakest learner to attain a higher level of achievement through well designed and implemented educational programmes. We should also ensure that those who are capable of achieving high do not achieve low.

4.9 Curriculum Evaluation

This is the weakest link of the Indian curriculum development scene. It involves the tryout of the curriculum and curriculum materials to find out their adequacy and appropriateness for achieving the objectives in advance of putting it into practice. This is seldom done and even where it is attempted, it is not done as it should be. The try out could be sequentially done *unitwise* as and when one is developed as also that the whole *curriculum*. As a matter of fact both the above types of tryouts are necessary when a completely new curriculum is being developed. But sometimes only a partial revision of the curriculum is desired and in this case only that part of the newly developed replacement of the curriculum may be tried out.

In all these cases, however, it is sought to find out, as to how far the various elements of the curriculum and the procedures and practices implied through it, are effective in achieving the objectives set. *More than one set of material and methods could also be tried* out in this process for identifying the most appropriate one. Questions like the following could be sought to be answered through the tryout.

- Whether the objectives of instruction set are within the competence of the learners to achieve?
- Whether one set of content matter or another is more adequate and or appropriate for enabling the learners to achieve the objectives?
- Which one of the various methodologies tried is more suitable to be adopted as compared to the others?
- What instructional materials or sets of them help the learners achieve the objectives better than others?
- Whether the scheme of evaluation is capable of providing valid and reliable result and whether the diagnosis made throught them can constructively help in the improvement of teaching and learning through the needed reinforcement etc., etc.?

The step is mainly contemplated to put the effectiveness of the curriculum to test before putting it into practice. The step of curriculum evaluation may no doubt mean substantial investment in terms of time, effort and money but it could save educational disasters which may mean losses multiplied several times over.

It may be mentioned that in an ideal scheme there should be a built in system of continuous review and revision (renewal) of the curriculum.

4.10 Conclusion

In conclusion it could be said that curriculum in the past has been a victimised outcome of social economic, political cultural and other influences. Serious efforts at the development of purposeful curricula to satisfy some of the felt needs are comparatively recent. Even when curriculum changes were contemplated and planned they were designed to fit into the existing organisational structure rather than to challenge it. *They were, furthermore, experience-based and any experimentation was foreign to the thinking on curriculum development.*

The proposals contained here are certainly not a cure for all the ills of curriculum development and implementation. They only give an approach for attacking the problems in the field. Several such approaches could be possible.

Curriculum development which has normally been an ad hoc outcome of unanticipated changes in the past, *could well be compared to unplanned urban development where, in course of time, we are forced to live with short-sighted and short-term decision-making.* Let us then rise in unison to rescue curriculum from the above malady and make it worthy of meeting the challenge of preparing our children adequately and effectively for the twenty-first century.

5

Generic Facets of Educational Objectives

5.1 The Purpose of Objectives

Objectives are the starting points of any educational process and their understanding is a basic requirement for all educational planners, educational administrators, teacher educators, teachers and evaluators to be successful in their mission. With the goal of alround development of personality, teachers in particular ought also have an intimate acquaintance with the three domains into which the objectives stand classified viz., *Cognitive Affective and Psycho-motor*, which have been touched upon in passing earlier. They are the facts and concepts related to the objectives of the different domains which are attempted to be presented here.

Derivation of objective, the first step towards proper development and statement of educational objectives, stands to gain in several ways, by subjecting them to a proper framework of classification. It helps to view them as parts of a system rather than in isolation. It also increases their usability by providing clarity about their interconnections. A proper classification to a great extent helps avoid overlap among similar objectives in a list. They have to be properly delimited and defined. This, also helps in ascertaining as to how far the various aspects of a major objective have been covered by their specifications. A well laid out system of objectives is a must for designing an effective educational programme comprising of curriculum development, instruction and evaluation. A system of classification is also essential for the pursuit of research, particularly in the fields of instruction and evaluation. Finally, a classification is very necessary for better communication among teachers on the subject of educational objectives without which all attempts at educational improvement may go waste.

5.2 A Snag in the Classification of Objectives

Each statement of an educational objective, as we know, has two distinct components—*the modification part* and *the content part*. It is not easily possible to evolve a logical scheme of grouping objectives in a way that they cover the requirements of both these components. The subject oriented classification will tend to lean heavily on content matter, whereas the behaviour-based classification will be mainly concerned with processes, particulary the changes expected to be brought about among the educands. Besides, it is also no easy task to synthesise demands of the different, categories of sources and evolve a balanced list. Such attempts have often ended in a very complicated list without much potential for practical application. Since the main business of education is to bring about a change in terms of behavioural outcomes, the choice naturally devolves upon the behavioural classification of objectives. While many attempts have been made in this direction much more has yet to be accomplished.

5.3 The Eight-year Study Model

One of the earliest systematic works on behaviour-based classification of objectives is witnessed in the evaluation programme of an Eight-year Study under the leadership of *Ralph Taylor*. Just for historical interest, the scheme of objectives as arrived at under this experiment is given below:

1. The development of effective ways of thinking.
2. The acquisition of important information, ideas and principles.
3. The development of effective work habits and skills.
4. The development of increased sensitivity to social problems and aesthetic experience.
5. The inculcation of social rather than selfish attitude.
6. The development of appreciation of literature, art and music.
7. The development of increasing range of worthwhile interests.
8. Increased personal and social development.
9. Improved physical health.
10. The formulation and classification of a philosophy of life.

The procedure adopted for developing this ten category model of objectives was curriculum analysis and the conference method. The curricular objectives of the *thirty schools* under the study were sifted and regrouped keeing in view their behaviour homogeneity. However, the experimenters kept an open mind and were conscious of the shortcomings of their model. They felt that "the classification of objectives would be improved as evidence accumulates regarding the social significance of different behaviour patterns and regarding the correlation and consistency among various specific reactions classified under the particular type of a behaviour". A conference of specialists, teachers and administration was finally used for vetting the list tentatively drawn up.

5.4 The Sources of Educational Objectives

The philosophy of life is, in fact, the main source of all facets of all our activities including education. Educational targets too get derived from this very fundamental foundation. The main of these are the:

- The *social order* and its diverse linkages with life e.g. we in India and the orient do not discard and reject the past, we assimilate it. This has important implications for life and also for education.
- The *economic structure* too, is an important determinant of educational targets which naturally differ in countries following capitalistic, and socialistic societies.
- The *political system* too exerts a powerful influence on educational targets and practices, demonstrating wide variation in democracies and dictatorships.
- The *cultural heritage* is again an undeniable factor that determines educational targets, which among other things involves pride in ones past.
- The *existing store of human knowledge* is another factor as we know many things now which we were looking for in the past. This masks a shift of ground and focus of our educational targets.
- Educational targets cannot also ignore the individuals for whom they are enunciated—their age, maturity level, previous knowledge etc.

5.5 The Levels of Educational Objectives

There is a distinct hierarchy among the educational target consisting of :

From top to bottom it implies a journey from *whole to parts* for example there could be many *aims* in a goal, many *objectives* in an aim and many *specifications* in an objective.

It also at the some time presents a phenomenon of a movement from *general to specific*. For example a *goal* could be 'making a good man'. Now this could have different interpretations in different situations and in different ideologies. An *Aim* in this very context could be 'making a good citizen.' Even this could mean differently in different societies. The allegiance of a good citizen in a dictatorship could be to the dictator, in a communistic state to the party, and so on. An *Objective* in the same backdrop could be making a judicious voter who will take an objective decision about whom to vote for. The next in the chain are *specifications*. They indicate the applied side of objectives giving *what a learner will be able to do to demonstrate to us that he has achieved a particular objective*.

This hierarchy can be diagrammatically presented as in Fig. 5.1.

It is at the level of objectives that targets become tangible and realisable through educational inputs and testable through evaluation for judging the quantum and quality of gain.

Specifications of different objectives in many ways, are competencies which become the basic ability elements for being focused upon for being achieved as also the basis for formulating evaluation situations and testing tools.

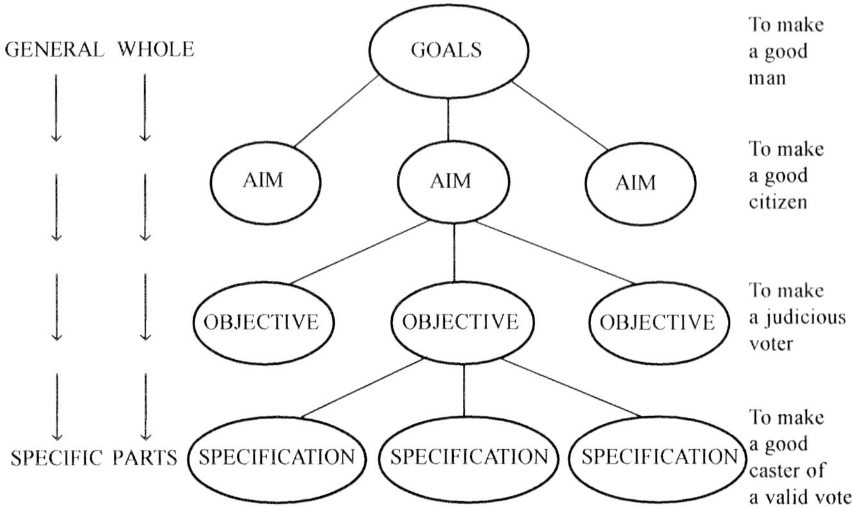

Fig. 5.1

5.6 The Statements of Educational Objectives

Objectives as mentioned earlier in fact indicate that level of targets which are tangible for being handled in educational processes.

The statements of objectives are, therefore, governed by some characteristic conditions. These are briefly enunciated below:

- Objectives have to be stated specifically in concrete terms, without vagueness or ambiguity.
- The statement of objectives have to have both the *modification* and the *content* components i.e. the changes desired to be realised in pupil behaviour (competencies) and the *content* through which they are proposed to be realised.
- Objectives must be aligned to the subject for which they are listed.
- Objectives must correspond to the age-group-and the level of abilities of the learners.
- Objectives ought to be stated in terms of pupil behaviour and not in terms of teacher behaviour ('to acquire' the ability of ... and not 'to help learners acquire').
- Objectives must be achievable.
- Objectives must be evaluable.

5.7 The Definition of Objectives

For purposes of being constructively utilised objectives do need to be broken down into parts. The parts ought to wear a behavioural garb in respect of the learners. These parts are called *specifications* and are derived, in answer to the question as to *'what would a learner will be able to do to demonstrate to us that he/she has achieved a particular objective'*. Let us take the example of the objective of 'understanding' in Social Studies.

Statements of the Objectives

To develop an understanding of facts, terms, concepts, principles, hypothesis, trends etc. in Social Studies.

Specifications of the Objectives

To demonstrate that a learner has achieved the above objective, he/she will be able to:

- discriminate
- classify
- compare and contrast
- identity relationship
- defect and correct errors.
- give examples

These specifications as already mentioned are competencies which need to be developed and which deserve to be tested for enabling us to know about the quantum and quality of growth among learners as a result of the educational inputs selected and provided.

5.8 Taxonomies of Educational Objectives

A taxonomy is a scheme of classification followed originally in biological sciences where plants or animals are arranged in increasing degrees of specificity (diminishing degrees of generality) on the basis of certain criteria, in a way that *each succeeding class appears to be telescoping out of or into the preceding one*, depending upon the direction of views, e.g., order, family genus and species. Likewise, when applied to educational objectives, the model should yield *hierarchically arranged objectives in ascending or descending order of complexity or difficulty*.

A number of models of classification of objectives have since been developed. The most convincing of these in the recent years has been the taxonomical model of educational objectives developed by *Bloom* and his associates. It has conceived and adopted a tripartite division of competencies/abilities corresponding to the three primary aspects of pupil growth-cognitive, affective, psycho-motor (knowing; feeling; doing).

The taxonomy of educational objectives as developed by *Bloom* and his associates, is basically a judicious combination of educational, logical and psychological classification systems. The distinction between different categories is educationally significant. The terms have been defined precisely in a manner that earlier meanings are logically consistent among themselves. Lastly, the classification is kept constant with the correct psychological findings about the mental processes. This classification employs a decimal enumeration system. This classification still awaits empirical evidence in its support although it has already been subjected to a fair degree of logical validation.

5.9 Objectives of the Cognitive Domain (Bloom's Model)

The Cognitive Domain represents the intellectual component of mental life and is certainly the most basic one, from the point of view of education. A variety of attempts have been made to classify mental processes and one may come across a variety of terms indicative of it, e.g., logical reasoning, reflective thinking, productive thinking and such others. *Guilford's three-dimensional model* (operations; contents; products) of the *Structure of Intellect* (SI model) may be of interest in this regard. It attempts to classify intellectual operations into a hierarchical order—cognitive, memory, divergent thinking and evaluation.

In Bloom's taxonomy these operations or processes have been divided and arranged into the following six classes/categories:

1. Knowledge
    - Knowledge of Specifics
    - Knowledge of Methodology
    - Knowledge of Abstractions.
2. Comprehension
    - Translation
    - Interpretation
    - Extrapolation
3. Application
4. Analysis
    - Analysis of Elements
    - Analysis of Relationships
    - Analysis of Organisational Principles.
5. Synthesis
    - Production of a Unique Communication

- Production of a Plan
- Derivation of a Set of Abstract Relationships.

6. Evaluation
   - Judging in terms of Internal Criteria
   - Judging in terms of External Criteria.

The six categories of behaviours in the above scheme are obviously arranged from simple to complex. They have been further defined in terms of more specific behaviours as under:

Knowledge is taken to involve the recall of specifics, universals, methods, processes, patterns, structures, settings, generalisations, etc. The basic psychological process in use is *remembering*. This is distinguished from the remaining five which are together called intellectual abilities for the simple reason that the latter requires "organised models of operations and generalised techniques for dealing with materials and problems."

Comprehension which is next higher in the category of objectives is considered as the lowest level of 'understanding' equivalent of knowing what is being communicated and using the material or idea communicated "without necessarily relating it to other material or seeing its fullest implications."

Application is the third category which pertains to "the use of an abstract idea in a particular and concrete situation" and thereby arriving at a solution of a problem. There may be some difference of opinion about the limited scope of this objective and as such the use of the term, application for it. This may be defended on the ground that the word may be given an ad-hoc meaning by defining it adequately to connote the use of acquired knowledge in unfamiliar situations.

Analysis forms the fourth category and connotes the breaking down of a communication into its constituent elements, in a way that relationships or sequence or both of the components, of a set of ideas are made clear. Some people treat it as an equivalent of the objective of critical thinking which is only partly true. Analysis is an important component of critical thinking but the latter is something more. Analysis may lead to the identification of elements, relationships or principles.

Synthesis is the fifth category of objectives and involves the ability to put together the elements or parts in a way that a new pattern emerges therefrom. It has elements of creativeness.

Evaluation crowns all the categories and calls for the most complex mental processes necessary for judging a material, method or communication against a standard, internal or external to it.

It may be mentioned that as in a hierarchy each higher entity in a taxonomy includes the lower one. This knowledge (information) is a part of 'understanding' i.e. understanding includes knowledge and similarly 'application' includes understanding, 'analysis' includes application, 'synthesis' includes analysis and 'evaluation' includes synthesis.

5.10 Some Other Taxonomies of the Cognitive Domain

Gagne's Taxonomy (Hierarchical Learning)

Reinstating
Discriminating
Identifying
Classifying
Demonstrating
Generating

Guilford's Taxonomy

(Structure of Intellect)
Cognition
Memory
Convergent Thinking
Divergent Thinking
Evaluation

Madau's Taxonomy

Knowledge
Comprehension
Application
Analysis
Synthesis
Evaluation

Decorte's Taxonomy

Perception
Recall and Reproduction of Information
Interpretation of Information
Convergent Product of Information
Divergent Product of Information
Evaluation Product of Information

Hannah's Taxonomy

Interpreting
Comparing
Classifying
Generalising
Inferring

Analysing
Synthesising
Predicting
Hypothesising
Evaluating

5.11 Objectives of the Affective Domain—Krathwohl's Model

There is often a greater lack of clarity and unanimity among educationists with regard to the statement of objectives of the *affective domain* than of the cognitive one. The terms like interests, appreciations, values, attitudes are often assigned varying shades of meaning. The term appreciation for instance, may extend from awareness to profound aesthetic impact with a large spread in between. Apart from other factors accounting for the "erosion in respect of affective objectives in education" it is no doubt the lack of clarity about their scope and meaning which really turns out to be a very grave handicap in their proper pursuit.

The taxonomy developed by Krathwohl systematises these objectives into five broad categories given as under—

1. Receiving (attending)
   - Awareness
   - Willingness to receive
   - Controlled or selected response.
2. Responding
   - Acquiescence in responding
   - Willingness to respond
   - Satisfaction in response
3. Valuing
   - Acceptance of a value
   - Preference of a value
   - Commitment.
4. Organisation
   - Conceptualisation of a value
   - Organisation of a value system.
5. Characterisation of a value or value complex.
   - Generalised set
   - Characterisation.

Receiving is the lowest or rather the most rudimentary category of affective behaviour. At this level the learner shows sensitivity to certain stimuli. It is like the teacher catching the learner's attention. Awareness, willingness to receive and the selected nature of attention are its important sub-levels.

Responding which is the next category, expects greater motivation and regularity in attention. It may also for practical considerations be described as 'interest' by which we mean a tendency to respond to a particular object or stimuli. Interest in turn, is evinced at three levels (1) compliance when expected, (2) voluntary response, and (3) response with a clear emotional tone.

Valuing is the third category which involves increasing internalisation of the sense of worth and identification with it. It indicates the motivation of behaviour not by deliberate desire but by the individual's commitment to the underlying value guiding the behaviour." This objectives may conveniently be called "attitudes". These objectives are "prime stuff from which the conscience of the individual is developed into control of behaviour."

Organisation forms the fourth category and connotes a system of values or attitudes. An individual's behaviour is not ordinarily motivated by a single attitude in isolation, but by an 'attitude complex'. Development of one's own code of conduct or standard of public life, may be an instance of the organisation of a value system.

Characterisation, the last of the categories, is reached when an individual is consistently found behaving in accordance with the values or attitudes he has imbibed, ultimately reaching a stage, when he has a consistent philosophy of life, of his own and an internal compulsion to pursue it.

The taxonomy of the affective domain may not appear quite hierarchical especially inasmuch as one order does not completely telescope into the other as a taxonomical characteristic, but surely presents an useful educational principle.

5.12 Objectives of the Psycho-motor Domain (Dave's Model)

The Psycho-motor Domain concerns itself with levels of attainment in neuro-muscular coordination. As the level of coordination moves up, the action becomes more refined, speedy and automatic. In this case five broad categories have been identified by R.H. Dave as given below:

1. Imitation
    - Impulsion
    - Overt repetition
2. Manipulation
    - Following direction
    - Selection
    - Fixation
3. Precision
    - Reproduction
    - Control
4. Articulation
    - Sequence
    - Harmony

5. Naturalisation
    - Automatism
    - Internalisation

Imitation accounts for the lowest level of psycho-motor behaviour. It starts as an inner urge or push or impulse. It is represented by "Covert inner rehearsal of the muscular system" which may be taken to be more of an action at the material level. Soon it may grow into an overt act with capacity to repeat the performance with very rudimentary coordination.

Manipulation is the next higher level of psycho-motor behaviour. It involves following direction, selecting certain actions in preference to others and acting accordingly. It marks the beginning of the fixation of operation and the end of initial fumbling in the manipulative actions.

Precision is the third category and is reached when reproduction of operations is carried out with speed and refinement, giving the learner the ability to control and adjust (increase, decrease or modify) his action in response to requirements.

Articulation which is the fourth category, can be said to have been attained when the learner is able to handle a number of actions in unison, keeping in view their sequence and rhythm. It involves coordination in action, i.e., right sequence in right proportion of time or at the right moment.

Naturalisation is the final stage which is the equivalent of perfect habituation ranging from automatisation to routilisation. At this level the performer does not expend any psychic energy in carrying out an operation. His actions are more or less automatic and mechanical and without any conscious thinking or planning, i.e., a mere reflex action.

The classification of objectives of the psycho-motor domain may not interest, in its entirety, the teachers of all subjects but in such curricular areas as writing, speech, driving, crafts, etc., it will find a very wide application. Unlike Cognitive and Affective domains the transfer value of an objective in the psycho-motor domain from one context to another may not be quite so pervasive.

Skills

That can be called a skill which

- is doable
- cab be physically observed in operation
- can be imitated
- involves the joint operation of the mind and the muscle
- has three basic characteristics of precaution, precision and proportion
- can be controlled at will
- can be manipulated
- in each subsequent attempt takes lesser time

- when repeated the quality of the outcome improves
- once learnt is learnt forever and does not need any revision or drill for retention (like swimming or cycling)

5.13 Interrelationship of Different Domains of Objectives

The tripartite division of instructional objectives into domains is not a water tight or an exclusive one. Firstly, the achievement in one domain is to a quite appreciable degree dependent on the learner's status in others. For instance, understanding (comprehension) may be a prerequisite for attaching proper value to an object or proper cognition, necessary for arousing proper interest. Similarly, interests and attitudes influence the quality of performance in both cognitive and psycho-motor domains. Comprehension again is a natural component of precision level in the psycho-motor domain and similarly interests can be traced to affective components of almost all the cognitive proficiencies. Thus, there is some degree of parallelism in terms of readiness relationship between various categories. Lower levels of each domain come relatively closer to each other, e.g., knowing, receiving and imitating are very much interdependent among themselves. In the higher categories too, there is discernible parallelism. A particular category of one domain, as already illustrated earlier, may correspond to one or more of categories of the other.

The implications of the nature of inter-connectedness are many. For example, while planning the instruction for realising an objective, it may be considered as to how best the corresponding objectives of other domains can be exploited, fed or even protected. The affective domain, it could be safely mentioned, has grievously suffered on account of the over emphasis on teaching for the so-called glorious cognitive objectives as 'critical thinking' and 'problem solving' without caring for the emotive reactions simultaneously arising out of such mental exercises. Of the dichotomy of 'mastery' and 'transfer' objectives, the effective realisation of the latter, which in fact is of real importance, will immensely be affected by the manner in which the interconnectedness among the objectives of different domains, is handled.

Pupils' growth in respect of the three domains, as a result of the learning experiences provided, is *simultaneous*. But every learning experience does not result in growth in all the domains and also in the same quantum in all the three domains. Thus, when a learning experience is planned and provided, it emits currents of growth in different domains, which finally settle down at different levels in the different domains. This variation in the potential of learning experiences for promoting growth leaves it to the initiative of the teachers to devise and offer an appropriate mix of learning activities for bringing about the desired behavioural changes and growth in the pupils in different domains.

It may also be mentioned that due to individual differences, the same learning experiences may result in different levels of growth in the three domains among different individuals. This highlights the need for individualised instruction.

The three taxonomies which could be called the CAP (Cognitive, Affective and Psychomotor) classification of objectives could be diagramatically presented as under in a composite model.

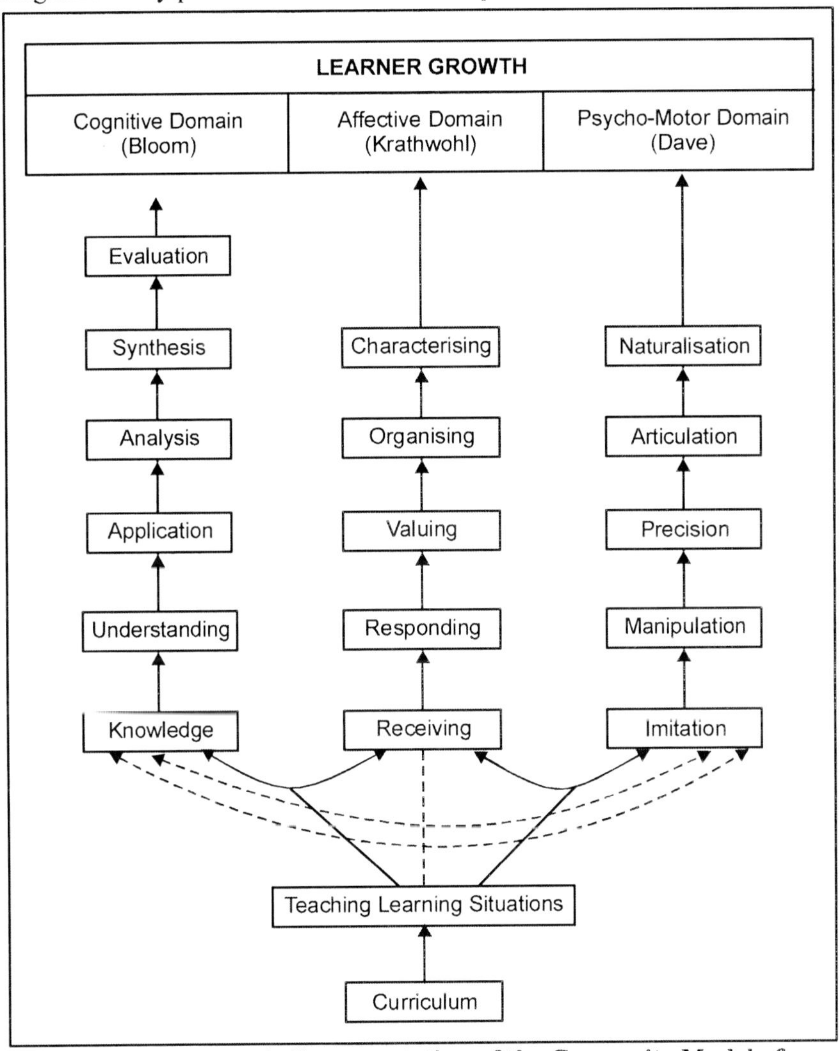

Fig.: A Diagramatic Representation of the Composite Model of Taxonomies of the Three Domains of Development

5.14 Some Examples of Manifestations of Different Areas of Growth

COGNITIVE	AFFECTIVE	PSYCHO-MOTOR
1. Creative Assignments	1. **Personal & Social Qualities**	• Yoga
2. Experimentation	• Cleanliness	• Games reports
3. Exploration	• Regularity	• Scouting and sports
4. Surveys	• Punctuality	• First Aid
5. Projects	• Discipline	• Swimming
6. Library Research	2. **Interests**	• Adventure activities
7. Participatory Learning	• Literary	• SUPW
8. Internet Surfing	• Artistic	• Gardening
9. Seminars	• Scientific	
10. Symposia	• Cultural	
11. Panel Discussions	3. **Attitudes towards**	
12. Fold Trips	• Teachers	
13. Case Studies	• School programmes	
14. Think-Tank Sessions	• School mates	
	• School/public property	
	4. **Values**	
	• Dignity of Labour	
	• Honesty	
	• Courage	
	• Courtesy	
	• Team Spirit	
	• Tolerance	

The usefulness of the taxonomical classification of instructional objectives is also sometimes disputed. It, therefore, appears necessary at this place to summarise below some of the uses to which it can be put particularly in the area of testing:

1. Since categories in the Taxonomy are arranged on the principle of graded complexity, the scheme is very helpful in identifying the meaningful level at which the learner is functioning, especially in view of "the upper and lower limits of the same category as well as in the context of the nature of the next higher and lower categories."
2. The techniques and tools of assessment can be relevantly decided upon, developed and deployed. Their categorisation thus becomes easy and clear. The form and typology, which has so much grip on the minds of the teachers now, can be very profitably replaced by the objective-based one, as a much desired change.
3. It will be helpful in translating into practice the principle of comprehensiveness of evaluation by ensuring proper realisation of the coverage of various aspects of pupils' growth: cognitive, affective and psycho-motor.
4. The evaluation of the evaluation devices in terms of their validity will be facilitated.

5. The evaluation may prove very helpful in arriving at the meaningful synthesis of various dimensions of pupils growth. Identification of areas of inter-relationship among the three domains may be of particular significance in this regard.
6. The logical nature of categorisation helps in identifying and grading teaching-learning situations, which can be an important source of selecting proper testing situations and deciding their sequence too.
7. Curriculum development and preparation of instructional material should profit from such a scheme of classification in many ways. Preparation and analysis of textbooks based on well defined objectives may prove to be a big improvement.
8. The classification through its well defined criteria "will provide a bridge for further communication among teachers, between teachers and evaluators, curriculum and research workers, psychologists and other behavioural scientists."
9. The taxonomy has also opened new avenues for research in education. To name a few, the re-evaluation of objectives should be the immediate reaction, such as finding out the relationship between different domains, categories and sub-categories. Empirical validation of the Taxonomies besides being a worthy research in its own way, will also open-up new vistas of work. The study of the problems of retentivity and recession in learning on different objectives may be an equally fruitful project. Teachers may also be motivated to undertake experimentation on objective-based teaching and testing. The scope is likely to become more wide and varied in course of time.

For purpose of the discussion that follows in this document, Bloom's taxonomy in the Cognitive Domain, Krathwohl's taxonomy in the Affective Domain and Dave's taxonomy in the Psycho-motor Domain have been taken as the basis as they are the most widely used ones. The above mentioned taxonomies of the three domains and no others are, however, followed in the '*letter*' but only in '*spirit*'. The adaptations it may be mentioned, are an outcome of the suggestions received in the course of discussions with a very large number of learners, teachers, teacher-educators, educational psychologists and sociologists, educational administrators, educational planners in India, spread over a span of more than five decades.

The main criteria for these adaptations was their suitability to the national environment in its various facets. Attempts were therefore made to check that the objectives identified for classification in each of the three domains were realisable through the curriculum, textbooks, educational resources, commonly available as also the competencies of the teachers and the learners to attain them.

In regard to the objectives of the *Cognitive Domain* they have been limited to the first three of the steps of Bloom's taxonomy, viz., knowledge, understanding and application with *analysis, synthesis and evaluation compressed and dovetailed into application.* This has been done because the average teacher is likely to find it difficult to discriminate between them and consequently to appropriately tackle them either for purposes of teaching for realising them or for evaluating them with the precision with which they have been originally enunciated by Bloom particularly so in social sciences.

The objectives of the Affective Domain again have also been condensed in the present document. They have firstly not been presented in the nomenclature proposed by Krathwohl but just limited to 'interests' and 'attitudes' and personal attributes which are commonly understood terminologies.

The objectives of the psycho-motor domain have been reduced to the muscular skills related to the subjects of study. Basically, these are such as require the abilities of '*precision*', '*precaution*' and '*proportion*' needed in undertaking activities like experiments, drawing sketches and diagrams, pursuing performing arts.

5.15 The Author's Contribution to the Taxonomies

As we have seen, the taxonomies of the Cognitive, Affective and the Psycho-motor domains present the phenomenon of vertical growth of the individuals in the three domains individually and collectively.

In the above context the author has expounded the theory of *sequential horizontal relationship among the three domains.* When anybody acquires some acquaintance (cognitive impression) about something, it often triggers an appreciation (affective impact) of the thing, learnt. The overflow of these feelings then moves beyond emotions propelling some fulfilling (psycho-motor) action.

This sequential horizontal relationship, among the three domains can be easily and effectively explained through a commonly observed phenomenon. We observe (cognition) some likeable characteristics of a child., we come to like them (affection) and then we instinctively hug and kiss it (Psycho-motor action).

The three taxonomies can be presented through the following composite model:

5.16 Taxonomy of Instuctional objectives of language and literature (H.S. Srivastava's Model)

While working on objective-based teaching and testing, the teachers of languages and literature, have repeatedly complained that the Taxonomies of Educational Objectives developed by different people did not satisfy the needs of languages and literature and that a separate taxonomy for this segment of curricular content needs to be developed.

The main hurdle in undertaking such an exercise, however, came from the unique nature of content (subject matter) of language and literature which differentiates it from non-language subjects, in a marked manner. In non-language subjects, themes of content demonstrate a scene of continuity , where one theme is built upon the other whereas in languages each one of them presents a stand alone identity.

The subject matter of languages and literature , as we know consists of Stories, Novels, Dialogues, Dramas, Essays, Letters, Biographies, Poetry etc. There is hardly any relationship among them, as each one of them is a unique entity by itself. At best, they can be compared or classified in a very broad manner in regard to the dates of their publication or their authorship or whether they are comedies or tragedies or whether their underlying/background settings are social or economic political or cultural or environmental and so on. These tags however exhale no definite clues about their content or import.

It was in the context of such an apparent non-amenability to clear-cult taxonomical paradigms of taxonomical classifications that the following list of instructional objectives applicable to language and literature was developed:

- Knowledge of the Elements of Language
- Comprehension
  - ➢ Listening Comprehension
  - ➢ Reading Comprehension
- Expression
  - ➢ Grad Expression
  - ➢ Written Expression
- Appreciation

While this list satisfied the characteristics of objectives in terms of their alignment with the subject, matter and its achievability and testability the list did not present a picture where the objectives were graded in terms of increasing complexity involving higher levels of mental processes. These set of objectives did not also demonstrate inclusiveness where each next objective covered the attributes of all the ones mentioned earlier.

With a view to overcoming these technical short falls a modified version of the objectives of language and literature, for brining the list closer to the concept of a taxonomy, was worked out as under.

- Knowledge of the Elements of Language.
- Listening Comprehension
- Oral Expression
- Reading Comprehension
- Written Expression
- Appreciation

this above list proposed to be designated as the taxonomy and languages and literature represents.

- the natural sequence of the acquisition of the listed abilities
- a graded complexity of abilities
- the needed inclusiveness of the next stated abilities covering the lower ones

Knowledge of the Elements of Language, however permeates all the abilities

It is also desirable to appreciate the coverage of the stated/listed objectives in respect of the three Domains of Development. This a presented through the following chart:

Coverage of Domains of Development through the Objectives of Language and Literature

Domains of Development / *Taxonomical Objectives of Language and Literature*	*Cognitive Domain*	*Affective Domain*	*Psychomotor Domain*
Knowledge of the Elements of Language	✓		
Listening Comprehension	✓	✓	
Oral Expression	✓		✓
Reading Comprehension	✓	✓	
Written Expression	✓	✓	✓
Appreciation		✓	

5.17 Salient Manifestations of the Objectives

- Knowledge of the Elements of Language
  - ➢ Vocabulary including basic semantics and stucture
  - ➢ Usage
  - ➢ Applied Grammar
  - ➢ Forms and formats of literature
- Listening Comprehension
  - ➢ Recognising the characteristics of speech sounds as also stress and intonation.
  - ➢ Following the sequence of the ideas listened, grasping the substance of what is listened.
- Oral Expression
  - ➢ Demonstrating correct pronunciation, stress intonation, accent and pauses

- using appropriate words, phrases and sentences for reaching out ones ideas to others
- maintaining proper sequence, speed and flow using conventional modes of address.

- Reading comprehension is envisaged to include:
  - Displaying reasonable speed in silent reading
  - Grasping the meanings of words, phrases sentences in their context
  - Locating key words phrases, sentences, important facts and ideas
  - Identifying the relationship between ideas facts, events characters etc.
  - Interpreting, inferring and evaluating the ideas, messages, mood of the writer and feelings expressed.
- Written expression
  - Using correct and appropriate words, idioms spellings (graphics), punctuations capitalization and connectives.
  - Maintaining of logical sequence in ideas, statements and in paragraphing
  - Following apt and appropriate forms and formats of written expression
  - Writing a neat and a legible hand with normal speed
  - Appropriately introducing the topic and ending it well
  - Giving a suitable title
- Appreciation
  - Appreciation is an overwhelming experience of a sensory reaction to beauty.
  - The unique and appealing beauty of words or of sounds of music or of works of art or of the softness of touch or of the buds of taste, constitute the prime genes of appreciation. Their delicacy refinement, tenderness, sensitivity and imaginativeness often leave us pondering and speechless.

Appreciation thus is an amalgam of supreme understanding, elated emotions and heart penetrating sentiments.

SECTION II
The Learning and Teaching Process

6

The Process of Learning

6.1 A Macro Overview

Teaching becomes successful only when learning takes place. It is, therefore, necessary for teachers to be conversant with the manner in which learning comes to occur among the learners.

As learning is the undisputed goal of teaching, it is also desirable to understand the phenomenon of learning—the factors that accelerate it and those that retard it, the conditions which make it easy and those that put road blacks, in its way, the situations which promote its success and those that don't.

Education is supposed to create:

— enablement
— empowerment and
— enrichment

and learning for inculcation of competencies, is the most important means for attaining these goals, through the modification it injects in the individuals, which result in enhancement of capacities as reflected through behaviour.

Three main types of interactions take place in educational institutions as a part of the teaching-learning process.

Teacher-Learner Interaction where the teacher normally plays a prominent role and the learner usually a passive one. In these situations *the concentration of learners is minimal.*

Learner – Learner Interaction, where the learners work in situations of participatory learning or group work or project work. In these situations *the level of 'concentration' rises/increases.*

Self-Self interaction or self-learning or auto-instruction which marks the beginning of self-directed learning, present situations where the challenges increase and *the level of 'concentration' is the highest.*

It, therefore, becomes an important function or responsibility of the teachers to make the learners independent of him by making them the '*subjects*' of education rather than letting them remain '*objects*' of education.

Technology too has come to play an important role in the teaching learning process. Technological aids, working models, video films are now being increasingly used, not just for augmenting knowledge but more so for providing insight into varied facts and phenomenon of the environment. *The television has added a new curriculum, on the educational scene, as an important supplement to the curriculum of the home, of the immediate environment, of the peer group and that of the school. The internet too is now offering the new source of enrichment curriculum.* It has, however, to be simultaneously appreciated that *technology can only at best be an enabler and is not the answer.* It can never replace the teacher though it can surely provide valuable reinforcements to the planned and designed programmes of instruction. Technology has surely to be adjusted and adapted to the maturity level of the learners and the institutional curriculum they are learning from. The technological resources and inputs have also to take care of the pre-requisites *of availability* and *accessibility.* Technological aids because of their versatile and universal applications have but to admit adaptation, as they can not be used at any time, at any place and by any individual. These aids to instruction, therefore, have to be relevant, efficient and utilised with accountability.

The delivery modes in education too have, of late, undergone a dramatic change and these changes have but to be taken cognisance of, for being relevant to the environmental transformations and transactions of curriculum. The methodologies pressed into service, therefore, have to cater to these demands and be open to other changes that may get ushered in, in course of time. The main of these according to present day demands are:

- Instructor-led Learning
- Distance learning
- Learning through CD-ROMs
- On line self-learning
- Video learning

The extensions and diversifications of techniques have not just become desirable but necessary, as education cannot survive in its present form and learners have to ultimately take over the responsibility of their learning from the teachers. In this context it will be *undesirable to take learners as customers and consumers of education by converting the philanthropic activity that education should be into commercial and a business enterprise.* The concept of 'Education for All' has therefore to receive our focussed attention.

There has also to be a *marriage of technology and pedagogy* for self-growth for influencing the process of growth in its wider context.

Irrespective of the variations in the methods of teaching, some of the common purposes to be served and challenges to be met by them are those of:

- Modernisation
- Globalisation
- Liberalisation
- Technologisation
- Professionalisation and
- Indianisation

The last of these, is the most important because education cannot succeed if it is alien to the social and cultural context and ethos as also the heritage.

The salient aspects of theory and practice of learning have been vary explicity and yet briefly enunciated by *Rajamal P. Devadas* in her book Methods of Teaching Home Science which is given below:

"How does Learning take place? What are the conditions which favour learning? Learning is change or modification that occurs in performance as a result of training and experience, (*McConnell*). Learning in school means, modifying or changing the behaviour of the pupils, in terms of achieving the goals. It is the process by which the pupil profits from past experience. According to *Skinner* learning "is a process of progressive behaviour adaptation." When learning takes place, some new technique or ability, based on past experience, develops.

Learning leads to establishing relationships between the stimuli and the responses, through a mental connection. Learning thus implies connecting ideas, events, phenomenon and so on. Man is the greatest of all learners, because he is capable of forming many connections. Good teaching based on the psychology of learning and adequate preparation, leads to numerous connections born out of effective thinking, planning and execution. Understanding the factors involved in the learning process is, therefore, important for the teacher as pupils respond to knowledge in different ways. When the teacher recognises the factors which favour learning, she will make the teaching-learning process efficient, accelarated and economical leading to deeper learning, by discarding the wrong steps and establishing the correct connections.

6.2 Principles of Learning

Hullfish and Smith have expounded five principles of learning. According to these authors, learning is:

1. *Motivated* when the learner has some stake in the activity.
2. *Geared* to the learner's level and compatible with his physical and intellectual ability.
3. *Patterned* when the learner can see meaningful relationships between the activity and the goal.

4. *Evaluated* when the learner has some way of knowing the progress he is making, and
5. *Integrated* with personal and social development, when the learner experiences satisfactory growth and adjustments.

6.3 Motivation in Learning

Motivation is the most powerful director of learning. In learning and living motivation is indispensable for success. Achievement in learning depends largely on how much and how well the pupil really wants to study and succeed and how far he is willing to put forth the investments in terms of human effort and energy to reach the goal.

Teachers use many approaches for motivating children to learn. *Compulsion, coercion, tempting with reward or praise and rousing their interest and eagerness to acquire knowledge are some of the common methods used.* Wherever all-round development of character and personality through voluntary self-activities, self-direction and self-expression are emphasised coercion and tempting will have no place. Pupils learn and develop best when they exert their utmost, when they energise their responses and behaviour and when they have dynamic relationship with their environment.

Teachers must learn the *art of stimulating and sustaining pupils' interest in learning*. A high degree of motivation helps in impelling pupils into action and ensures their active participation in learning activities. Mere repetition does not lead to learning. The repetition must be purposive and active. It must enlist the involvement of the pupil. The teacher needs to direct the learning process through such a positive motivation.

Richardson has formulated the following principles linking teaching and learning.

Learning

1. results from the active involvement of the learner,
2. begins with the learner's present achievement,
3. increases its effectiveness with motivation,
4. occurs through various channels,
5. bases meanings of words and other symbols on experience,
6. takes place in the total organism in response to the total situation, and
7. varies with individual differences in respect of needs and abilities.

In *Thorndike's* view, the laws which operate in the learning process are those of *readiness, effect and exercise including frequency and recency*. If the pupil has been prepared to learn through meaningful suggestions, he is ready to learn. The *law of readiness* then operates. If an effort brings success, reward or satisfaction, it is likely to be repeated. If the size of the incentive or reward increases, the efficiency of learning may also increase, provided the motivation continues. This illustrates the *law of effect.* The speed of performance depends on the satisfaction-value of the reward. 'Adaptation', 'adjustment', 'regulative change' and similar terms describe successful learning, indicating effect. Repeated effort gathers strength making repetition easier. This is the *law of frequency.* The act that has been performed recently has an advantage of being easy to repeat. This is the *law of recency.* The laws of frequency and recency together constitute the *law of exercise.* However, as the learning ability depends upon the stages of growth reached by the nervous and muscular systems. Mere exercise or drill alone cannot effect learning.

6.4 Maturation and Learning

Maturity has an important bearing on the learning process, particularly the maturity reached by the central nervous system and the muscular system. As the organism matures, the innate potentialities unfold themselves. In the development and functioning of the brain, adequate nutrition during pregnancy and early childhood plays a dominant role. The degree of maturation necessary for a particular training to be effective, is usually called 'learning readiness'.

Thyne points out four features of learning in terms of behavioural outcomes:

(1) In each learning situation the learner learns to do something. This is the feature of behaviour;

(2) Also previously he did something differently—hence there is change of behaviour;

(3) The change of behaviour occurs in a particular kind of situation and

(4) Finally the old and new behaviour do not merely happen in the situation—each is occasioned by, or is a response to it. To learn is to adopt a new response to a situation.

There are four requirements for learning to take place; cue, force, promptness and reinforcement. Cue means, "In any instance of learning, there must be a series of situations showing the 'cue' of that instance. The teacher has to ensure a series of situations containing the cue. For example giving the page numbers in the references assigned to the pupil. Behaviour has two aspects: form and time of beginning. The learner must make his response in terms of these two which constitute the situation, which offer '*force*' for learning to take place. The situation must make the learner react and elicit a response." In any instance of learning, the 'cue' must have 'force'. '*Promptness*' ensures that the response which the cue evokes has the specified form. In any instance of learning, a 'prompt' response must appear in one or more of the successive situations. In the school, the 'prompt' is usually in the form of instruction form the teacher. '*Reinforcement*' implies that the specified form of 'response' must be tied to the 'cue'. Learning will occur only when all these four functions are fulfilled.

6.5 Conditioned Learning

Conditioning is a form of learning in which the capacity to elicit a response is transferred from one stimulus to another. Conditioning means the establishment of a connection between a response and a stimulus which may not have a known or a natural connection with it. Conditioning represents learning at a simple level. The principles of conditioning in learning were first established by *Pavlov*. He was conducing some experiments on dogs. Food as we know is a natural stimulus to the salivary reflex. Pavlov demonstrated that the dog can be made to salivate to any stimulus associated with food, such as resonating a tuning fork. Since the secretion of saliva, which is a reflex action, resulted from the dog's response to the stimulus of the tuning fork, Pavlov designated such reflexes as 'Conditioned reflexes'.

6.6 Trial and Error

Clayton describes that as early as 1898, *Thorndike* published a theory of learning, based primarily upon animal experiments, such as the cat in a box. Later he expanded and developed this approach with applications to school situations. The unit of demonstrated or displayed behaviour was a relationship, an association or connection between sense impressions and impulses to action. Faced with a situation, the learner will engage in a number of responses eventuating in the one that 'solves' the problem. In repetitions of the situation, the incorrect responses will diminish and the correct response will become fixed. Learning, therefore, is concluded to be a trial and error process. In the initial trials, there are a large number of errors, but as trials are repeated, there is no error and the result is a success.

6.7 Insightful Learning

Kohler put a chimpanzee in a cage and suspended a banana from the roof outside the cage. Two sticks were placed inside the cage. Neither of the two was long enough to reach the banana. After some unsuccessful attempts, the monkey incidentally found that one stick fitted into the hole of the other, but not properly. This gave the animal a bright idea. It joined the two sticks firmly together and got the banana. This was not an exploratory type of learning involving conditioning or trial and error, but a sudden flash, leading to insight. 'Insightful learning' is common among human beings.

6.8 Learning by Imitation

Learning by imitation, happens by observing others doing things which one finds difficult to do himself and imitating them. Imitation helps in curtaining errors, supplying cues for the learner. Speaking, writing, playing and numerous other skills are learned by observing others and repeating what they do. The learner imitates the person he admires, one whom he would like to resemble. He identifies himself with the role model in the sense that he wants to be like him. According no *Nunn*, "Imitation is but the first stage in the creation of individuality, and the richer the scope for imitation, the richer the developed individuality will be." Imitation is never a complete reproduction. There is always some variation indicating choice, preference for details and creativity.

6.9 Remembering and Forgetting

There are several factors and practices which influence remembering and forgetting. Remembering is an active process. Remembering is important for the learner because by remembering what he has learnt, he can recall and learn more. Studying some material at a stretch is known as *massed learning*. When the material is learnt with intervals of rest, the method is called *distributed learning or spaced learning*. It has not been established that distributed learning is better than massed learning since unspread learning often leads to confusion.

Learning should proceed from the *simple to the complex*, from *whole* to parts from general to specific, from concrete to abstract. Learning a lesson as one whole unit is known as '*whole learning*'. Dividing the lesson and learning into the smaller units is termed *part learning*. Whole learning is more advantageous to the pupil, since he can comprehend the whole. However, if a passage is too long, dividing it into meaningful subgroups (paragraphs) will facilitate learning.

More often a learned material is repeated, (through drill) the better is the retention. The pupil must be encouraged either to often recite or review, the lessons learnt.

The meaningfulness of a lesson to be learned is the most important feature affecting the rate of learning and the amount of retention. *Guilford* demonstrated that *the more meaningful the material is to the learners the greater is its retention.* Retention over various intervals of time, is greater for substance learning than for rote learning. Factual information is forgotten faster than the ability to explain, interpret and apply general principles. Therefore, *Guilford* has stressed the use of concrete rather than abstract materials and direct experience rather than second or third hand experience, particularly with young children.

All lessons should be made as meaningful as possible. It is purposeless to ask children to spell words, which have no purposeful meaning for them. Scientific facts are rapidly forgotten, unless reinforced by relevant experience. Dates and names are valueless as isolated facts. They must be incorporated into units which have significance for pupils. Meaningful organisation of material can be developed by attention to similarities and differences and by emphasis on the who, what, when, where and why of relationships.

Curves of forgetting generally show greater forgetting of verbal lessons as compared to those of motor skills. *Ebbinghaus's* pioneer work on learning and forgetting with the nonsense syllables which he invented in order to have learning tasks free of previous experience, showed a rapid initial drop followed by a gradual slide to nearly complete forgetting. The curve of forgetting varies considerably depending upon the extent to which school work has meaning, its relatedness and organisation. There are also situations when overlearning or occasional recall occur.

6.10 Transfer of Training

Mastery of one skill may facilitate the learning of another skill. This is known as *transfer of training (learning)*. *Thorndike's* experiments and experiences have proved that transfer of learning is not a universal occurrence.

The distinction between retention and transfer, rests upon the similarity or difference between the test situation and the learning situation. *When the situation in which learning is being tested replicates the situation in which it was learned, retention can be measured, but when the situation differs, transfer of training is being measured.*

The following factors appear to influence learning and its transfer:

1. The perceptual clarity of the task, in points of relevant cues and appropriate responses.
2. The meaningfulness of the material and the understanding obtained.
3. The context in which the skill or knowledge is acquired.
4. Conditions contributing to, or reducing the interference between tasks such as similarity of stimuli or responses, and degree of overlearning.

Ultimately, each aspect of the curriculum must be seen as part of the total curriculum—the situations which provide learning experiences including those outside the school and its prescribed courses used for teaching and testing situations. They also include those that cater to individual differences, motivations, interests, attitudes, achievements and development.

6.11 Optimising Learning

Lacey's guidelines based on the principles of learning, emphasise that pupils learn most effectively when:

1. teaching is within the context of their previous experience.
2. an emotionally and intellectually stimulating environment is present.
3. they feel secure with the learning situation and have respect for the teacher.
4. multiple, concrete and first hand experiences are available as bases for concept formation.
5. they see the whole situation as well as the various parts in relation to the whole.
6. they are engaged in activities calling for critical thinking and problem-solving.

7. they participate and share actively in selecting problems and goals which have meaning for them.
8. learning experiences are planned in a meaningful, sequential pattern, in which every learning activity has a definite objective.
9. there is provision for differences in meeting the individual abilities, interests and needs.
10. meaningful practice reinforces sensory experiences.
11. the teacher plans learning experiences as carefully for attitudes and appreciations as for knowledge and skills.
12. learning gained in the classroom leads to purposeful action related to it and transfers readily to out-of-school situations, and
13. they participate in the evaluation of their learning experiences and receive emotional and intellectual satisfaction and a sense of achievement.

Since learning cannot be separated from teaching, good guidance and effective procedures are required of the teacher. She needs to apply knowledge of the principles of both teaching and learning, in planning the educational activities and more particularly for relating them to life experiences with a view to making the pursuits concrete and meaningful to the learners.

And above all it has to be accepted and realized that education admits only evolution and no revolution. Furthermore, human learning is a slow process. Where after birth animals take a few hours to stand on their feet, human children take a few months. In this context the transition from oscillation of thoughts from commencement to their consolidation and stabilization is a rather prolonged process in early years.

7

Energising Instruction

Learning, is the core determinant of growth and the sole path of progress. Our main effort, therefore, ought to be to make it *enabling empowering and enriching.*

7.1 The Fundamental Foundations

As already mentioned in passing earlier objectives are the anchor points of both learning experiences and evaluation. As the teacher must be thoroughly acquainted about 'both these' they are being briefly discussed in this context below:

The most important understanding, which the theoretician and practitioner of education ought to develop, is the intrinsic two-way relationship between the instructional objectives, learning experiences and evaluation techniques. Teaching is planned so as to achieve the objectives set in advance and evaluation techniques help us know the extent to which the inputs provided have been effective in helping pupils realise attain the desired goals.

Objective-based instruction and objective-based evaluation thus ought to form the crux of all educational programmes and practices of educational institutions. The relationship is generally presented through the following well-known diagram by Rolf Taylor :

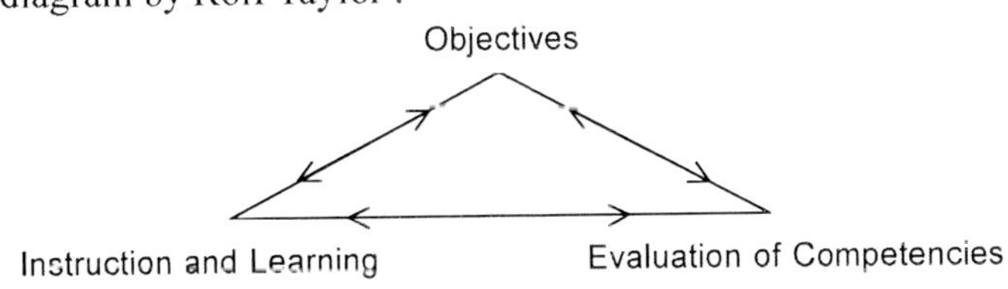

Diagram 7.1

First of all let us examine the mental processes involved in the achievement of instructional objectives. The whole process of instruction indeed ought to be geared to this end. Tracing the steps of the process, we can say that *teaching* becomes successful only when learning takes place. *Learning* takes place through experiences. *Experiences* consist of the absorption of ideas through different senses. *Senses* react to external situations (*stimuli*) for absorbing ideas. These situations are made up if learners' activities which are thus the starting points for the attainment of objectives The manipulation of teaching learning activities with a area to realising the desired objectives are 'Methods of Teaching'.

Based on the gains of participation, in the teaching-learning activities and processes, the evaluation instruments are designed for assessing the degree of the realisation of the expected goals. The analysis of performance reveals the shortfalls in performance or hard spots in learning if any. The process is then reversed and the learning experiences are examined, revised and re-provided for the effective realisation of the goals. If it is considered necessary even objectives are modified, to make them realistic—both achievable and evaluable.

Objectives, have two specifications the *'competency'* specification and the *'content'* specification. Both these specifications converge on to a central point which we call *teaching-learning situations*. These situations as the synthesis of the two aforesaid specifications of objectives, become the basis for designing instructional programmes and evaluation strategies in respect of both the content and competency specifications of the objectives.

The extension of the model also shows the relationship between evaluation and learning. This process can be expressed as under :

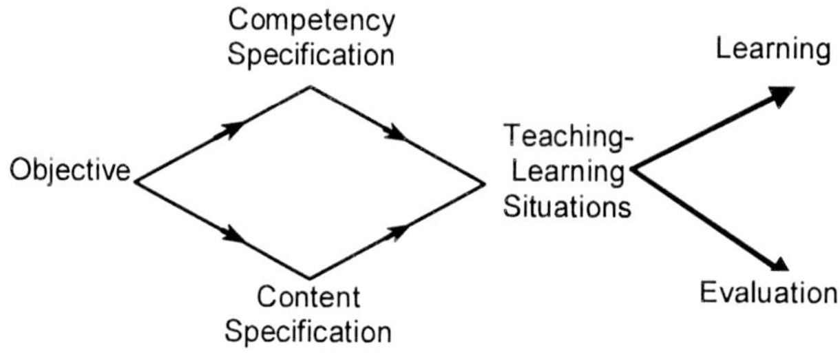

Diagram 7.2

Coming back to the learning process, it could be stated that it is not possible to provide all the possible activities in a particular instructional programme for all learner groups. A selection is imperative. The selection is primarily made on the basis of some considerations, like, the objectives desired to be achieved, the time and the resources available and the maturity level and background of the learners.

In order to clearly visualise, the relationship between objectives and learner's activities, let us for a while study the following table, giving the activities and the corresponding objectives that each can help achieve and try to draw some conclusions from it:

PUPIL ACTIVITIES	*OBJECTIVES*
Execution of Practical Work	Understanding, Skill
Organising an Exhibition	Interest, Appreciation, Application, Skill
Excursions /Field Trips	Knowledge, Understanding
Discussions	Understanding, Critical thinking
Lectures	Knowledge, Understanding
Dramatisation	Comprehension, Interest

The generalisations which can be easily drawn from the above table are as under :

- Different activities lead to the realisation of different objectives or conversely it is not possible to realise all the objectives through a single activity.
- For the achievement of any one objective, it may be necessary to employ one or more activities or conversely one activity may, at the same time, lead to the achievement of more than one objective.

7.2 Principles of Objective-Based Instruction

These generalisations lead us to some of the very important principles of objective-based instruction. These are:

7.2.1 *The Principle of Relevance*

This implies that the teaching-learning activities chosen for being pressed into service, should be relevant to the objective and possess the potentiality of achieving it. As it is not possible for all the activities to help in the realisation of all the objectives, they will have to be carefully selected to conform to the needs of the situations.

7.2.2 *The Principles of Concomitant or Collateral Learning*

This implies that activities when undertaken by learners, do not help in the realisation of only a single objective. Indeed they act in varied directions and while deliberately attempting to develop a particular objective, they may also help achieve some other objectives as well simultaneously, in an incidental manner.

7.2.3 *The Principle of Adequacy*

This implies that the activities selected should be adequate for achieving the desired objectives of instruction, comprehensively. This adequacy in respect of activities is achieved through the selection of relevant activities in adequately sufficient number, the frequency of their repetition and the spacing of offering these learning experiences.

7.2.4 *The Principle of Variety*

As a corollary of the above three principles, it could be said that for accomplishing the desired objectives, it is necessary to choose and use a variety of activities.

7.3 Instructional Approaches

The above principles lead us, almost naturally to a discussion on teaching methods for curriculum transaction which could be defined as *the systematic organisation of activities that result in learning and thus in the achievement of the desired objectives of instruction.*

Teaching methods can be sub-divided into two categories :

(a) *The Standard Methods* of Teaching, and

(b) *The Specific Methods* of Instruction designed for achieving certain emergent purposes.

The standard methods of instruction are quite well known. The activities to be pressed into service in the process of instruction, through them are almost fixed. These designated activities are followed sequentially almost in a ritualistic manner. The objectives that are possible to be achieved through such methods are also commonly known.

The specific methods of instruction on the other hand, are a product of teachers' ingenuity for achieving the specific purposes which may emerge in the course of teaching or those that the teacher may deem necessary. These are original in their nature and involve a unique organisation of activities with a view to achieving specific goals desired to be realised by the teacher in the process of instruction. They do not admit any rigidity either in the sequence of the steps or in the number or kind of the activities to be used.

Objective-based instruction would mainly follow the latter of the two methods, though efforts can be made to incorporate some of the features of the formal methods of instruction as well.

7.4 Planning Enriched Objective-Based Instruction

Objective-based instruction can be divided into the following main operational steps:

- Statement of instructional objectives.
- The preparation and use of objective-based instructional material.
- Planning instruction in keeping with the objectives.

  This planning may consist of the preparation of:

  (a) a year's plan
  (b) a term's plan
  (c) a unit plan
  (d) a class period plan

In advance planning for objective-based instruction, the preparation of an yearly plan is very important. It is the first step for *preparing a time-budget* for covering the course, as a teacher is allotted only a given number of class periods for covering the given specific quantum of the subject matter. As an initial step of planning, the whole content area is divided into different sub-units and allotted class periods in terms of a *time-budget* in the instructional programme. Here the measure of emphasis will be determined by the degree of difficulty of the theme proportion of resources, energy, time etc. proposed to be pressed into service for achieving the objectives. This plan can be *hypothetically presented* through a table like the one given below based on the supposition that there are six major units of content to be covered and that eighty class periods are available for accomplishing the task.

Domains of Development →	*Cognitive Areas*			*Affective Areas*		*Psycho-motor Areas*	*Number of Class Periods*
Objectives → ↓ *Units of Content*	*Knowledge*	*Under-standing*	*Application*	*Interests*	*Attitudes*	*Skills*	
U_1	✓				✓		15
U_2		✓		✓			10
U_3	✓		✓			✓	25
U_4		✓			✓		15
U_5	✓		✓				10
U_6	✓	✓		✓		✓	5
Total number of available class periods							80

The next step in the planning of instruction is the preparation of teaching units. These units are to be generally prepared by experts with the help of teachers, and are supplied to teachers. Teachers, however, should always remain the masters of the teaching operations and must never become slaves of the teaching units handed down to them. Teachers are supposed to make use of these units according to their specific needs and requirements. Resourceful teachers can also prepare their own teaching units, if they have time and facilities. The preparation of lesson-plans is the subsequent step. From a teaching unit a teacher can prepare lesson-plans for each class period according to need and convenience to fit into the overall time budget.

It will not be out of place to re-emphasise here that *educational objectives as mentioned earlier are derived from several primary sources, chief of which, are the level of psychological development of the child, the social order, the economic environment, the political system, the cultural heritage and the existing store of human knowledge in the society in question.* From the overall educational objectives, are derived the *stage-wise objectives* which become the basis for curriculum development of the different stages of education. From the stage-wise objectives, in turn are derived the *subject-wise objectives* of teaching which become the basis of the development of the curriculum plans of particular subjects for a particular stage. These subsequently help and guide the preparation of unit-plans and lesson-plans. Taking the processes in the opposite direction it could be said that the achievement of the different lesson-wise objectives leads to the achievement of unit-wise objectives, the achievement of different unit-wise objectives leads to the achievement of different subject-wise objectives, the achievement of the subject-wise objectives leads to the realisation of stage-wise objectives and these finally lead to the achievement of overall objectives of education.

The above discussion leads us to conclude that there is a parallelism between testing and teaching-learning which can be diagramatically represented as under :

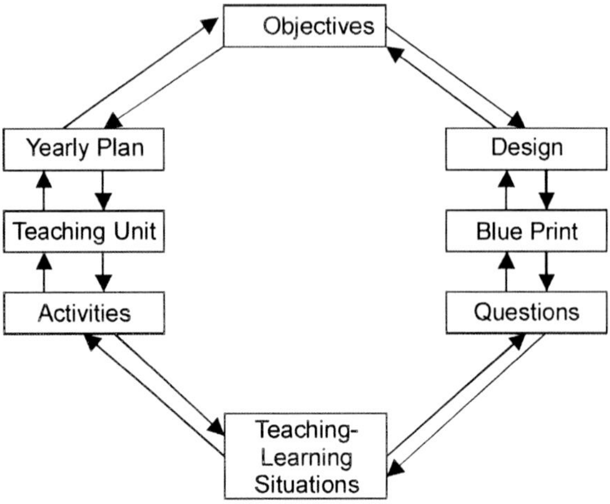

7.5 Nature and Purpose of Instructional Material

Suitable instructional material is an essential prerequisite for ensuring enriched instruction. There has, of late, been a phenomenal explosion of knowledge. In a good many cases different subjects and topics have assumed new dimensions and meanings. In many places, however, there is a paucity of aids and materials having relevance to related classroom instruction. Syllabi in different subjects are also often very sketchy and generalised in nature. They do not indicate the exact scope of subject-matter desired to be taught and tested. Until 1960's when NCERT came into being textbooks also used to be very deficient in many respects.

New types of instructional materials and ways of structuring the content of different subjects and topics of study, leave nothing which is not teachable. Methods of instruction, however, well-conceived will also remain ineffective without a solid grounding in the subject-matter, which is basically offered by instructional materials. Instead of giving only some recapitulatory questions at the end of the chapters, possible projects, surveys, library research, and references about possible web-sites ought also be given and related exercises built into the content of the related chapters. The books should also give teacher guided and computer assisted curriculum transaction.

Furthermore, evaluation also will fail to appropriately test the objectives, unless the objectives like understanding of major ideas, skills and attitudes are drawn from the solid base of the subject-matter. Activities too in order to be purposeful must fit into the context of what is to be taught. These activities will lose their significance unless teachers have a complete perspective of all the dimensions of the subject-matter.

The main available source of subject-matter to both teachers and learners is instructional material. Instructional material to be effective has but to incorporate enriched content material, which is helpful to the teacher in curriculum transaction. It also ought to contain guidelines for the teacher not only on 'What to teach?' as also on 'How to teach?'

Instructional materials can be developed both for the teachers and for the learners. For teachers they take the form of Resource Units, Teaching Units, Reference Books, Teacher's Handbooks and Curriculum Guides, etc. Instructional materials for the learners comprises of textbooks, supplementary books, workbooks, etc. Both teachers and learners also make use of some common material like textbooks, atlases, internet etc.

At this place the difference between Teaching Units and Resource Units also needs to be clearly appreciated. Resource units contain basic information from which a teacher can make a selection on the basis of his need. A teaching unit on the other hand lays down specific guidelines about the content and process of education related to the unit of teaching in question which is a part of the curriculum. The teaching units have a direct relevance to the syllabus prescribed as also to the periods of instruction allotted to the particular teaching units and to the classes to be taught. The preparation of teaching units is a crucial exercise and needs both the mastery of the subject-matter as well as the skills related to instructional methodology. Teaching units should not duplicate the content of textbooks nor should they be a mere compilations of materials culled from advanced books. They have indeed to be specially tailored to specific needs.

The syllabus of the entire year is first to be split into a number of viable units. Each one ought to be autonomous in some ways—in respect of subject-matter, a sequence and relationship with what has gone before and what is to follow in the scheme of instruction should not be overlooked. One teaching unit may be further split into more than one teaching lessons or class periods.

This assumes particular importance in professional courses where there is almost exclusive focus on the development of competencies related to application of knowledge in life/work situations.

The contents of teaching units are merely suggestive. The teachers may use them flexibly according to the needs and exigencies of actual classroom situations. Length of descriptive statements is not a guiding criterion of a good teaching unit. Its usability and the support it offers to the teachers which are the real yardsticks for judging its utility.

Such freedom and flexibility is required because of variations in the students'

• Needs • Abilities • Work-Style • Inter-personal Skills • Exposure

7.6 A Suggestive Format of an Instructional Unit

The format of the teaching unit is not rigid. It also need not be uniform in all the subjects and at all levels. However, a broad outline is suggested below.

7.6.1 *Introduction*

The introduction of the teaching unit should bring out the significance of the topic, its conspicuous character or novelty, its implications and relevance in life. It is to be based on what the learners have studied before and also becomes the basis of the content of the following units.

7.6.2 *Specific Objectives*

A teaching unit must indicate specific objectives of the topic to be taught. These will comprise the understanding of major ideas, application of related knowledge, in unfamiliar situation development of skills, the development of desired interests and attitudes as expected outcomes of the learning of the unit in question. The formulation of specific objectives is based on the general objectives envisaged in the study of the particular subject.

The formulation of objectives has to be precise, clear and their wording ought to indicate what is significant for learning in respect of the content unit in question. Formulation of objectives is also very crucial, because they give a sense of direction and a perspective to our entire approach of presentation of content, incorporation of activities and evaluation. They should indeed be stated in terms of 'specifications' of the objectives, as to what a learner will be able to do, to demonstrate that s/he has realised the objective in question.

7.6.3 *Content Analysis*

The content analysis given in a teaching unit as mentioned earlier should not merely reproduce the content given in the textbooks. It should unfold details more vividly and in the correct perspective, which will make teaching graphic and powerful. It may contain extracts from original sources or enriched materials which may not be within the easy reach of the teacher. The content may even contain materials not necessarily falling within the precise preview of specific major ideas, but which may provide appropriate links in the continuity of its sequence or in supporting it.

Major ideas, which are, in a way, basic concepts come to be the basic learning points, which are supposed to be internalised by the learners while some peripheral things could be permitted to be forgotton. Some examples of 'Major Ideas' in social sciences are given here under:

- Ashoka's administration symbolised a centralised monarchy.
- Raja Rammohan Roy brought modernity to Indian education.
- A citizen has both rights and duties.
- Industrialisation has brought problems in its wake.
- Early civilisations grew in river beds.
- Scientific developments have not always been for the good of mankind.

The content should also be regularly reviewed and revised to be authentic and up-to-date. If it deals with controversial issues, it should present the different conflicting view points objectively. If it has a generalisation, it should be fully substantiated by supporting data. The content ought to err on the side of comprehensiveness rather than on that of too much simplification or generalised form of global presentation.

7.6.4 *Teaching Hints and Activities*

Instruction in order to be effective must be objective-based and center round *activities*. These activities should be purposeful. They should flow out of the content aimed at the realisation of objectives. Suggestions in this regard must be specific and in the context of the subject-matter. They should necessarily outline the process of instruction, the teacher's role as also the learner's activities and the approaches to their execution. If discussion is suggested, the stages of its actual conduct and various possible questions and issues to be deliberated upon, ought to be broadly indicated. The hints to teachers should be specific. Assignments projects, surveys whenever suggested need also be broadly outlined. They should be creative and not routine and repetitive.

7.6.5 *Evaluation of Competencies*

Evaluation is an integral part of instruction. It has to be continuous and built into the total teaching-learning process. It ought to be objective-based and comprehensive covering both scholastic and non-co-scholastic aspects of learners growth. It should also be valid (accurate) reliable (dependable), objective (just), and practicable (feasible). The questions should not merely test memory. Teacher's mastery of the subject-matter and about the rules for framing different forms of question and other tools of evaluation however, is essential for framing questions properly. In evaluation various procedures and tools of evaluation should be utilised in a bid to fully realise the instructional objectives, in the *Cognitive, Affective* and *Psycho-motor domains*.

7.6.6 *Reference Material*

This section of a teaching unit should indicate the reference material including books which the teachers/learners may consult on the topic. The list should not be unduly ambitious. It should be complete—containing full specifications of authorship and publishers, year of publication, edition, relevant chapters, pages etc. for being easy to be accessed.

7.7 Conclusion

To conclude, it may be said that enrichment of instruction for improved learning will remain a vague slogan until we impart to our teachers greater competence and mastery in the use of instructional materials through *pre-service and in-service teacher-education programmes*. Development and supply of skillfully prepared teaching units is an important step in this direction.

Objective-based evaluation and objective-based instruction are the two sides of the same coin. Preparation of good teaching units needs the cooperation of the teacher, the pedagogue, the subject expert and the evaluator and this ought to be solicited in letter and spirit.

A diagramatic representation of objective-based instruction is given in Diagram 8.5.

7.9 Objective-based Instruction: A Diagramatic Representation

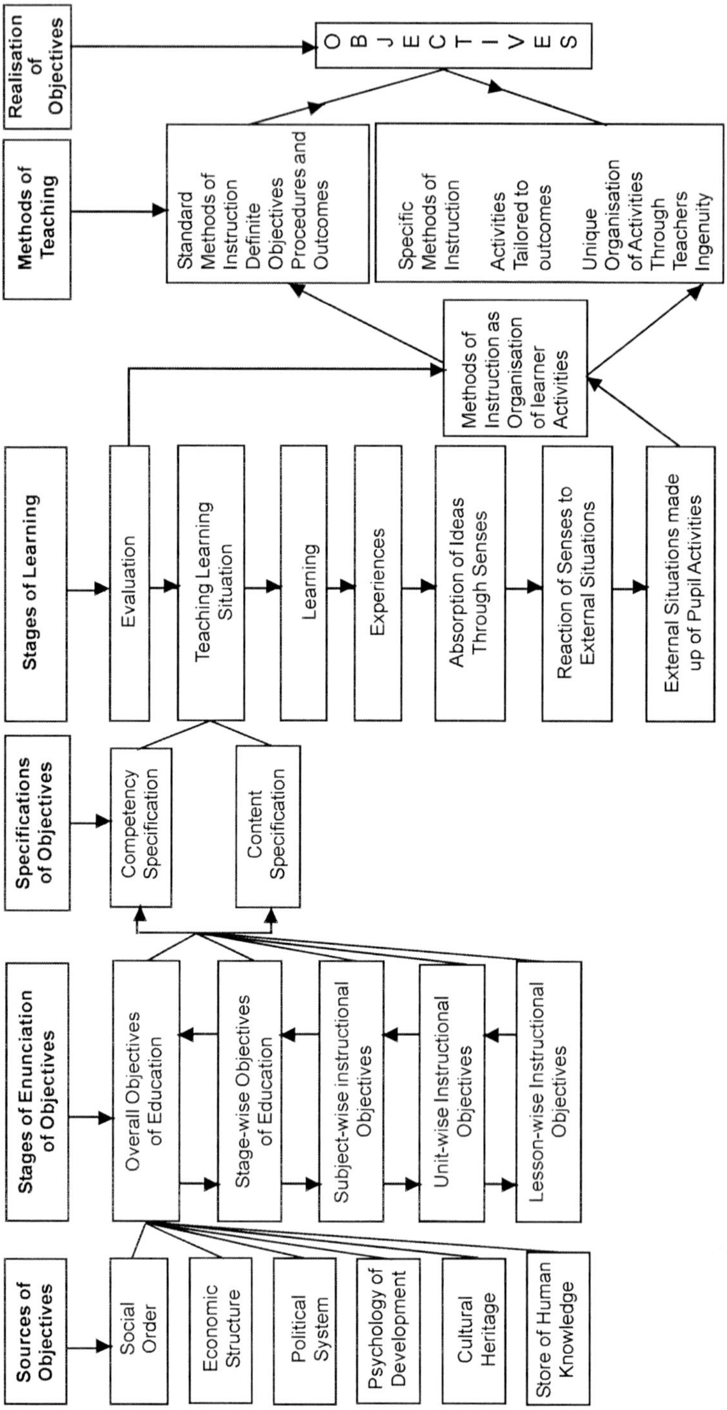

Diagram 8.5

8

The Concept of 'Prep Index'

An Approach for Quantifying Qualitative Outcomes of Education
(Example: Evaluation of Instructional Effectiveness)

8.1 The Need

Educational evaluation is a process of estimating and appraising the degree and dimension of achievement and abilities.

Evaluation of educational practices is a process of estimating and appraising the proficiency of educationists in conducting educational programmes. In other words, it is a process of appraising the application of educational postulates into practice.

In some situations the outcomes of education are available only in qualitative terms and the outcomes of evaluation are expected in quantitative terms particularly for purposes of rating grading or classification. To get over this problem an approach is being proposed and suggested here for quantifying qualitative outcomes of education.

8.2 Scope of Evaluation of Educational Practices

Educational practices and the activities can be broadly classified as under:

- Curricular activities related to the subjects of instruction, which are organised with a view to achieving the objectives of the cognitive domain.
- Activities related to the co-scholastic areas or those related to the other educational programmes and practices. The purpose of organising these activities is to ensure those aspects of pupils' growth, which though important goals of the instructional programme, cannot be achieved through the teaching and learning of subjects alone. These could relate to the affective and psycho-motor domains of human development.
- Activities related to diagnosis, prognosis, review, motivation, guidance, evaluation etc. The very title of each of these activities itself explains the purpose and importance of their position in the curriculum.

8.3 Purpose of Evaluating Educational Practices

There may be several purposes or functions for which the evaluation of educational practices may be taken up. The area of *Teacher Proficiency* is being selected here to illustrate the proposed approach. Three *purposes of Teacher Education Programmes* are being stated here by way of an example:

- To discover the degree of competence developed by the teacher in initiating, organising and improving the educational practices and to diagnose the strengths and weakness of learners for further guidance.
- To make a suggestion about the likely educational practices which a particular teacher can best organise as a regular teacher in a school.
- To certify the teacher competencies about the level of his proficiency in initiating and organising a particular educational practice.

8.4 Methodology of Evaluating Educational Practices

Objectives

A good Teacher Appraisal Programme attempts to find out the degree of proficiency attained by the teachers in the various programmes and practices incorporated in the various programmes of the institution. It is, therefore, essential at the outset to identify the most prominent of teacher competencies to be subjected to evaluation, these are lasted below:

- An understanding of the subject to be taught, the objectives of teaching it and the methods and techniques best suited for teaching it.
- Familiarity with the different philosophies of education and to acquire the ability of evolving a sound philosophy of his own.
- An understanding of the different aspects of pupils' development and behaviour and the factors related to them.
- An experimental attitude towards teaching and faith in the teaching profession.
- A motivation for one's professional growth.
- Acquisition of skills in planning and executing teaching-learning activities through observation, and actual teaching under observation/ supervision.
- Familiarisation with the salient features and problems of Indian education with reference to the different stages of general education, i.e., primary, secondary, university or professional education.
- Ability to organise activities related to both scholastic and co-scholastic

areas as also other programmes and practices.

- Acquisition of the knowledge of evaluation procedures and the ability of developing and administering tools for evaluating pupil behaviour continuously, comprehensively and for applying measures for improvement.

The above illustrative list can be further elaborated and some additions can surely be made to it.

Evidences

In order to evaluate teacher competencies it is necessary to collect evidences about the professional growth of the individual teacher in relation to the objectives. For this purpose a teacher will have to consider issues such as the following:

- What techniques and tools should be employed for evaluating different abilities in a given situation.
- What method should be used for obtaining evidences so that a variety of expected educational outcomes can be incorporated in the scheme of evaluation. This would also involve the sampling of situations.
- How much time should be spent on each task.

Taking the illustration further *to the specific area of classroom teaching*, it could be said that this area of evaluation comprises the following aspects for evaluation.

- Class management:
- Pupils' co-operation
- Teacher's expression
- Teacher's subject-matter competence
- Activities incorporated in the instructional programme.
- Use of aids
- Evaluation.

These aspects of evaluation should be very clearly specified. Their enumeration should cover the entire gamut of the subject. They ought also help him in locating the most adequate tool for the assessment of each of the aspects. This would also imply the use of a variety of tools as the same tool may not prove to be effective for evaluating all the aspects of each area.

Developing Evaluative Criteria

For each aspect of evaluation detailed out, it will be necessary to develop evaluative criteria to make the assessment specific and accurate.

Taking the point still further, it could be said that if *subject matter competence* of the teacher is taken as an aspect of evaluation, its evaluative criteria could be:

- Correctness
- Relevance and
- Richness

It will then be in respect of each of each of these evaluative criteria that the degree of proficiency of a teacher will be judged.

Collection of Evidence

After having developed the evaluative criteria for each area of evaluation, the next natural step will be the collection of evidences for evaluation on the basis of the identified criteria.

One of the most common techniques for the collection of evidences in the present situation will be *planned observation*. Other possible techniques could be interview, assessment of records of the process of execution and the outcome. In order to be able to collect usable evidences, it will be necessary to select or develop appropriate tools.

Taking the illustration still further it could be said that if subject matter competence is the aspect to be evaluated and if its correctness, relevance and richness are the criteria for evaluating it, the evidences could normally be collected from the following sources:

- Lesson plans for evaluating the degree and kind of preparation made by the teacher for teaching the particular lesson.
- Performance in actual teaching situations.

Evidences so obtained could be summarised in qualitative or quantitative terms. Qualitative evaluation based on the summarisation and interpretation of the evidence collected, is quite common. It can be obtained from the study of the lesson notes, the observation of lessons and the prepared teaching aids.

Evaluation in qualitative terms is not only possible but is also likely to prove of greater practical utility though it is not usually attempted probably because of the natural resistance to change. But in view of its scientific foundation, *a quantitative assessment of proficiency in educational practice based on qualitative evidences is likely to yield a more commonly acceptable measure*. It will also make comparisons possible and easier to make. Such a conversion of qualitative evidences into quantitative indices has, however, to be based on a scientific basis.

Summarisation of Data

Summarisation of data—So that the data collected could be used for educational ends, it is necessary that it may be appropriately summarised and interpreted.

Summarisation of data as already mentioned could either be in qualitative or quantitative terms. In qualitative terms it could focus on a particular individual aspect in respect of a specific ability. In quantitative terms, it could be summarised through a tool like a *rating scale* on which ratings could be awarded to different individuals for the degree of their accomplishment in a particular aspect of evaluation.

8.5 PREP Index and its Derivation

How a quantitative measure of a qualitative outcome could be obtained is illustrated below. The proposed tool is a Rating Scale. The following description further stretches the example of subject matter competence of a teacher already enunciated earlier.

A nine-point rating scale with five points defined is devised for evaluating each of the aspects on the basis of the abilities assessed on identified evaluative criteria. The following is an illustration of such a scale developed for assessing subject matter competence.

8. – Fully correct, completely relevant and very rich

7.

6. – Rare evidences of incorrectness or irrelevance and richness

5.

4. – Usually correct and relevant and moderately rich

3.

2. – Several evidences of incorrectness and irrelevance and poor content

1.

0. – Mostly incorrect, irrelevant and very poor content

Such scales will need to be devised for all specified aspects of evaluation. The ratings on these scales could then be translated into a profile. Thus while evaluating a complete lesson suppose it is found that particular teacher has been rated as follows on nine-point rating scale for in respect of different aspects;

Class Management	5
Pupil's Co-operation	3
Expression	4
Subject matter competence	7
Activitics incorporated	5
Use of aids	3
Evaluation	4

These ratings could then be translated into a profile like the one given below :

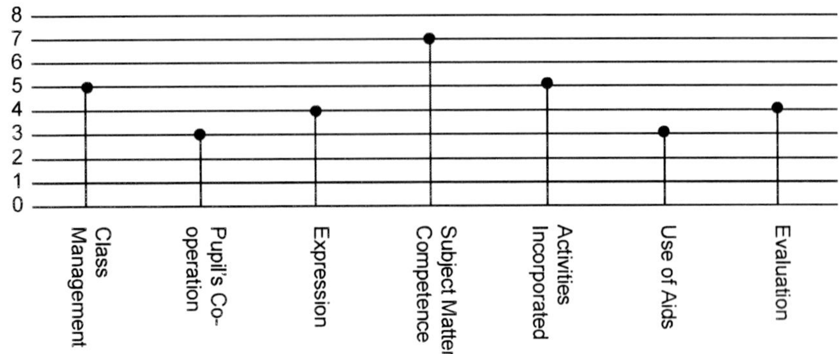

Such profiles will prove to be of very great help not only to the evaluator but also to the teacher himself for making his own self-evaluation. Giving profiles from time to time, will enable the teacher to judge for himself, his own strengths and weaknesses in specific aspects of evaluation and the progress that he may have made between one point of time and another in respect of each one of them individually.

The representation on these profiles could as well be quantified by the following method to arrive at the *Index of Proficiency in Educational Practice* (PREP Index)

Suppose there are 75 marks in all out of which teacher has to be evaluated and the different weightages to each of the aspects of evaluation are as given in the table as follows. Suppose also that on each of these aspects of evaluation the respective scores obtained out of eight (the points 0-8 on the scale), are also as indicated in the table, the PREP INDEX will be calculated as follows:

S. No.	*Aspects of Evaluation*	*Weightage to Aspects*	*Scores on the Rating Scales*	*Weighted Scores*
1.	Class Management	10	5	50
2.	Pupil Co-operation	5	3	15
3.	Expression	20	4	80
4.	Subject-matter Competence	10	7	70
5.	Activities incorporated	10	5	50
6.	Use of aids	10	3	30
7.	Evaluation	10	4	40
	Total	75	31	335

Total of weighted scores $= 50+15+80+70+50+30+40 = 335$

Maximum scores out of which the total weighted scores have been obtained $= 8 \times 75$

(8 being the maximum point of scales and 75 the total weightage to all the aspects of the particular area of evaluation)

$= 600$

Score = 335/600

PREP INDEX = 335/600 × 100 = 55.83

Thus 55.83 is the Prep Index of the particular teacher in regard to teaching competency.

In the same manner as explained above, *'Prep Index' or the Index of Proficiency (PR) in Educational (E) Practice (P)* could be calculated for each aspect of evaluation and will help the evaluator in the different ways in which this data can be used.

8.6 Use of Evaluation Data

Evaluation data, as we know, could be either qualitative or quantitative. Both these forms of data can be used for a variety of purposes. These are:

Diagnosis

Educational practices are incorporated in institutional programmes with a view to achieving some well defined educational objectives. The achievement of these objectives leads to learner growth in desirable directions, in organising the various school programmes and in conducting educational practices, to ensure pupil growth as enunciated through the objectives. The degree to which he is successful also needs to be evaluated. The primary purpose is to identify the strengths and weaknesses of a particular teacher so as to guide him in making better progress and in achieving higher successes.

Self-Evaluation and Guidance

Evaluation of educational practices, particularly in regard to the development of profiles and derivation of the *Prep Index*, in respect of each aspect of evaluation for a particular teacher, serves another very important purpose of self-evaluation and self-guidance. This also provides him motivation for achieving better success on subsequent occasions.

The evaluator also finds himself on a better footing in assessing the teacher on the basis of the evaluation data referred to above and not on any conjectures. As the evaluator would specifically know a particular teacher's hard sports, he can be more precise and more effective in giving him guidance.

Certification

Certification in regard to the degree of competence achieved by him in different areas of evaluation is also one of the most important functions of evaluation data. The derivation of the PREP INDEX will again prove to be of a more valid measure of proficiency than the arbitrary assessments based on vague perceptions which are very often attempted. Certification on the basis of this data will not only be more valid and reliable but also more meaningful to the employer for being used for different purposes.

Prediction

The evaluation data could also be used for the purpose of prediction as to what a particular teacher is capable of accomplishing.

8.7 Conclusion

Evaluation of educational practices used to be mostly undertaken in the past in an arbitrary manner, endangering both the reliability and validity of the measurements. The development of a Methodology for Evaluating Educational Practices has therefore been a long felt need. The fore-going discussion is an attempt at 'developing' such a methodology which could be applied to all educational practices and even in other disciplines Evaluation done on the basis of such a methodology will, it is hoped, yield data which will be more authentic, specific and meaningful than the one arrived at through the usual arbitrary conclusions of a few individuals who may find it difficult to overcome their biases while making assessments.

This could as well be a valuable approach for assessing practice-teaching lessons in teacher's colleges. The format of the profile could be printed in a corner of each page of the criticism book and the faculty members observing the lesson could just put in the dots and the learner teacher may then calculate the Prep Index. This may be in addition to the written observations.

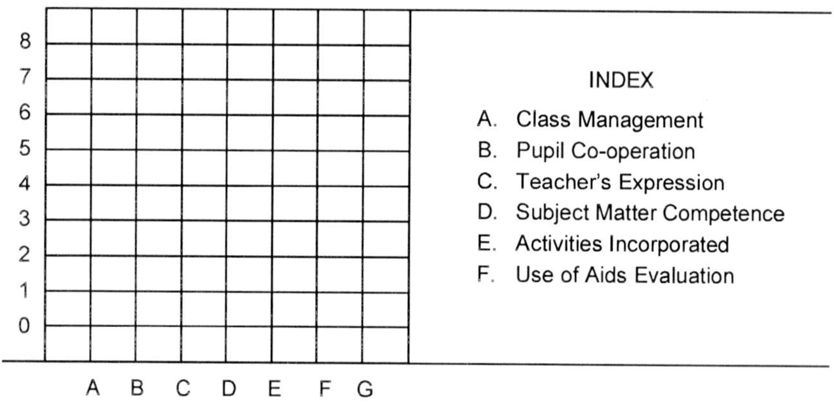

PREP INDEXs

The final annual index could also then be calculated on this basis and become a valid source for making a conclusion, about the final grade of the learner teacher for the examination.

Adapted from the chapter contributed by Dr. R.H. Dave & Dr. H.S. Srivastava for "Evaluating Teacher Effectiveness" brought out by the ETS, Princeton (New Jersey), U.S.A.

8.8 Methodology of Evaluating Educational Practices—Graphical Presentation of Steps

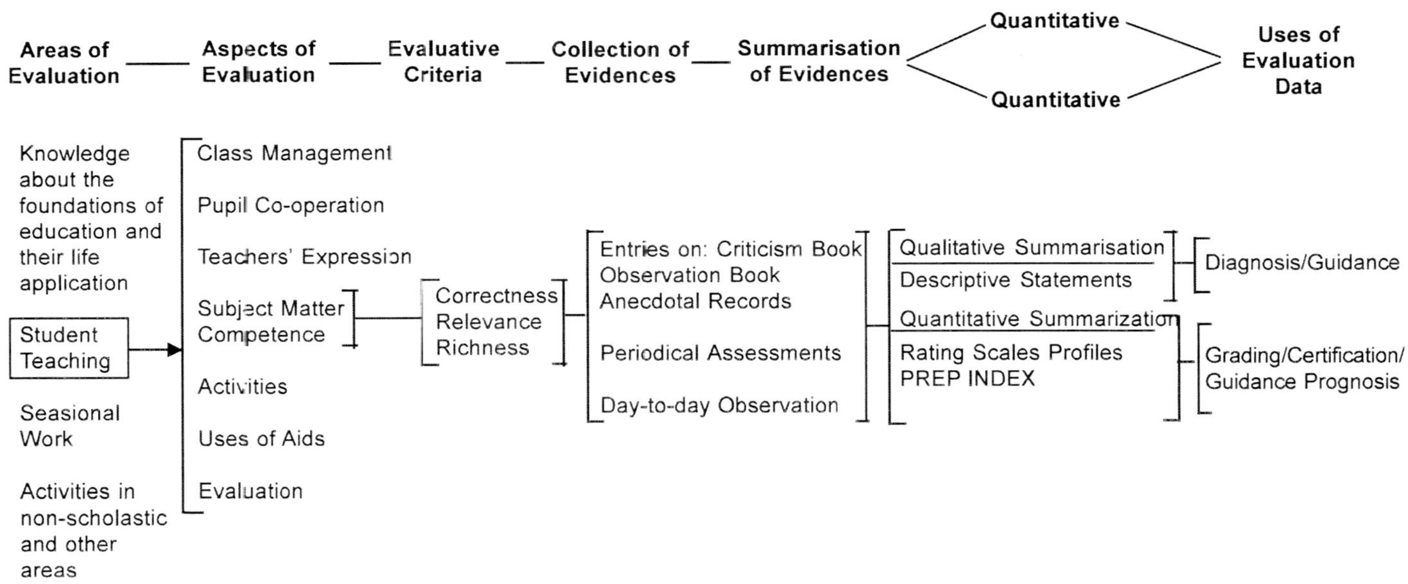

* Selected as illustration for explaining different steps of the methodology

Diagram 8.1

9

Determining and Designing Course Contents

Determining and designing of course content cannot be an adhoc affair based on biases and opinions. It has but to be a logical systematic venture.

9.1 Steps in the Development of Course Contents

The main elements of curriculum development can be represented through the following diagram:

Guiding Philosophy
↓
Course Objectives
↓
Course Framework
↓
Course Material
↓
Instructional Methodology
↓
Support Material
↓
Evaluation

9.2 Manifestation of Course Content

Course content in the above context, is part of "Course Framework" which translates the courses in specific terms giving:

- level/class at which the course is to be pitched.
- graded – with correspondence and alignment with what has gone before and what has to follow subsequently in the subject concerned.

- outline of the subject matter in the depth and detail in which desired to be pursued.
- time budget (both for teaching and learning).
- Instructional methodology desired/possible to be pressed into service along with a list of possible activities from which the teacher could choose like projects, surveys, exploration, experimentation etc.
- recapitulatory questions/or end-of-the-topic-tests.
- consolidation/enrichment exercises internet references etc.

Thus in nut shell the course content is not just a list of topics and subtopics to be covered (taught and learnt).

Course content, as enunciated above is determined and delimited by History, Geography, Economy, Politics, latest developments in the field, level of scientific and technological input, business and industrial policies, standard of education, time available.

9.3 Instructional Considerations for Detailing Contents

While detecting course content it proves facilitating for both the teachers and the learners if while listing possible activities, it is also indicated whether a particular activity is likely to be more educative if it is pursued—

- as a group or an individual activity
- inside the school/class room or outside
- as a theoretical and or practical exercise
- with conventional or unconventional approaches.

9.4 Treatment of Different Aspects of Content

It will be important to also indicate whether a particular activity has to be—

- only technology transacted
- just technology assisted
- only teacher transacted

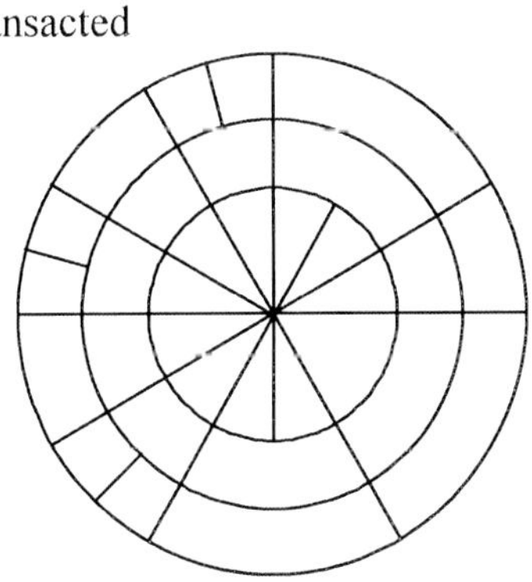

It also needs to be appreciated that the content from one level to another normally follows a *concentric approach* where at each higher level the same theme is dealt in greater depth and detail at subsequent levels, addition and deletion of themes is also witnessed in subsequent levels. Furthermore, in each subsequent level, there could also be branching of course content as well.

In the progression of content from one class to another the possibilities of integration among different subject is consciously and deliberately pursued.

9.5 Salient Features of Course Content

Apart from differences all the courses are expected to demonstrate some fundamental characteristics like

- unity
- balance
- gradation
- coherence
- logical continuity
- increasing complexity/difficulty of competency

9.6 Distance Education – A Gap-Filling Mode

Courses for the Distance Education mode ought to display a slow and a steady pace. There will need to be stock-taking at each step and revision exercises punctuate the learning process. Attention capturing pithy statements which the learners would be able to retain easily shall prove very helpful. Supplementing learning reinforcement exercises will help realise the objectives more easily and fast.

Introduction of client friendly innovations like the *"on demand examinations"* do deserve attention. Effort for making the system more scientific and fool proof will no doubt be necessary. *Computer generation of parallel question* papers is the most crucial aspect in this regard. In this context it has also become necessary to provide vocational courses; through the distance education mode particularly those that lead to equipping individual for self-employment.

9.7 Warding Off Conceptual Confusions

It is quite a common phenomenon that people use technical words catch-words and slogans. Only a couple of examples can prove the fallacies of such instances.

Among these 'semester system' is one. It is a course covered within half of an academic session and this is where it gets its name from. *A semester course however is a coherent unit with an independent identity.* A semester course is one of the many available to be chosen from by the learner. Invariably a semester course carries credits depending on its extensive and intensive dimensions in regard to the work-inputs expected to be inverted as given below.

1 hour per week per semester of class work – 1 credit
2 hours per week per semester of lab-work, project work, library work, survey work etc. – 1 credit

The credits are possible to be earned over a period of time and kept by the learner as *a bank balance*. When a number of credits earned gets to be equal to those required for a degree or a diploma, the learner can claim that degree from the qualification awarding examining agency. While the above is the technical meaning of a semester course, in some places a years prescribed course is divided into two parts and each one is called a semester course. These courses are subjected to the same treatment as the traditional courses except the name. The examinations too are of the same old fashioned type and there is no concept of earning of credits.

One other such concept is that of "Comprehensive and Continuous School-based Evaluation" (CCE) which emerged as a rebellion to the concept of "Internal Assessment" where a certain percentage of the total marks were allocated for the school to award from say 20% for work and attainments in school. The marks awarded out of this allocation were arithmetically added to the marks obtained by a learner out of 80% marks in the external examinations. The well-intentional proposal mooted in good faith, soon started being misused at unscrupulous hands for boosting marks and was withdrawn one by one from wherever it was introduced.

The concept of CCE that then emerged was that of school-based examination be not just limited to academic areas but extended to the coverage of co-scholastic areas as well, which though important for success in life were not possible to be covered through external examinations. Furthermore, as both external examinations and school-based evaluation tested different things, *a separate independent certificate of CCE as a supplement to that of external examinations was mooted.* This certificate was supposed to be issued by the schools on a format prescribed by the Board. Above all the Certificate of Board Examination in this instance was supposed to carry a footnote that the school certificate be also studied for judging the total personality of the learner.

It needs to be specially mentioned in this regard that academic achievement is the only common area evaluated by both the school, and the Boards, but even in this the external examinations test it through question papers and school evaluation through projects, surveys, assignments etc. With the abilities tested being substantially different in the two cases the results of the two do not admit any logical justification for being added, as is often done in some places.

10

Some Insights into Curriculum Transaction

While there are a number of well-known theories of teaching and learning and well established conventional and un-conventional methodologies of instruction, they can be implemented better through a general understanding of pedagogy, psychology and technology.

10.1 A Operational Definition of Education

Education in the life-long perspective, is a process of human transformation in respect of:

- human enablement
- human empowerment and
- human enrichment

for the attainment of a better and a higher quality of life. Better quality of life deals with the external universe and a higher quality of life with the internal universe. The two could also be called "material" and spiritual".

10.2 Challenges of Education

In this context, the challenges of education are:

- modernisation
- globalisation
- technologisation
- professionalisation
- Indianisation

All these have to be conceived in terms of—

- a global perspective and
- a local perception

While transacting the curriculum we also need to appreciate that *while over the time "facts" to be transacted have increased, "concepts" have not.*

The compelling demands for the development of competencies related to employability and entrepreneurship have also necessitated the reduction of attention and work load on theoretical aspects and increase on practical aspects. In this regard, the practice of soliciting *community support* has also to yield place to *community involvement* in the designing of content and process of education.

10.3 Vocational Facet of Education

We have also, therefore, to think of developing not just the academic but more so personal, social and vocational abilities/proficiencies traversing the sequential stages of

- vocational awareness
- vocational orientation
- vocational training
- specialised training

aimed at *learning to learn* and finally *learning to earn.*

10.4 Types of Interaction in Teaching and Learning

Yet another focus will need to be on the nature and kind of interaction involved in the teaching-learning process where our methodologies may be imbued by two-way interactions. The *teacher-learner interaction* is normally a one way interaction where learner concentration is minimal. The *learner-learner interaction* has a higher degree of learner concentration. But when the *individual interacts with himself* the level of concentration is maximum. We must therefore make our methodologies a judicious mix of teacher-learner, learner-learner and learner-self interactions.

We will also, therefore, be called upon to demonstrate an outstanding kind and degree of both foresight and insight because *planning needs foresight and implementation needs insight*.

10.5 Life Management Skills

In the entire process Life Management Skills of

- Time management
- Health management
- Stress management
- Financial management
- Environmental management

will have to occupy the central focus.

Gender equality, too, will need to be accepted appreciated and practised because *men and women are only different, not better and worse.*

Flexibility for adaptation will also have to be built into the methodologies as specific teacher-designed strategies will need to supplement the standard methods.

The activities incorporated will need to display adequate variety to incorporate

- Competition for progress and
- Cooperation for strength

10.6 Goals of Instructional Methodologies

To sum up the instructional methodologies are expected to be

- interest evoking
- imagination tickling
- curiosity arousing
- expectancy generating
- action triggering

11

Using Questions for Teaching

[*Some Examples Related to School Education*]

11.1 Introduction

Teaching and testing are two basic components of every instructional programme. They are dovetailed to the instructional objectives which provide directions for both. *Teaching is the criterion behaviour against which testing is validated.* Testing on the other hand also validates the whole teaching-learning process by providing relevant evidences about the degree of its effectiveness in realising the objectives. Thus teaching and testing not only motivate learners' learning, but can also be used as instruments of effective instruction, and its further reinforcement through a built-in feed-back mechanism.

Questions are mainly used for testing the achievement of learners. At the same time it is not unusual to find learners solving the question papers of previous years before the examination. As the questions in traditional public examinations used to be generally repeated and tested rote learning, learners memorised answers to expected questions in order to pass the examinations. In this chapter an attempt is made to highlight the *role of questions in classroom instruction*. Examples from some selected subjects of the curriculum have been taken to indicate the objective, specification, topic, problem, assumed previous knowledge, teachers' activities, pupils' activities and some other additional tasks. The teacher should ensure that he prepares his learners adequately for this type of questions by suitably adapting his teaching. The test items presented in regard to different subjects will give them an indication of how he may shift the emphasis in teaching-learning procedures from rote memorisation to real internalisation of learning.

Every teacher should however keep in view specific instructional objectives while teaching and testing, which should go hand in hand. Test items are normally used for determining the attainment levels of learners. While using any such item in the classroom, the teacher himself should be very clear about the objective on which it is based, and also about the kind of expected learning outcomes. This will make him look back to the knowledge already imparted and also to fill-in the gaps in learning. In the light of these gaps he can reinforce his teaching for improved learning on the part of learners.

Use of question is one of the means the teacher can profitably use in classroom situations. However, it must be borne in mind that testing in this context is only a supplement and not a substitute for teaching.

Some Examples

Some examples in different subjects on this unfamiliar theme were developed by the then Examination Reform Unit of the NCERT way back in 1977. A few of these have been summarised and are being presented here.

11.2 English

Topic

The Happy Prince: (Author: Oscar Wilde)

Question

If God had asked His Angel to bring only one most precious thing from the city instead of two, what would he have brought? Give reasons. Your answer should be limited to about 100 words.

Objective

- The learner reads the story entitled 'The Happy Prince' with comprehension.
- The learner writes answers to questions based on the text correctly and effectively.

Specific Learning Outcomes

In respect of the above story:

◆ *Comprehension*

The Learner:

- locates important events, facts and ideas.
- reads between the lines.
- identifies relationship between objects and events.
- critically examines and evaluates events, actions, ideas, and feelings in the light of their outcomes.

◆ *Expression*

The Learner:

- uses appropriate vocabulary and structures.
- culls and presents only relevant ideas and facts in logical order.
- avoids unnecessary repetition.

- organises ideas, facts, etc. appropriately into paragraphs and other forms of presentation.
- displays imagination in writing.

Previous Knowledge

For being able to answer the above question, it is assumed that the learners are:

- thoroughly acquainted with the story 'The Happy Prince'.
- acquainted with various events that occur in the story.
- able to appreciate the values of love, sacrifice, and service.
- able to organise their ideas and thoughts in a logical order.

Teaching-Learning Activities

- The learners will be asked to read the story 'The Happy Prince' silently in the class.
- They will then be asked the above questions.
- They will be guided to identify significant events in the story.
- The likely reasons for bringing the two possible objects by the Angel will be discussed in the class.
- The learners will debate on the significance of the two possible alternative decisions on the part of the Angels.
- The learners will critically examine and evaluate both the possibilities and reach their own conclusions.
- The teacher will guide them in substantiating their respective points with examples from the story.
- The teacher will help the learners in expressing their ideas effectively.
- The teacher will help them in arranging and organising details in a logical sequence and coherent presentation so that the answer becomes effective.
- The learners will then write the answers to the above question.

Follow-up Activities

The teacher may plan to undertake one or more of the following activities:

- The teacher, while correcting the answers, should note their mistakes and discuss them in the class.
- He may ask the learners to write an imaginary incident in which the little swallow again helps the 'Happy Prince' in his service to humanity, in the event of the lives of both of them restored to them.

11.3 Physics

Topic

Relative Density-Law of Floating Bodies

Question

A cork weighing 10 grams can just sink into water. When a load of 40 grams is placed over it. What will be the relative density of the cork?

Objective

The learners apply their knowledge of law of floating bodies, in the current hypothetical situation.

Specific Learning Outcomes

The learner:

- analyses the situation to identify the principle underlying in the given problems.
- makes some hypothesis regarding laws of floating bodies etc.
- establishes relationship between mass of displaced water and the cork with the load placed on it.
- predicts the effect of increase or decrease in load placed on the cork.

Previous Knowledge

- Definitions of density and relative density.
- Archimedes' principle.
- Density of water is 1 gram/c.c.
- Mass = Volume × Density.

Teaching-Learning Activities

- The teacher presents the problem listed above after teaching and experimentally demonstrating Archimedes' principle, laws of floating bodies etc.
- The learners try to understand the problem, analyse it and try to know what is given and what is required.
- The teacher helps the learners to analyse the problem further and formulates the following hypotheses:
  - (i) The weight of the floating body is equal to the upward thrust of the liquid.
  - (ii) The volume of the displaced water is equal to that of the body inside water.
  - (iii) The upward thrust is equal to the weight of water displaced.
- On the basis of the above hypotheses, the learners find that the mass of water displaced is equal to the total mass of the cork and the load placed on it i.e. (10 + 40) gms. = 50 gms. Hence, the volume of the displaced water = 50 c.c. which is, therefore, the volume of the cork. The learners finally find that the relative density of the cork = 10/50 gm/cc. = 0.2 gm/c.c.
- The teacher asks the learners as to what will happen if more load is placed on the cork.

- The learners will on their own find that since the mass of the body is greater than that of the displaced water, the body cannot float, but will sink completely.
- The teacher asks a further question of the learners as to what will happen if a weight less than 40 gms. is placed on the cork.
- The learners argue that in above case the weight of the body (cork) being less than that of the displaced water, the body will float and some portion of the body will be above water.
- The teacher advises the learners to remember that Archimedes' principle cannot be applied if the liquid is not in equilibrium.

Follow-up Activities

The pupils:

- arrange the experiment to get the results checked and comment on arrangements made by other friends.
- prepare similar questions taking other factors as unknown: volume, mass etc.
- comment on questions prepared by friends. For example, if the problem is to find the relative density of the load put over the cork, then it cannot be solved.
- prepare similar questions taking a liquid other than water and then realise that the one additional data viz. the density of the liquid is needed to solve the problem.
- try to solve similar types of more complicated problems like a situation when the cork is immersed in a mixture of two liquids whose densities are known.

11.4 Chemistry

Topic

Halogens and Halides – Preparation of Hydrogen Bromide Gas

Question

Sodium Chloride reacts with: 'Concentrated Sulphuric acid to give (HCl) Hydrogen Chloride gas but Sodium Bromide does not give (HBr) Hydrogen Bromide gas under similar conditions'—Give reasons for this behaviour.

Objective

The learner applies his knowledge of properties of halogens to the given unfamiliar situation.

Specific Learning Outcomes

The pupil:

- analyses the given unfamiliar situation regarding the behaviour of Sodium Chloride and Sodium Bromide towards concentrated Sulphuric acid.
- establishes the causes and effects of such a dissimilar behaviour of Sodium Chloride and Sodium Bromide.

- makes all possible types of interpretation for such a behaviour of Sodium Chloride and Sodium Bromide.
- tests all possible interpretations.
- draws correct conclusion regarding the behaviour of NaBr towards concentrated H_2SO_4.

Previous Knowledge

- All metallic chlorides on being heated with concentrated Sulphuric acid liberate Hydrogen Chloride gas.
- Sulphuric acid is an oxidising agent.
- Chlorine is a gas, bromine a liquid and Iodine a solid at room temperature.
- Bromine and Iodine vapours on being passed through water yield brownish and violet brownish solutions respectively.
- The colour of bromine vapour is reddish brown and that of Iodine vapour is violet.

Teaching-Learning Activities

The teacher poses the problem and demonstrates the effect of heating.

- A mixture of concentrated Sulphuric acid and solid Sodium bromide in a boiling tube and passing the evolved gas into water.
- A mixture of concentrated Sulphuric acid and solid Sodium chloride and passing the evolved gas into water.

The pupil observes the two experiments demonstrated by the teacher.

The teacher helps the learners to write the chemical equations of the experiments demonstrated by him and interpret the difference in reactions of Sodium chloride and Sodium bromide with conc. Sulphuric acid.

The pupil writes the chemical equations of the reactions involved in the demonstrated experiment as:

$NaCl + H_2SO_4 = NaHSO_4 + HCl$ .... (1)

$NaCl + NaHSO_4 = Na_2SO_4 + HCl$ .... (2)

$2NaCl + H_2SO_4 = Na_2HSO_4 + 2HCl$ (by addition of (1) and (2))

$NaBr + H_2SO_4 = NaHSO_4 + HBr$ ...... (1)

$NaBr + NaHSO_4 = Na_2SO_4 + HBr$ ...... (2)

$2HBr + H_2SO_4 = 2H_2O + SO_2 + Br_2$ ...... (3)

$2NaBr + 2H_2SO_4 = Na_2SO_4 + 2H_2O + SO_2 + Br_2$ (By addition of (1), (2) and (3))

The teacher helps the learner to recall the information for the identification of gases evolved in the experiments.

The pupil hypothesises and gives all types of alternatives:

- Sulphuric acid may be impure (a)
- Sodium bromide may be impure (b)

- HBr may decompose at room temperature (c)
- HBr may react with Conc, H_2SO_4. (d)

Drawing correct conclusion by discussion of the four hypothesis marked a, b, c and d above.

- The teacher displays Analar H_2SO_4 bottle marked with all analysis data and certificate of its purity to convince the learners that H_2SO_4 was not impure and the learners discard the hypothesis (a).
- The teacher displays Analar NaBr bottle marked with all analysis data and certificate of purity to convince the learners that NaBr was not impure and they discard the hypothesis (b).
- The teacher conveys to the learners that HBr is unstable at room temperature and its due to this that HBr is not kept in laboratory because it will decompose. The learners agree and draw conclusion as in hypothesis (c).
- The teacher refers to equation # above and the learners come to the right conclusion that H_2SO_4 reacts with and oxidises HBr agreeing with the hypothesis (d).

Follow-up Activities

- The learners design experiments to ascertain the evolution of bromine by heating different bromides with concentrated Sulphuric acid.
- The pupils try to find similarities in the reactions of KI and KBr on heating with conc. H_2SO_4.

11.5 Biology

Content Unit

Levels of Organisation: (Concept of cell, tissue, organ and system)

The illustration given here deals with the concept of cell, tissue, organ and system. The question that follows is only one example of only one type which can be made use of in teaching as described below. The purpose is to emphasise and explore the possibility of using a question as a device of teaching. It is only through the discussion of relationships in each alternative that learners arrive at the correct answer and learn about the concepts involved.

Questions

The relationship between cell and tissue is almost similar to the relationship between:

A. ptyaline and starch.
B. liver and the gall bladder.
C. carbohydrate and fat.
D. ectoderm and endoderm.
E. organ and the system

Objective

The learner comprehends the concept of cell, tissue, organ and system with respect to human physiology.

Specific Learning Outcomes

The pupil:

- recalls different levels of organisation of life and recognises the structure of cell and of different tissues and organs of the digestive system.
- identifies relationship among cell, tissue, organ and the system.
- compares different units of life.
- cites examples of tissues, organs and the system.
- observes and interprets correctly the given diagram or a slide showing transverse section of some organs.
- draws inferences about the given or observed situations involving different types of relationship.

Previous Knowledge

Learners are already familiar with the following:

- The cell as the basic unit of all living organisms.
- Elementary idea of tissue.
- Elementary idea of digestive system.
- Proximal constituents of food.
- Structure of multicellular animals like coelenterates.

Teaching-Learning Activities

- The teacher poses the above problem in the class.
- He explains the relationship involved in the cell and tissue for further clarification. He helps the learners to recall that cell is the basic unit of life and the tissue is composed of a group of such cells. Therefore, cell is a component of the tissue which is a larger unit of life.
- Pupils study the problem, recall the structure and function of cells and tissues. They also try to identify relationship between the two concepts and may give different answers to the problem stated.
- The teacher analyses the responses; takes note of the various categories of answers and discusses each choice with the learners to enable them to establish relationship in each case. He educes with the help of learners that in alternative 'A' the relationship is that of an enzyme and the substance digested; in 'B' it is that of a production and a storage unit; in 'C' it is that of two constituent units or components of a common substance (food) while in 'D' the relationship is spatial, i.e., external and internal positions of an organ.
- Pupils make comparisons of the relationship between cell and tissue with each of the relationship observed in each of the cases A, B, C

and D and recognise that none of these relationships is similar to the one between cell and tissue.

- Pupils are especially asked to study the choice 'E' which may be the plausible answer in this case. They examine the functional relationship between organ and system.
- Pupils find out the different organs that go to make up a system just as cells go to make up a tissue. Thus they establish that the relationship between a cell and tissue is the same as between organs and the system thereby arriving at the correct choice.
- Teacher then asks pupils to interpret the relationship between tissues and the organ on the basis of relationship established by them between organ and system.
- Pupils interpret the overall relationship among cell, tissue, organ and system.
- Teacher then shows to the class different charts of animal and plant organs showing different tissues and cells comprising the tissues, for learners to observe and identify the various levels of organisation.

Activities in the practical class

Teacher guides the learners to open the viscera of the frog and helps them to:

- observe the various organs found inside the body of the frog.
- recognise some organs which form one system e.g. digestive system and see which organs combine together to form that system (digestive system in this case).
- examine the microprepared slide of the T.S. of one organ made up of various tissues (e.g. stomach).
- interpret the internal structure of the stomach and infer relationship between tissues and organs.
- In the prepared slide of T.S. of stomach, the learners examine one layer under the high power of the microscope and find out similar type of cells in the layer and draw inference that a group of similar cells form a tissue and tissues form the organ.

Follow-up Activities

- Pupils are asked to examine simple or isolated cells of an animal like Amoeba or a plant like Chlamydomonas.
- Pupils would examine a group of cells forming simple tissue, say in Hydra.
- Pupils may be asked to examine different tissues in an organ in any microprepared slide, say T.S. of intestine and report their observations regarding relationship between the two.
- Teacher suggests to his pupils to prepare a chart depicting a particular system of an animal as also the organs, tissues and cells separately indicating relationship among them.

- Learners are asked to discover and record other similar relationship that they might observe or locate from different sources.

11.6 History

Content Unit

Egyptian Civilisation

Question

Into which social classes was the ancient Egyptian society divided? In what manner does this social division differ from that of the caste system of ancient India?

Objective

The pupil develops an understanding of the basis of the social division of ancient Indian and ancient Egyptian societies and their characteristics.

Specific Learning Outcomes

The Pupil

- recalls
    - (a) the social, economic, cultural and political conditions of the two countries in ancient times that influenced their social order.
    - (b) the different social divisions of ancient Indian and ancient Egyptian societies.
- identifies
    - (a) the social hierarchies of each one of them, in both the societies.
    - (b) the similar and dissimilar features of the social divisions of the two societies and is able to substantiate the same through examples.
- critically examines and evaluates the strong and weak points of the two social divisions

Previous Knowledge

The pupil has already acquired the knowledge of the following:

- The conditions from which the two social orders emerged.
- The milieu in which the two civilisations flourished.
- The situations, conditions and the circumstances that led to the emergence of the two social systems.
- Social divisions in ancient Egyptian society and their characteristics.
- Social divisions in ancient Indian society and their characteristics.
- Difference and similarities between the social divisions of the two ancient civilisations.

Teaching-Learning Activities

A number of teaching-learning activities could be undertaken. A suggestive list out of which the teacher could choose from, are indicated below. The teacher should, however, feel free to press into service any other activities which he may deem desirable for realising the objectives.

The teacher divides the whole class into two groups, and initiates a discussion in the class on the related themes like:

- "Circumstances that were responsible for the emergence of the divisions in the ancient Egyptian and ancient Indian societies".
- "The basis of the class divisions in both ancient Egypt and ancient India and the purpose it served". The teacher corrects and supplements the information given by the groups.

The teacher organises a debate on the following issues like:

- In the opinion of this house the class division of ancient Indian society was more flexible than that of ancient Egyptian society.
- In the opinion of this house the permanent nature of the classification of ancient Egyptian society was an impediment to social cohesion.
- In the opinion of this house the social divisions both in the ancient Indian and ancient Egyptian societies were evils for which no advantage could be claimed.

The pupils locate with the help of the teacher the location and extent of the two ancient civilisations on the world map.

The teacher gives concluding remarks supplementing the information not given by the learners and penetrating deep into the heart of the problems to throw light on the salient features of the two societies.

The learners are also then encouraged to put questions to supplement their information. The questions could be first answered by the pupils from the class and then supplemented by the teacher.

Follow-up Activities

Group projects on ancient Indian and ancient Egyptian civilisations entitled "Greater India and Greater Egypt" could also then be undertaken by the learners.

The teacher suggests references to the pupils for further reading.

11.7 Geography

Content Unit

Geography of India: Climate (Monsoons)

Question

Compare and contrast the summer and winter monsoons in India with respect to their causes, direction of winds, duration and areas of occurrence.

Objective

The learners exhibit an understanding of the role of the monsoons.

Specific Learning Outcomes

The learner:

- discriminates between such terms as summer and winter monsoons. South-west and North-east monsoons. Advancing and retreating monsoons, in the two cases bursting of monsoons etc.
- interprets climatic data presented in different forms.
- analyses the effect of the northward shifting of the thermal zone in the summer season and its retreat in the winter season.
- compares the effect of the shifting thermal equator on the surface weather and conditions in the upper atmosphere.
- establishes relationship between temperature and pressure conditions in the atmosphere in summer and winter.
- establishes relationship between distribution of rainfall and various factors which affect their regional distribution.
- draws inferences about the sources of air-masses and direction of winds.
- selects relevant facts to explain the similarities and dissimilarities in weather and climate conditions in different parts of India.
- predicts weather conditions in different parts of the country during winter, summer and monsoon seasons.

Previous Knowledge

It is presumed that the learners already know the following:

- The latitudinal and longitudinal position of India.
- Major relief regions of India.
- Seasons.
- Distribution of summer and winter temperatures and its relationship with pressure systems prevailing in different regions.
- Relationship between pressure systems and wind systems.
- Ferrels law.
- Cyclones tropical and temperate.
- Seasonal and annual distribution of rainfall.

Teaching-Learning Activities

- Teacher illustrates with a relief map, rainfall map and temperature map of India, the temperature and pressure conditions of India in the different months, and the shifting of the centres of low pressure pockets.
- Learners observe the facts and explain the changes in wind direction in relation to the occurrence of the monsoons.
- Teacher poses the problems of the vagaries of rainfall distribution in the country in all seasons and explains the relationship between intensity of low pressure and 'bursting of monsoons' and the march of the monsoon winds in the country.

- Learners identify on maps regions of heaviest rainfall in the different months and explain the real difference in occurrence of rains from June to September on the west coast and October to March on the east coast.
- The teacher highlights the phenomena of 'reversal' or 'retreat' of monsoon conditions and its relationship to distribution of temperature and pressure conditions. Thus the classification of monsoon winds as summer and winter, wet and dry or North-east and South-west is explained.
- Learners identify from a world climatic regions map the other areas which experience monsoons and the causes of such an occurrence. They differentiate the Indian monsoon from the Malaysian monsoon and the Japanese and North Australian monsoons.
- Learners identify from temperature and rainfall data of a few places in India, the regions, of which they are representative.
- Teacher organises a discussion on the effect of monsoons on growing seasons in different parts of India and the problems created by monsoons, of flooding and erosion and steps to counteract such destruction. Similar discussions on the role of monsoon in respect of (i) irrigation facilities (ii) forestry (iii) crop production, (iv) distribution of population etc. could also be arranged.

Follow-up Activities

Practical work

- Preparation of maps of India showing seasonal distribution of rainfall, temperature, pressure wind direction, particularly during the spans June to September and March to October.
- Preparation of maps of the Indian Ocean showing distribution of pressure and direction of winds in different periods especially January, March, May, June, September and November.

Discussions and Group Work

- Effect of seasonal variation in rainfall on crop production.
- Problem of famine following failure of rainfall in different parts of India and steps taken to counteract this.
- Relationship of forests and rainfall.

The above illustration is just one of the many approaches in which a question could be tackled and used as an instrument for teaching. The other activities which have potentials for using a good question as instructional material are (i) self-study or assignment (ii) group study project (iii) classroom discussions on topical news etc.

SECTION III
Some Conventional Instructional Methodologies

Introduction

A teaching technique, method or approach connotes the manner of curriculum transaction. There are many of these and such a one should be selected for a particular teaching situation which:

- is aligned to the concerned age-group,
- is found to be of interest by the learners,
- is based on the previous knowledge and experience of the learners,
- is within the ability of the learners to pursue,
- can motivate children for further learning on their own,
- enhances pupils' competencies by imparting enablement, empowerment and enrichment to the learners,
- encourages learning initiatives of self-directed learning among learners, and
- help in the realisation of instructional objectives.

Thus not all methods are suitable for all situations. The choice of a method will have to depend among other things on the learners being addressed, the teachers own abilities, the facilities available.

Some of the main of the commonly used of these are described below alongwith their diverse manifestations and the approaches of their effective use.

12

The Lecture Method

This '*Tongue and the Ear Method*' is by and large the most widely used method of teaching and learning and consists of dispensing of information by the teacher to the learners. The teacher is *active* and the learner is *passive*. The method conceives that the completion of the prescribed course content by the teacher, in this fashion, is the main purpose of education. The teachers proficiency is judged by the quantum of information transmitted and not by its assimilation by the learners. *Teaching thus becomes both the means* and *the end and learning not conceived as the core concern.*

The lecture method is the most economical method. More information can be transferred to a large number of learners in a given period of time than by any other method. To be fruitful the lectures must be supplemented by some other methods or activities. Active participation of the learners, in the process of learning helps in augmentation, acceleration and internalisation of learning.

Socrates distrusted the lecture method on the ground that the lecturer puts ready-made ideas into the minds of pupils without giving them a chance to explore and experiment for drawing their own conclusions and thereby discover their own potentials. In fact we want and expect the learners to become *adventurers, explorers and discoverers*. To *Socrates* questions are a powerful means for triggering thinking besides being powerful instruments of evaluation. The Socratic method aims at leading pupils (through self-evaluation) from '*unconscious ignorance to conscious ignorance*' through an ironic or destructive stage of questioning and then on to 'truth' through a constructive stage of further questioning.

There are two essential steps involved in the lecture method:

- Lecture Preparation
- Lecture Presentation

12.1 Lecture Preparation

Preparations for using the lecture method of teaching are not easy by any chance. It means the collection and compilation of information from different sources. Systematic organisation and sequencing is an important subsequent part of this exercise.

The prescribed course content and the maturity level of the learners is the basic foundation of this endeavour. *What has gone before and what is to follow determine the direction and dimensions of preparation.*

Time Budgeting is yet another basic necessity because the course has to be completed within the time available. The number of lectures that can be delivered is thus determined on the basis of the total time available. This in turn becomes the basis of the decision about how much of the content can be contained in a lecture.

The teacher has also to identify *the hard spots in learning*, in the subject matter, covered through a lecture and be amply prepared for clarifying the related ideas and material for overcoming them.

The teacher has also to collect the latest references, statistics, information about latest developments beyond the text books for enriching the process of his teaching to enable learners to overcome the related hurdles.

12.2 Lecture Presentation/Delivery

To make an impact, the presentation has but to be effective. And to be effective it has to have some *distinct characteristics*. Some main of these are described below:

- A lecture though called a lecture, should not just be a one way traffic but *an amplified dialogue with learner participation*. Studding and punctuating the ideas with examples and augmenting them with new ideas can save them from being reduced to monotonous monologues as they often become.
- An *attention capturing introduction* can also prove helpful in retaining pupils' attention and this has to be very carefully prepared.
- Couching the lecture in appropriate words and catching phrases are useful fodders for whetting the cutting edge for the learners.
- *Speech and delivery* are other criteria for success and this implies clarity of thought, simplicity of words, as also good pronunciation, intonation, articulation and above all fluency.
- *Graded sequence* of presentation which may carry learners from known to the unknown, from concrete to abstract, from general to specific, are well tried prescriptions for effective teaching.
- *Emphasis on anchor points* and definitions even at the cost of repetition become important measures for assimilation of knowledge. This is also of great help to the learners jotting down points to remember.

- Proceeding to the *next point* after making sure that the *previous one* has been well understood is a confirmatory test of teaching. This could be ensured by recapitulating what is taught through pointed questions and cross questions. In fact the learners too ought to be encouraged to ask questions to clarify any misgivings they may have. The clarifications given are, in fact, a better methodology than just lecturing and the teacher should welcome interruptions by learners in this regard.
- Alertness of learners has but to be ensured in the course of lectures and one of the easiest methods is to ask questions in the course of the lectures and these questions should be so distributed over the class as to keep learner attention althrough, with a constant apprehension that the next question may be asked of any of them.
- A *congenial* is conducive to learning. It should always be a friendly atmosphere that should permeate the learning environment. It is desirable in this context to address learners by name.

There are also some ***don'ts*** in this regard. The teacher should never try to show off by mentioning facts and terminology which the learners cannot understand. He should address learners in their face, watching their eyes and their forehead wrinkles which are great indicators of their having understood or having not understood the ideas communicated. The teacher should neither chew nor swallow words. He should also not speak to himself but to the class. The lectures from a pulpit or a public dais are to be differentiated form those in the classroom. A clergy-man or a political leader can call it quits after a lecture which a teacher cannot as the lecture is a means to the end of learning and not an end it itself. A teacher has but to ensure that he has communicated what was necessary and that it has also gone down the throats of the learners. Even enabling learners to learn and understand is not enough, they should also be empowered to use that knowledge gained in unfamiliar situations. The teacher therefore has to work with that ultimate goal in mind.

13

The Discussion Method

There are issues where there is a likelihood of differences of opinion or problems admitting different solutions or some conceptual confusions needing clarifications where some consensus is required to be obtained. These are to be put up for discussions.

13.1 Purposes Served by Discussions

- permit learners to freely express their viewpoints
- stimulate group thinking
- enable learners to agree to differ from other co-learners.
- promote public speaking.

13.2 Teacher's/Leader's Role

Discussions must always have a leader, a role which the teacher could assume himself or he may delegate that position to some learner.

In case it is necessary or is considered desirable, a class may be divided into groups for discussion on the theme as a whole or on sub-themes and each may have its own leader.

The leader in such situations would need to execute the following responsibilities:

- ensure that everybody gets an opportunity to speak and to be brief
- honour the time limit
- pacify heat in contradictions.

13.3 The Process of Discussions

A discussion starts with an introduction by the leader, who must make a thorough advance preparation not just for presenting the theme, but more so for the needed unforeseen interventions and for making the concluding remarks. The theme should be presented comprehensively, highlighting the differing view points.

In the course of discussions it is always the leader who is addressed and not another member of the group as a part of the *discussion decorum and etiquette*. Speakers should be given a clear idea of the time constraint and be tactfully reminded/interrupted whenever necessary.

The leader should also not allow the discussion to get derailed. Deviations from the focus of the discussion needs to be promptly checked.

The leader should not necessarily intervene after each observation unless absolutely unavoidable. The learners should take their turns one by one. The leader should resist the temptation for repeated intervention and go on jotting points. He may make his balancing concluding observations at the end to save himself from imposing his views on the group. A black-board or white board summary, in telegraphic language, is always helpful for highlighting the conclusions or focal points. This is helpful in consolidating and internalising learning.

No learner should ever be snubbed but listened to with respect. Freedom of speech and an informal ethos, are guarantees for the success of discussions. Humour always eases tense moments and deserves to be inducted like 'commas'. In the event of confusions the black-board or white board should come to help.

13.4 Pre-requisites for Effective Discussions

With the goals clearly defined and the road map drawn, the discussion should at its close impart to every participant a feeling:

- of having contributed to the joint effort.
- of taking the conclusions convincingly as his own.
- of having gained a clearer picture of the situation than before.
- of realising that there are also points of view other than his own.

Discussions imply both listening and speaking. Listening has to be patient and speaking relevant. Being attentive to whatever any member of the group speaks and to understand what is meant to be conveyed by the speaker, enables a pin pointed and meaningful response, which is always appreciated by everybody.

Logical presentations and responses always need the marshalling of ones own arguments. Ones own classify about the term of discussion is very necessary and for this some self study is always called for. In fact a habit of general reading, always comes to the aid of everybody and this ought to be constantly pursued.

14

Demonstration

14.1 Introduction

Demonstration as a method of teaching is used in practical subjects like Physics, Chemistry, Biology, Mathematics, Geography, Home Science etc. It is used by itself or as part of a lecture.

Demonstration by the teacher or a professional or a learner demonstrates to the learners the steps of the *process* in executing a task for ensuring the quality of the outcome or *product*. Experimentation on ones own is the follow up of demonstrations.

Demonstration is able to explain the do's and the don'ts of the process of performance or a practical task, more convincingly than any oral description, because *demonstration is an action picture*. An old *Chinese proverb says that one picture is worth a thousand words* and demonstration, therefore, is much more than that.

14.2 Demonstration as a Teaching Device

Demonstration as such is a valuable teaching device and as an action-cum-demonstration lecture, it brings to the fore the precise relationships between theoretical foundation on the one hand apparatus, materials, articles, machinery and appliances and the methods of handling them. On the other *Necessary precautions in avoiding damage and accidents, of avoiding wastage, of the meticulous maintenance of equipment, of their orderly placement for ensuring ease in locating them when required also get automatically highlighted during demonstrations.*

Demonstrations serve as models of laboratory work by the learners independently. They bridge the gap between theory and practice, stimulate thinking and motivate further learning through exploration and experimentation on the part of the learners.

Demonstrations require special seating arrangements for the learners so that everybody can see the process of operations. Specially designed class-rooms with rows in stair-steps, semi-circular in shape are considered appropriate as in an amphitheater.

14.3 Preparation for Demonstration

In preparing for demonstration, the demonstrator must brush-up his theoretical knowledge about the theme and its relationship with other themes going before and coming after it, to be able to answer questions learners may ask. This will also give him the confidence in performing the experiments for the demonstration. He should also be relaxed and friendly in the course of the demonstrations and should also display an infectious vitality and enthusiasm.

An *inventory* of the equipment required for the experiments must be made and a *checklist* for checking not just the availability but also their workability should be ensured while it is often proposed that the best of equipment should be used for demonstrations it is desirable to use, the like of the same which the learners would be using in real situations. This will impart greater confidence to the learners when they perform the experiments and practical exercises on their own.

14.4 Pre-requisites for Demonstration

The most appropriate height of a demonstration table is supposed to be 75 cms or 30 inches. The length and width of the demonstration table would depend on the kind of demonstration. Usually the traditional demonstration halls mentioned earlier have large-sized fixed tables with taps and sinks and drawers. Appropriate lighting and seating arrangement will need to be ensured for adequate visibility of the micro-level details of the micro-level details of the demonstration. A rehearsal of the total operation about how to begin, how to proceed and how to conclude is a valuable preparatory step. This practice about what to say and what to do, will lead the teacher to better success.

The main steps of preparation in this regard will, therefore, be:

- preparation for the presentation (oral).
- arrangement of the apparatus/equipment to ensure easy accessibility.
- checking seating, lighting and other arrangements.
- rehearsal of the total operation.
- the wordings of the questions.
- the stepwise development of summary in bullet points.
- the special points of significance and relationships to be highlighted.

In case it is possible for the learners also to do some experiments/or parts of experiments simultaneously, it can be a useful teaching method.

The demonstrator should also simultaneously clarify all misgivings of learners, for a clearer understanding and for avoiding any subsequent confusions.

14.5 Limitations of the Demonstration Method

Demonstration as a method of instruction, also has some limitations. It proves to be an expensive proposition financially. It also takes quite a lot of time. Furthermore, it presumes that all learners learn at the same speed. It is, therefore, that it is proposed that demonstrations and practical work by studens should go on simultaneously. But advantages outweigh the shortcomings as experimentation and demonstrations consolidate learning.

15

Observation

Observation is basic to learning, enquiry and discovery. It is the process through which pupils can be stimulated to think and learn.

Observation helps:

- to develop the ability to see phenomenon and processes as they exist and operate and to note important details, which otherwise might be overlooked.
- to develop an objective approach and to participate efficiently in individual or group work.
- not just to 'see' but also to critically perceive and realise what they see. This augments what they learn from the book.

Directed observation can be carried out by an individual learner or by small or larger groups. Individual observation offers broader experience as a learning technique, than group observation, since greater amount of competency, independence and responsibility, get engineered among learners through a critical observation. Participation in activities such as field trips, video films, exhibitions, promote group observation.

15.1 Preparation for Making Observations

The pupils ought to be given an orientation about the situation in which observation has to be made and a list of what exactly they have to observe. In fact giving them a list of things to be observed is very helpful.

Some situations in which observation has to be made may be natural and others contrived or simulated. Specific activities facilitate learning through observation. Sometimes for consolidation of learning, drill by way of repetition of activities may be necessary. Repetition may also be needed for arriving at self validated or self-confirmed generalisations which finally culminate in abiding learning.

15.2 Process of Observation

All observations must be recorded without lapse of time immediately and accurately. Observation sheets/schedules prove helpful in this regard as the fact/phenomenon observed can be entered easily and quickly in the relevant column, which may even save future labour of classifying information.

Attention is the key to accurate observation, which leads to learning. Children should not talk among themselves during the process of observation. Learners should also be asked not to maintain a casual detached attitude while observing. No questions may be asked by the observers or the teacher or the other learners in the course of observation as the *phenomenon observed are mostly fleeting*. All question, doubts, apprehensions may be jotted down to be presented during the discussion time allocated for discussing the observations.

Observations made should be discussed after the process is over. In this session all the things observed by all the learners may be listed and their similarity on a particular issue, may then be summarised and conclusions drawn to reinforce the understanding of learners about the observations made by them. When their observations are confirmed, by others too, that will not only give them confidence about the accuracy of their observations as also in their ability to draw conclusions on their own in subsequent situations.

15.3 Observation of Individuals

They are not just the facts and phenomenon that are to be observed but also the behaviour of the learners themselves. In fact many aspects of personality, need only observation so as to be evaluated. The areas of personality attributes, *attitudes and values* etc. can only be observed, in different situations. These situation have therefore but to be provided by the institutions in a systematic manner. These situation should not look like external unrelated interventions but built into the entire teaching learning process as an integral part.

The areas of physical competencies in outdoor co-curricular co-scholastic activities too require only observation for being judged. In fact the ways in a learner behaves in different situations unmistakably reveals many traits and attributes of the individual besides the level of proficiencies attained in them.

The insight that observations provide are authentic evidence for being used for different purposes.

As a subject for evaluation, they also require different types of assessment tools like *rating scales* and the collection of evidences would require *anecdotal records* for prompt, on the spot recording of the kind and degree of attainment.

16

Problem-Solving Method

Any method of solving a problem scientifically, involving thinking, reasoning planning and execution by following logical steps, is a scientific method. The process of problem solving results in the development of *cognitive abilities, affective qualities, psycho-motor skills*. It is in this context that the 'Problem-Solving Method' is called a scientific method.

RISK explains problem solving as "*a planned attack on a difficulty, perplexity or problem to find a satisfactory solution*". ROSS interprets problem solving as an educational device whereby the teacher and the pupils attempt (in a conscious, planned and purposeful manner) to arrive at an explanation or solution to some educationally significant difficulty.

A problem occurs in a situation in which a felt difficulty to act is realised. It may be a mental difficulty or a physical one, slowing or blocking the path of progress for reaching the goal. It may therefore impress upon the learners (who may meet it) as needing a solution and is recognised and realised by them as a challenge to be picked up and squarely met.

16.1 Characteristics of a 'Problem'

A problem in an educational setting ought to possess and actually possesses some distinct characteristic spelled out below:

- *Emergence from a live educational setting*: The problem is normally related to life or education and is, therefore, normally within the ambit of common experience of the learners.
- *Focussed in nature*: The problem identified as the subject of instruction/learning ought to be clear, definite, understandable, interesting, aligned to the age group of the pupils, within the capability of the learners to tackle through the knowledge they already possess. Above all, it ought to be thought provoking.
- *Of practical utility*: The problem should have a practical value and the outcomes/solutions ought to be taken to be of practical utility by the pupils. This would motivate the pupils to demonstrate diligence and perseverance in investing efforts for solving them.

- *Related to the curriculum*: To be pursued purposefully the problem must be a part of the curriculum (objectives, content, content/support material, methodology and evaluation) to realise the goals which, is the prime concern of the learners.
- *Within the operational range of the time budget and resources available*: The process of problem solving as a method of teaching/learning should not put unnecessary strain on the finances of the institutions. At the same time it should also be possible to accomplish the total task, within the available time.

16.2 Approaches to Problem Solving

Basically, there are two main approaches to problem solving with different and contrasting procedures:

- the inductive method, and
- the deductive method.

The *Inductive Method* carries the thinking process from particular to general situations. Conclusions by way of generalisations are arrived at from particular principles and concrete situational examples. An example of inductive problem solving could be that "As Vitamin C dissolves in water and is easily destroyed by heat, a generalisation could be drawn that all foods rich in Vitamin C should be cooked in minimum amount of water, for the least possible amount of time and with minimum possible heat."

The *Deductive Method* carries reflective thinking from general to particular/specific. For example when learners find that in dry summer the desert coolers substantially bring down temperatures inside the rooms, they draw the inference, through deduction that the heat outside leads to the evaporation of the water of the cooler pads and thus causes loss of heat which makes the air passing through the wet pads cooler, which in turn cools the rooms.

In classroom situations, simulated/hypothetical problematic situations could also lead to integrative learning and in this manner reinforce the knowledge and the skills among the learners.

Two other important methods also help reinforce the problem solving method and could be safely mentioned here, in passing.

Heuristic Method: Heurism is derived from the Greek concept of 'Heurisken' which means finding out. This can be an important approach for problem solving or for the discovery approach. It aims at making learners more observant, accurate, truthful, thoughtful and dexterous. The method lays the foundation of self-education and helps promote the spirit of enquiry and research among learners.

Discovery Method: Problem solving involves scientific enquiry which is a search for truth and knowledge. The emphasis in problem solving too is on discovery/search of something so far unknown or unfamiliar rather than mere acquisition of existing knowledge. This scientific method is also referred to as the discovery approach to teaching and learning. The method was spearheaded by Piaget in Switzerland and Brunner in Cambridge Massachusetts.

Learning by discovery also implies experiencing a sense of achievement and personal aggrandisement. Discovery is the identification and recognition of a relationship between:

- an idea and an observation
- two ideas
- two relationships

BRUNNER mentions four following advantages of learning by discovery:

- increase in intellectual potency
- shift from extrinsic to instrinsic rewards
- learning the heuristics of discovery
- memory processing

16.3 Steps of the Problem Solving Method

The main steps involved in using the Problem Solving Method could be listed as under :

- *Sensing or selecting the problem*: The teacher should help the learners to identify the problem to be solved by analysing the hurdles and handicaps posed by it. Necessary motivation for solving it should also thus be generated among the learners. Learners should also be enabled to be alert in spotting and recognising the problems as and when they crop up in different situations.
- *Defining (Interpreting and delimiting) the problem*: The problem selected should be fully understood by the learners. The nature of the problem should help in charting the path for overcoming it. The feasibility of the action plan is governed by the ability of the learners and the availability of the needed resources.

  Hullfish and Smith suggest the following questions to be raised in defining a problem:

  - What exactly is the problem? Can it be broken into sub-problems?
  - Does the problem bear any similarity to any of those encountered in the past?
  - In what fundamental ways is the problem similar to others
  - In which ways does the particular problem differ from the others
  - What do differences imply—new approaches?
  - Is it necessary to redefine the problem in view of the above?

- *Collecting and evaluating relevant information/data*: After the problem has been defined and interpreted in collaboration with the learners, they should be prompted to list the information needed for solving it and to commence the process of its collection. With a view to initiating this, the teacher may identify:
  - the sources from which the information can be collected—books, documents, reports etc.
  - the personnel—experts and functionaries to be consulted.

  The collected information should then be checked for its:
  - appropriateness and relevance,
  - adequacy and
  - applicability in the given situations of the problem.
- *Formulating alternative solutions and selecting the most suitable one*: Different possible approaches for solving the problem could then be listed and their pros and cons discussed. This process of churning would enable the identification of the one most suitable. Tentative solutions could also thus be arrived at.
- *Arriving at the final solution*: The next natural step is to pool together the possible solutions. These may then be discussed thread bare from different angles, for reaching a decision about the approach/solution to be pursued. At this point, teacher's indepth knowledge and ingenuity will be called for, for guiding learners to reach apt and appropriate judgemental inferences.
- *Testing the validity of the solution arrived at*: The validity of the solution finally reached at, could be arrived at through:
  - the application of the hypothesis to new situations
  - further exploration, experimentation and investigations
  - additional investigations for gathering new information.

  Teachers constructive help and guidance would but be necessary throughout the process of problem solving.

16.4 Problem Solving and Project Method

Inspite of a host of similarities the problem solving and project methods do stand out prominently in respect of marked differences.

Problem solving requires a solution in thought or action or both. Project Method on the other hand aims at the successful completion of a task or unit of work.

Problem solving could be taken up as project work but a project cannot always be a problem solving exercise.

16.5 Merits and Limitations of Problem Solving Method

The pursuit of the Problem Solving Method imparts valuable personality attributes to the learners. The limitations of this method however, mainly relate to logistics and the perpetual paucity of resources.

The Problem Solving Method prompts pupils to learn by doing, a process through which they learn to think, to reason and in the process to develop initiative. They also acquire valuably desirable work habits and self-reliance. As problem solving requires a higher order of mental abilities, it also helps learners develop mental self-discipline.

The main *limitations of the problem solving method* are that it is time consuming both for the teachers and the learners and hence cannot be used extensively and frequently. Paucity of resources too often become hurdles in using it. Quite often when problem solving is used as a method of teaching the elaborate and intensive focus it requires, turn out to be the only mental activity with others relegated into the background and in fact they get grossly neglected.

The teacher has, therefore, to use his discretion in establishing the needed balance among different methodologies of instruction. He has particularly to guard against the situation when he may assign problems without the problems coming from the learners as that kills their interest.

17

The Herbartian Steps

17.1 Historical Overview

John Friedrich Herbart (1776-1841), the German educational philosopher was both by birth and education an educationist. His grandfather was the Rector of a Gymnasium (a German School) at Oldenburg, Herbart's native town. His father was a lawyer and Privy Counsellor there. Herbart's mother is known to be a rare and a wonderful woman, who was able to assist her son with Greek and Mathematics and provide direction to his educational pursuits.

Just before graduation he became a tutor to the three sons of a Swiss Governor. During this span of two years (1797-1799) he was required by his patron to prepare a bi-monthly written report about the methods he used and about the progress and conduct of his learners. This was Herbart's only experience in Pedagogy.

While in Switzerland Herbart met Pestalozzi and was greatly impressed by the educational principles propounded by him.

Then on resuming his interrupted university course he developed his own ideas from Pestalozzianism and put them into writing as well.

Following this, he lectured on pedagogy at the University of Gottingen from 1802 to 1809 and brought out his book 'General Pedagogy'. In 1809 Herbart was called upon to the chair of philosophy at Konigsberg as practically the successor of the illustrious Immanuel Kant. Kant died in 1804 and was succeeded by Traugott who resigned in 1809 to accept the chair at Leipzig.

It was at Konigsberg that Herbart took to documenting his ideas to become the first example of being an educational psychologist and philosopher, developing the educational process from the point of view of a teacher with the evolution of his concept of the '*apperceptive mass*' as the core doctrine of his educational philosophy. According to him it is in accordance with apperception that a teacher can secure the interest and attention of the pupil to any new idea and have him retain it. The teacher can make or modify his apperception masses or system of ideas in such a way that it can be apperceived or incorporated with the old in educative instruction.

17.2 The Originally Proposed Steps

The spirit of Herbartian steps to instruction propounded by the philosopher are widely used in different parts of the world until this day. They are:

- clearness (absorption)
- association (reflection)
- system (coherence)
- method (application/active reflection)

17.3 The Subsequent Adaptations

Subsequently Herbart's noted disciple ZILLER divided the step of 'clearness' into 'preparation' and 'presentation' and a more recent Herbartian REIN added 'Aim' as a sub-step to preparation. The names of the other three processes have also now been changed by subsequent Herbartians for giving greater lucidity and significance to them. The formal steps of instruction are now given as:

- Statement of Aim
- Preparation
- Presentation
- Comparison and association
- Generalisation
- Application

These steps are based on his concept of three primary functions of the mind as knowing, feeling and willing and incorporate Herbart's concepts of 'apperceptive mass', 'concentration' 'correlation' and multisided interests and project his philosophy that to 'instruct' the mind is to 'construct' it.

The above steps could be described as under:

- *The Statement of Aim:* What we today call the expected learning outcome is stated in clear terms. These are relevant to the subject of study, the age group of the pupils, and are to be both achievable and testable.
- *Preparation*: Before starting to introduce new ideas it is necessary to mentally prepare children for the new intake. What the children already know is to be related to what is planned to be taught to them. The most common and also the most appropriate method is to ask them some questions about their previous knowledge which may logically or sequentially lead them to the new one. This step has essentially to be a brief one.
- *Presentation* consists of relating and connecting new information with the old one, by dividing it into sections if necessary. Links between what is already known and what is purported to become known, as also the subsequent areas of content, have thus to be established.

The degree and quantum of learning, desired to be imparted by the teacher and acquired by the learners is an important decision to be made at this stage.

The subject matter becomes the focus of attention of both the teacher and the taughts. The presentation made by the teacher has but to be logical, sequential, clear, and focussed, involving lecturing, narration, description, demonstration and discussions participated by pupils. Repetition is also resorted to for internalisation of learning and the themes are also attempted to be integrated with those of other subjects and with life for creating, promoting and retaining the interest of the learners in the subject. Developmental questions play an important part in this process.

- *Comparison or Association* is the stage for consolidating learning by attempting to relate old knowledge with the new through comparisons and contrasts for establishing closer relationships between the two. The process is also aimed at arousing pupils motivation to know more, curiosity for learning more, about the theme as also for leading them to think creatively.
- *Generalisation* is the stage for putting together through *recapitulation* (revision) the facts and principles dealt with, during the earlier stages and for drawing of inferences and generalisations about them with the teacher remaining in the background. Such learner-based initiatives make learning abiding.
- *The Application stage* attempts to demonstrate to the learners that knowledge acquired has a vital relationship with life. The mind of the learners at this stage shuttles between specific facts and phenomenon to generalisations and back to the specifics. At this stage the learners ascend from the individual to the universal stage of knowledge and are enabled to acquire the ability for applying the generalised knowledge to specific unfamiliar individual situations.

17.4 Conclusion

Through these steps which go by his name Herbart it is attempted to demonstrate that philosophy is not just a macro-level concept but can also be applied at the micro-level as well.

Herbartian steps, in fact, present a blended amalgam of the principles of teaching and learning. That is why, they have been holding the ground for nearly two centuries now. Being easy to understand and practice they are a valuable guide for the teacher in preparing a teaching plan. Based on psychological principles they present the outline of a sequential action plan of day-to-day teaching.

As they have been *tested by time, suitably modified with experience* they propose a practicable approach to teaching.

In course of time it has been realised that within the time available to the practicing teachers, it is not possible to follow the Herbartian Steps. Therefore a simpler set of steps, incorporating the spirit of these steps has come to be evolved and is being followed even by a number of teacher training institution. These are

1. Objectives
2. Activities
3. Evaluation

Just as with the passage of time modifications have been introduced in the steps, they can be further altered to suit emergent needs. Their value however, will still remain.

SECTION IV
Some Unconventional Instructional Methodologies

Introduction

Emancipation from Rigidities of Formal Education

Formal education, has somehow come to imply mainly the use of the traditional methods, the main of which have been discussed in the preceding section on conventional techniques of teaching. Besides, there are also some other *unconventional methods*, the use of which is more an exception than the rule. These approaches nevertheless possess a powerful potential for imparting learning, which is easily digestible by the learners, to become an internalised part of themselves. This is because most of them involve the active involvement of learners in the process of the acquisition of knowledge and other competencies. These methods also enrich the learners because they become *participatory crusades of learning*, where individuals are enabled to learn through the joint outcomes of their individual efforts or the labour of their teams and the contributions that each one makes to the learning programmes.

As the approaches are basically learner-based, the teachers stand to gain, by way of saving on their time and effort in dishing out information to the learners. This must, therefore, be an additional motivation for the teachers to use them for economising on their work load, and at the same time, successfully reaching their sole goal of ensuring abiding learning on the part of the learners.

Furthermore, the freedom and flexibility that these unconventional strategies allow both to the teachers and the taughts, does not shackle the learning process by any rigid rules or standardised procedures. This is something that often turns the frequently caused pain of learning into a joyful pursuit.

Some of the main of these approaches are attempted to be discussed in the following pages in general terms. The teacher should feel free to make the needed adaptations in them to suit the special needs of their specific situations.

18

The Project Method

The Project Method is based on pragmatic philosophy of experience and experimentation propounded by *John Dewey* and *Kilpatrick*, which brought a new dynamism in education. It transformed the dull monotonous and often purposeless class-room teaching into one that made it vibrant and imparted vitality to it. Dewey said that '*Education should not only be for life but through life*'. He was keenly aware of the gap between a pupil's life in school and his life in the society. He insisted that in an efficient educational system this gap should be bridged. The project method is an attempt to bring society and the local community closer into the school.

William Kilpatrik defines the project as a "unit of whole hearted purposeful activity, proceeding in a social environment." *Stevenson* defines a project as "A problematic act carried to completion in its natural setting." *Ballard* states that "a project is a bit of real life that has been imported into the school." A *project is thus related to real life, its problems and their solutions in the social environment.*

18.1 Types of Projects

According to *Kilpatrick* projects can basically assume four forms:

The Producers' Type: In a producers type of project the emphasis is on actual production or development of material, or an object or an article.

The Consumers' Type: This type of project consists of various experiences like reading listening and evaluating things.

The Problem Type: This type of projects involve problem solving requiring the exercise of mental processes.

The Drill Type: This type of projects involve learning mainly by repetition of the processes like learning vocabulary, spellings etc.

18.2 Principles Involved in the Project Method

The principles governing the project method are:

Purposefulness: A project must be meaningful and purposeful to the learners. This offers incentive and motivation to the learners to learn and yields them the satisfaction and gratification at having been successful in accomplishing the tasks.

Activity centredness: A project is woven round some activity and offers opportunities to learners to learn by doing by getting involved in the activities. They are also required to plan, think, evolve strategies of functioning and in accomplishing tasks independently, with an urge for innovativeness in self-designed strategies culminating in a sense of achievement and flulfilment.

Life centredness: A project is planned around an actual life situation which is specially created/simulated in the school environment. The situations so created enable children to demonstrate their special abilities competencies, ingenuity capacities and talents.

Based on experience: Experiences lead to abiding learning, as the learning that so accrues, is self-acquired. The child also learns the value of team work and participatory learning and the resulting social and democratic values.

Freedom: The process of learning through the project method, offers full freedom to children to exercise their initiative and ingenuity in planning and executing the steps of the process on their own. Such freedom enables children to express themselves fully and freely. Incidentally this also helps them develop a sense of accountability for their activities.

Utility: Utility of the knowledge and experiences gained, through personally initiated and executed tasks, yields children the satisfaction of having realised something on their own, which is of utility in life. This imparts meaningfulness to the educational ventures undertaken.

18.3 Steps in the Project Method

Quite like some other approaches, in Project Method too children learn by doing. The teacher's job is to provide a situation which may give pupils a spontaneous urge, to carry out the project according to their interests, attitudes, aptitudes, competencies etc.

Project situations can be both inside the classroom and outside. Situations and settings for the execution of projects can be provided through:

- conversations on different topics
- discussions on different themes
- pictures
- video films
- story-telling
- excursions
- educational tours

With the seeds of situations sowed, the steps of proceeding on the projects have to be pursued, which are as under:

18.3.1 Proposing and Purposing a Project

The teacher proposes a project and enunciates the purpose. The latter serves as a motivating device as the children discover its usefulness and its compatibility with their respective interests and capacities to work for.

18.3.2 Planning the Project

Planning could be ideally done by the learners themselves but in regard to the younger folk, some hints could be offered by the teacher, who may keep on watching them do things on their own. In fact the learners may be encouraged to think of alternative approaches for realising the same goal and then to select the one that they consider as most appropriate. This paves the way for the internalisation of the idea that there could be multiple solutions to a single problem. This serves well in later life situations where an individual has but to learn to be flexible in weighing situations for taking ones own decisions.

The learners also come to learn that whatever they may have planned, need not always be rigidly followed even if the plans do not work. The concept of 'mid-way corrections' for realising success is a valuable mental attitude of accepting the need for making changes in plans and finally making them.

18.3.3 Executing the Project

The freedom of project execution too is the prerogative of the learners. It gives them the joy of doing things on their own, as per their self-developed plans. Distribution of responsibilities among themselves is another valuable step which enables learners to put in their best to their respective (often self-chosen) tasks. While the project execution goes on, the teacher mainly remains an observant on-looker, ensuring that the learners get all the materials they need and that all precautions are in place, so that they do not get hurt in any way. He has also to establish a balance between the over-enthusiastic and the comparatively less interested learners. Encouraging and guiding the latter can yield them confidence and enthusiasm to work and effectively contribute to team effort.

18.3.4 Evaluating the Project

While evaluation is considered to be a teacher's activity the learners can also be motivated to assess their own efforts and the resulting outcomes themselves making them their own rivals in striving for excellence.

The teacher should try to evaluate the project from the academic angle, diagnosing and identifying the outcomes of the project in real terms by way of the development of competencies by the participants, cooperation in team work, voluntary willingness to make a contribution to the project while in process, identification of gainful outcomes in terms of the developments and whetting of *interests* and *abilities*.

The learners too can undertake a self-evaluation of the gains, the new things learnt, the capacities improved, the insights into various operations gained, the improved level of confidence in oneself and motivation for further improving ones competencies. The teacher should in fact lead them to such realisations.

18.4 Shortcomings of the Project Method

Project method though a great educational innovation does suffer from some shortfalls the main of which are stated below:

It is a *time consuming* method of learning and teaching. It is also *not applicable to all the subjects and all the themes therein.* The teacher cannot always think of completely original themes for projects and therefore quite often they become repetitive.

18.5 Conclusion

Inspite of the shortcomings, the project method remains a very useful method of imparting abiding learning through personal experiences. Its great value in concept formation and the development of valuable life-relevant attitudes cannot be underestimated.

19

The Laboratory Method

19.1 Learning by Doing

We all learn by doing. The laboratory method helps learners to learn by doing. In experimental subjects experience in the laboratory becomes an important segment of pupils' total experience. It is the best method of providing a clear understanding of any process. Laboratory experience under teachers' supervision is the first step for the development of manipulative and managerial skills among the learners. Personal involvement in experimentation promotes the development of a spirit of inquiry, capacity for reasoning, exploration for purposes of acquiring the needed information and objectivity in observation as also faithful recording of observations, and rational deduction of inferences.

19.2 Support Material for Laboratory Work

The laboratory method even in science subjects, suffers from the handicap of the availability of sufficient items of apparatus for offering hands-on experience to all learners but now thanks to the NCERT, some Science Kits have been developed. Each kit has apparatus for twenty learners to perform experiments individually. The basic idea behind prompting this venture is to provide inexpensive aids for experimental science education. In these kits, every item of glass apparatus which could be converted into plastic has been so converted, eliminating the fear for their replacement in case of breakage, if it was glass and thus of repeated financial investments. The fundamental premise for developing these aids/items of experimentation is to educate learners in *concepts* rather than insisting on *accuracy* of results.

The Science kits are also a way of reaching the rural schools where adequate infrastructure is not available. The kit has taken the form of a box with a handle at the top. This can be stowed in any corner of the classroom thus eliminating the need for a special cup-board for storing the equipment. The apparatus is all stored in the drawers and chemicals on the shelves of the kit box. The kit has two doors, both in the front. One has hinges that brings the inner door from top to bottom and this can serve as a demonstration table. The outer cover is hinged in a manner that it opens up on one side. This side that opens up is painted black and can be used as a black-board, where even that is not available. Now however things have improved. The innovation of the development of science kits however, still remains an ingenious thing for overcoming constraints and handicaps.

As experimentation is usually time consuming, it is desirable to allot two consecutive class periods for it.

19.3 Types of Laboratory Methods

The laboratory method could assume three forms:

- Experimentational
- Observational
- Productive

The *experimental mode* helps explain, illustrate or to prove principles by enabling learners to explore, experiment and draw conclusions on their own. These conclusions become abiding acquisitions of the learners. This mode also helps in creating in learners an instinct for verifying facts and phenomenon.

The *observational mode* is again based on personal deductions not just based on experimentation but also on personal observations. Exploration becomes the chief means for making observations. Observations of this type could be illustrated by the inferences on characteristics of growing children of different age groups.

The *productive mode* consists of creating a tangible outcome like the production of a simple item like a pin tray in wood work, a candle in wax-work or a frock in tailoring (home science).

The laboratory method starts and ends with activities. It starts with an introduction by the teacher establishing a relationship between theory and practice. The pupils are enthused to make and promptly put down their observations as they make them. The laboratory method could be used both for individual and group teaching. The latter, however, is a common practice.

A *first aid kit* is, however, a perpetual part of all laboratories for meeting emergencies.

19.4 Process of Laboratory Work

In performing experiments learners are always advised to go strictly by the oral instructions given by the teachers and the directions contained in the manuals and instruction cards.

In the process of experimentation, the teacher goes round and supervises the work of individuals or groups and helps those that need it. If there is a common mistake being committed, he draws everybody's attention and makes necessary suggestions.

19.5 Post Experiment Discussion

After the process of experimentation is over, discussions are the concluding step. The common experiences and differences of opinion are discussed and the teacher finally helps them to get to accurate conclusions.

20

Programmed Instruction

20.1 The Purpose of Programmed Instruction

Programmed Instruction promises to increase the effectiveness of mass instruction. Through this approach individualised instruction is possible to be provided to pupils in a more effective manner than what is possible for any single teacher to do.

The uniqueness of programmed instruction lies in the fact of its not just being a device of teaching but more so as a scientific approach applicable to different levels and sectors of education.

Skinner and his colleagues at the Harvard University conducted research experiments to study the behaviours of pigeons. They managed to teach these docile little creatures to master certain tricks and also to play a form of Table Tennis.

The basic principles guiding the experiment of teaching pigeons were:

- If rewarded whenever a pigeon made a right move, it learns a new one more quickly.
- A complicated feat must be taught through small steps and just one at a time with each subsequent step being graded to become an easy one.

20.2 The Structure of Programmed Instruction

Skinner once visited his daughter's fifth grade Mathematics class and noticed that pupils' attention wandered away from the inefficient classroom instruction. He grew indignant at what he saw in the classroom and developed a fifth grade Mathematics course based on the principles used in teaching pigeons and other small animals.

In programmed instruction, *the subject-matter is broken down into a sequence of small steps*. The sequence and steps must be determined much more carefully and skillfully than what is possible for an ordinary learner to do. The steps must be small enough for the learner to move from an easier one to the next more difficult one easily, with a minimum of error. *Mistakes are costly, as they have to be unlearned.* Trial and error learning must be reduced to a minimum. The ideal programmes would result in no mistakes. Constant success reinforces past learning and motivates further effort.

Programmed instruction may take many forms depending upon the subject, and the objectives desired to be achieved. The most common form in academic subjects is to present certain carefully-worded data in a '*Frame*' or viewing space. Each Frame calls for a response.

In programmed teaching/learning, a school subject is broken into simple, easy graded progressive steps and presented as questions, which the pupil must answer. The pupil would be kept active with the process of continuously answering the questions. The reward would be that of knowing at once if he was right or wrong, and if the subject was programmed in its sequential logical order, he would rarely be wrong. The learner would need to work alone, concentrating on the questions as they emerge, writing his own answers. A mechanical device or a '*teaching machine*' is a device used for the purpose. It presents an exercise or a problem to the learner, induces him to respond and reveals to him whether or not his response is correct. Many machines require that incorrect responses be corrected before the learner can be allowed to continue and move ahead. Most teaching machines use the tutorial or the *Socratic method.* They ask questions, wait for answers and then let the learner know whether or not he is right. They induce the learner to think and work for himself. This is how the 'Teaching Machine Movement' came into existence. Instruction by '*Teaching machines*' *is called programmed learning or self-instruction.* The material may be presented through any device—a machine or a book.

20.3 The Operations of Programmed Instruction

In general, programmed material consists of a series of small units called '*Frames*'. Each Frame is based on the previous knowledge already possessed by the learner and each Frame attempts to add a small increment to this knowledge. Each Frame contains one or more blanks to be filled in by the learner in a sentence—completion fashion. The blank in a Frame calls for a response that the learner is able to make either because he learned how to make it, in the settings of the previous Frames or because it is made possible by the study of the Frame currently confronting him. The learner reads each Frame and then fills in the blanks. The learner type of reading required by a Frame ensures active and continuous manipulation of the ideas, described through it. This type of concentrated and focussed reading reinforces learning in contrast to passive reading, without a need for active manipulation of the ideas that make up the subject-matter.

The genesis of programmed learning can be summarised thus:

- Small steps
- Thoughtful reading
- Active responding
- Immediate confirmation
- Reinforcement
- Self-paced learning

There are different styles or systems of programming. The *'linear'* programming, associated with the work of *Skinner*, is a single track programme because the learner goes directly in a straight line through the material from beginning to end. The *'intrinsic'* programming associated with the work of *Crowder* is a branching programme. It is a method of programming material that directs the erring pupil along certain corrective pathways, before he is permitted to proceed to the next step in the programme. Introducing remedial or explanatory loops of review passage into a programme helps the learners who need them, while the swifter learners can skip the entire practice.

Research findings show that programmed instruction helps to accomplish *consolidation of learning at every level*, from pre-school to graduate or professional level. It is useful for slow learners as well as mature superior learner. It can teach a variety of subject-matter, such as mathematics, statistics and language and a variety of skilled, behaviours like, rote-learning, paired associated learning, application of formulae, formation of concepts and 'thoughtful' reading etc.

20.4 Conclusion

Developing a 'programme' is not easy. It requires not only mastery of and insight into the subject but also meticulous planning thorough preparation and sound training. The nature of the programmed instructional material is such that *it cannot be easily transplanted from one setting/environment or country to another*.

One of the important factors in the use of programmed material is, that programmed material *need not substitute the textbooks or the teacher* as only certain parts of a text is programmed. The textbook could thus remain largely intact.

Teaching machines can never replace human teachers, however indispensable they may become. Factual learning which comprises the content of most programmes is only one means to some important cognitive processes, associated with intuitive, judgemental and problem-solving behaviour.

21

Think-Tank Sessions

21.1 Connotation

Think-tank sessions imply joint/*collective loud thinking* by a group on a common issue or problem. The theme selected could be real or hypothetical.

21.2 Requirements

Normally placards, with questions, phrases and statements or slogans on the selected topic are prepared with the help of learners. These are such as to force people to think.

21.3 Physical Arrangements

Learners sit in groups (circles or semi-circles) to deliberate in-depth on the given theme. Each group has its own placards on the same theme.

21.4 Purpose

Reflecting in-depth on an issue or a problem, analysing it, delving into the causes (if any), discussing implications, suggesting alternative solutions, pondering on the pros and cons of each solution in terms of immediate outcomes as also long range impact and identifying the most suitable one, pre-occupy the learners as they engage themselves in dialogues to exchange views without any heated debate or argumentation.

21.5 The Process

Learners are divided into groups of 10 or 15. The purpose is explained to them along with the working dynamics. The learners are required to do reflective thinking. Each learner may explain the meaning and connotation of the contents of his/her placard. Placards are also circulated among different groups for encouraging different view points on the same issue. New ideas also thus get generated.

21.6 Expected Gains

It is possible to get different view points on the different facets of the same theme. With every learner desirous of saying something new, it becomes a *race in creativity of thought and speech.* Learners are also enabled to appreciated about how the same problem, can be viewed from different angles. It also helps impart to the learners the most valuable *conviction that theirs is not the only view,* and also not essentially the only correct one. With no inhibitions, learners are also able to come out with their thoughts which they may not normally express. This prompts them to experience the exercise their right present without any reservations their own respective opinions about different facts and phenomenon.

Think Tank Sessions basically are exercises in collective thinking on a given issue. Though different members of the team may hold different view points, because of the different exposures and experiences they may have had, they entertain the common mission of charting the most appropriate road map for reaching the same goal. In fact, different view points enrich the thinking process, as the suggestions are invariably constructive and forward looking.

The realisation of likely pitfalls and a discussion about the gravity of each, in regard to their potential for dislocating the proposed plans, gives valuable pointers for avoiding them through care in advance planning.

The development of placards on the identified theme also becomes a valuable training ground for being *creative with eye and ear catching brevity.* To squeeze the content of many sentences into small slogan like statements is by itself a valuable ability to inculcate, which can stand people, in good stead, in life.

Furthermore, when one coins a catchy statement for a placard, he follows a particular line of thinking the interactions that follow enable the individual to learn about other possible meanings and interpretations of what he has written as well. This process and the discussions that follow enlighten everybody in the group and by so learning from others, one acquires a greater clarity about his own notions.

Furthermore, 'Think Tank Sessions" also successfully offer to each member of the group, a sense of cohesion and unity as a team working towards the same goal. The outcome, in terms of conclusions thus does not remain any single individuals work but that of the entire group. The group as a whole, takes it to be its work with a sense of achievement and satisfaction.

This also creates a sense of interdependence among members who then have *no egoistic hesitation in consulting others*. Such attitudes are conducive for welfare of the institution, agency or organisation the individuals work for. The, so emanating personal harmony also naturally results in professional harmony.

22

Seminars

22.1 Connotation

A seminar is an in-depth discussion on a topic under the guidance of a teacher or a leader.

22.2 Requirements

Being an indepth discussion, a seminar is normally preceded by an extensive, indepth study of the theme in advance from different sources.

22.3 Physical Arrangements

A circular or a semi-circular seating arrangement for an in-house seminar is considered appropriate. For formal seminars, there may be a dais for experts to sit and rows or round tables seats for the audience in the front.

22.4 Operational Steps

The date for the seminar and the topic are announced in advance. Normally, the learners jot down their misgivings (if any) about the different aspects of the theme earlier. Some of them may even prepare a brief presentation about their explorations.

22.5 Process

The teacher or the leader briefly introduces the topic and coordinates the discussions, allowing time to everybody to have a chance to speak. The thematic organisation is also the leader's responsibility. S/he also makes inputs/ corrections wherever needed, and ensures that the major aspects of the theme are covered.

Different ideas and points of view are then presented and discussed threadbare, covering the minutest of details. For everybody, it is an opportunity for clarifying ones conceptual confusions.

22.6 Expected Gains

Even though the whole class/group may participate, the situation in seminars is informal, and learners have no reservations about expressing their opinions. The cross-fertilisation of ideas is very educative as everybody is eager to share whatever new s/he may be knowing about the topic, or whatever opinions s/he may be holding about it.

The theme being a part of the curriculum, the learning so acquired is unique and more enriching and abiding than classroom teaching or individualised learning.

Seminars normally display an academic inclination. With the prior timely announcement of the theme everybody may have had an opportunity to study the theme. In the process, he may also have jotted down his own misgivings about which he needs classifications.

The study of different books and materials by the learners may also have exposed them to different view points of the authors. The presentation of these view points naturally enriches the deliberations of the seminar.

While a consensus may or may not be possible, to be arrived at, a seminar does become a platform for participatory learning. The discussion at the seminar becomes such an enriching experience that no learner normally wants to miss a seminar while he may not mind missing a lecture.

The threadbare analysis of the theme in question, through contribution pouring in form all sides, enables the participants to gain from the labour and explorations of their other peers, which they on their own may never be able to do.

It is always useful to ask each learner to write briefly about the points they may have made in the course of the seminar. A small group could them be constituted to arrange the ideas sequentially in a logical order in the form of a summary paper. The sources from which different ideas may have been culled out will be valuable reference points for those who may like to know about the particular aspects of the theme.

Seminars offer a valuable opportunity for *library research* and help inculcate the ability of *learning how to learn and self directed learning*. The ample scope for showing off ones own exploits, is by itself a powerful motivation for the learners to acquire indepth knowledge and to present it before the whole group/class/seminarians. These presentations of individuals, often leave good impressions on others about the deligent and intelligent homework done by the individual and enhances his prestige in the group. This becomes an incidental gain.

23

Panel Discussions

23.1 Connotation

A small group of persons are selected to discuss an issue among themselves. The panelists could be both outside experts and/or faculty members.

23.2 Physical Arrangements

There is normally a dias where the coordinator and the panelists sit, and there is the audience. Panelists normally do not exceed five.

23.3 Requirements

The chairman/coordinator directs the presentations. He also sets time limits for the panelists to speak, and provides the links between the presentations of different panelists. He initiates the discussions and also concludes it.

23.4 Process

A topic is decided in advance. Panelists who are experts in the field are selected and invited to present their view points on the identified theme. After the chairman has introduced the panelists and the theme he asks each one of them to make brief presentations. Threads from the ideas expressed are then picked up, and discussions start among panalists. Sometimes even after the introduction of the theme, if it admits different view points or controversies, the discussion starts straight away with inputs coming from different panelists. Towards the close, sometimes, the audience is also permitted to ask questions which are responded to by the panelists.

23.5 Expected Gains

It is an opportunity to hear experts speak out their ideas on a theme. The differences of opinion on the subject come to the fore, and as points are normally made with reasons they are very enriching.

'Panel' discussions are normally organised on themes where view-points may be varied. A Panel Discussion provides an opportunity to the members of the audience who could be learners, to analyse the ideas and facts for themselves and draw their own conclusions.

Panel discussions are held on specialized themes and the panelists are experts in that field. Quite naturally, the experts would be having different experiences and backgrounds which will come to bear on the presentations they make.

Sometimes as a matter of planning the different panelists may be requested to focus on specific facets of the theme of discussion which may be allocated to them in advance. This helps avoid avoidable duplication. However, the main theme being the same some overlap is bound to be there. But, the panelists, on their own, try to avoid it on the basis of the presentations of earlier panelists.

The discussions among the panelists after the presentations are basically technical and the learners as the audience have to pick up things relevant to their needs. Sometimes when the panelists enter into technicalities quite a few things go over the heads of the audience, the learners. It is therefore desirable to brief the panelists in advance for remaining within the range of understanding of the learners for whom really the panel discussion has been arranged.

It is however always desirable to record the presentations and the deliberations. These presentations being by specialists are surely likely to be of interest and use to others working in the field. With the permission of the panelists, these could be widely circulated, after editing by the panelists themselves.

While selecting the panelists it is always desirable in the setting of an educational institutions not to include known rivals among the panelists who may contradict everything that the rival may state. This vitiates the ethos and destroys the purpose of the discussion by becoming a wordy battle ground.

After the presentations, discussion and the question answer session, time must be saved for brief concluding statements by the chairman.

24

Symposium

24.1 Connotation

A symposium is a discussion on essays prepared and presented by some selected individuals (learners or experts) on a particular theme/topic.

24.2 Physical Arrangement

It could be a semi-circular arrangement or a classroom setting.

24.3 Requirements

Learners or experts are selected, and after being assigned the topic, are asked to prepare brief papers for presentation. As normally the total time available for a symposium is limited, they are asked to prepare brief presentations as per the time budget.

24.4 Process

The learners or experts who have prepared the essays on the theme make presentations one by one, as called upon. As the presentations are made, the others jot down the things to remember and the questions to ask. The rest of the period is devoted to questions and answers.

24.5 Gains

The topic being the same, each speaker is anxious to prepare the best essay by consulting the largest possible number of sources. The exercise thus motivates learners (in an institutional symposium) to undertake library research. As the time is limited, they also learn to be brief in their writings, so as to include everything that is relevant, in the smallest possible space. The essay has to be drafted as a speech and so has to have new facts, convincing arguments and reasoning. Stage shyness is also got over in this exercise of public speaking/reading. Those who write and read papers also incidentally get the needed training in responding to questions orally. So, besides written expression, oral expression too finds an opportunity for being demonstrated, of which promptness to marshall arguments to respond is an important part.

It is desirable to ask learners to write essays by turns. The teacher could initially come to the help of those who may not be proficient in writing and speaking, and enable them to subsequently do things on their own.

A symposium is basically *an all learner affair*. The selection of a theme well in advance is necessary for the learners to prepare their own essays for presentation. In symposia the themes selected are mostly those of common interest reflecting common concerns/problems.

Quite naturally each learner selected to write an essay and to present his own point of view and the approach for solving the common problem. *Practicability of the suggested solutions* will, of course, be the central focus. No theoretical impracticable approaches will therefore be appreciated. As each one would have a stake in the solutions suggested he will analyse it in the context of his own interests. This will make it necessary for the suggestions to satisfy the majority if not all.

As this will involve presentations on the basis of written essays those writing them will need to ensure all the requirements of written expression. To add to this, the ability to present a reasoned point of view will also be called for. The pros and cons of different possible approaches will also need to be examined and the final solution suggested, will also have to be supported by arguments. This will be no easy task and need originality and creativity.

It will be desirable not to select the same learners for writing essays and presenting them every time. Learners should take turns in executing this valuable learning exercise which has many things to teach learners.

After the presentations have been made there should also be an open house for the audience to raise questions. Those who may have made presentations could jot down the points raised related to their respective presentations and then each of the four or five should respond. The concluding note however should be given by one of the teachers. This teacher should try to balance different view points and focus on points of agreement rather than points of disagreement.

A symposium thus becomes an instrument for training learners in library research for collecting and compiling information for drafting it in an organised manner and for making a public presentation.

25

Library Research

25.1 Connotation

Library Research implies systematic exploration and investigation for discovering/establishing facts on identified themes.

25.2 Requirements

Access to a library with books on the selected topic and access to internet as also availability of time for exploration are pre-requisites for library research which involves:

- Consultation
- Taking notes
- Systematic organisation
- Summarisation

25.3 Process

The theme is identified and given to the class. The class has then to be divided into groups not by choice but by selection. Each group is allotted a sub-theme to work on. Time-table for collection of material, group presentation, class discussion and summarisation is decided in advance and intimated. The groups then go about their business. Each learner takes his notes about significant points from the books/documents studied or from the internet surfed.

The learners then come back to their respective groups, where the collected material is pooled analysed, synthesised and evaluated for the preparation of the group reports. The points of the group report are jotted down and the member of the group with a facile pen prepares the draft of the group report. The report is then read to the group and approved by it. This is then presented by the writer/group leader.

The Group Reports on different sub-topics are then presented by the Group Leaders to the total class and discussed. The suggestions made, and the ideas that emerge in the course of the discussions are incorporated in the group reports and a final report on the whole topic weaving-in the different group reports is prepared and formally written.

This report and any other material which may have been prepared by the groups is then put up in an exhibition.

25.4 Expected Gains

Library research is a valuable experience in both individual and participatory learning which saves teaching-learning time, and at the same time is enriching. It is good training for the concept of *Frontline Curriculum* where say 90% syllabus remains relevant for four or five years and 10% changes every year or two. As no books are available for this 10% of the syllabus, *teachers too become co-learners with learners in the process of exploration.* Learners, while browsing through books, are able to realise the richness of the topic. They also learn to analyse ideas, synthesise them and evaluate them. This also often motivates them to learn more about the theme.

Library Research is always an enriching exercise. In fact the old time practice of allocating library periods in the timetable served a great motivating force for children to explore the world of books. He may not necessarily read every book in the library but "browse" through it. This will imply looking through the table of contents and turning the pages just like that for identifying an interesting chapter an attractive picture or an educative diagram. It is quite likely that the learners, would be able to find some chapters of books or books themselves for further study.

This in fact will be the beginning of self-learning which is an important attribute for success in life.

Library Research is surely not an aimless exercise of browsing through the books but a focussed one, before the theme is taken up in class and necessarily after the theme has been completed. Collection of additional knowledge about the same theme will surely be an enriching exercise as it would help the learner gain further insight into the topic which will make the content more meaningful to him,

Consultation of other textbooks for the same class and the same subject not prescribed by the school could be a very valuable exercise. Learners for example could select the exercise in mathematics textbooks for purposes of drill for the mastery of the theme.

Consultation of children's encyclopaedias would surely be a useful exercise in widening the knowledge horizons of learners.

The magazines subscribed by the school library could lead the learner, to some interesting reading material which may motivate the learners for further whetting his interest in self reading, self learning and learning how to learn.

26

Photo Language Session

26.1 Connotation

Photo-language sessions involve giving expression to thoughts, ideas, feelings, emotions evoked by photographs or pictures.

26.2 Requirements

The collection of photographs, pictures related to the selected topic is the first step, as everybody looks at the pictures attentively, and tries to mentally analyse what they depict and reflect on them in terms of the ethos of their contents. The atmosphere naturally is reflective, because what is attempted to be caught are thoughts and feelings that the pictures or photographs exhale.

The time for viewing these pictures or photographs is also *rationed*, say two or three minutes, so that all the learners are able to view them closely. The class is then divided into groups of say ten learners each, who are normally seated in a semi-circle for watching the set of pictures presented to each group.

26.3 Process

As mentioned, sets of pictures/photographs related to the central theme are given to each group. The leader of the group shows the pictures/photographs given to the group one by one. Learners are given time to observe them in silence and jot down in telegraphic language the things they observe. The leader then asks the learners to give their reactions to the details observed in the pictures without any inhibitions or reservations. The learners then individually write their observations. These observations are then compiled picture wise. The pictures and photographs are then circulated to the other groups where the same operation is repeated. All the groups then come together. Each picture or photograph is then presented one by one and each group presents its report on that one by one. The variation in the perception of different groups about the same picture or photograph are by themselves enriching experiences. If time permits a discussion on each could also follow.

26.4 The Gains

The exercise promotes the habit of close and critical observation and the ability to mentally translate the depictions/details into feelings, and these into words. The exercise empowers learners to reach out their thoughts to the affective domain and thereby to sensitise the learners to certain needs and situations. This also helps learners to channelise emotions and to communicate them.

Photo-language Sessions sound like something new but even in the good old days there used to be a question on **Picture composition** in language question papers.

The broad purpose in the two exercises is the same i.e. the translation of one form of presentation into another. Even in mathematics this type of translation exercises from one form of presentation to another among tables, diagrams and graphs bar/pie diagrams is quite common.

The Photo-language Session focus on language for interpreting the contents of pictures. The projective techniques in Psychological Testing like the *Thematic Apperception Test* uses the interpretation of pictures for judging attributes of personality.

Coming back to Photo-language Sessions, it could be said that this involves the varied interpretations of the contents of the pictures by different individuals. The exercises involve the power of intricate observation of pictures for giving them a meaning. The different observations on the same picture enable learners to learn about the points they missed to observe and interpret. This thus becomes a learning exercise in focussed observation by itself.

With all the pictures, aligned to the common themes the scope for differences in interpretation does no doubt get narrowed down, but still some elements of it do remain.

The ability to write what one sees and feels about it is the main ability attempted to be developed.

The exercises become difficult because of the depiction of emotions and likely related activities. This requires not just close observation of details but also of the expressions and gestures depicted by the pictures.

To be able to do that, one must have a good backup acquaintance with vocabulary and usage for which extra reading becomes a stand-by asset.

27

Surveys

21.1 Connotation

Surveys connote detailed study by collecting information tabulating it and analysing it to discover some new facts, or to reinforce the existing knowledge, or to confirm and verify some stated idea or principle.

27.2 Requirements

Selecting a topic and allotting its facets to different groups.

27.3 Physical (Seating) Arrangement

Informal and flexible.

27.4 Process

Dividing the class into groups and the teacher holding separate meetings with different groups to explain to them the objectives, areas of exploration, places to be visited, information to be collected and people to be interviewed, tables to be prepared the diagrams to be drawn etc.

The groups may be given *specific time budgets* for doing the job.

The learners may individually maintain notes of the things they observe, the things they learn and the conclusions they draw. Groups then make their presentations to the whole class (all the groups) and prepare a written report for exhibition along with tables, charts etc. prepared in the course of their work.

27.5 Gains

The learners do not receive information collected by someone else but collect it on their own, which by itself is very aggrandising. They learn how to collect, tabulate, and interpret the information they may collect for drawing their own conclusions. This makes the inferences more meaningful to them. They experience the thrill of discovery and also come to realise that team work can do many things which individuals by themselves cannot singly do. They also gain faith in their conclusions and take the established principles to be really true and valid, having been experimentally verified by them.

Surveys as such are a valuable teaching devices. They enable children to acquire first hand knowledge form *primary sources*, to compile and organise it and to draw their own conclusions form it. The so derived inferences become the self-earned part of an individual's knowledge and being so, turns out to be his abiding permanent treasure of knowledge. *The Engel's Law of Consumption in Economics* for example if memorised it can slip out of the memory after some time, but if it is derived though a survey of different levels of people (say an executive, an office assistant, a labourer) about the proportion of their income they spend on food, clothes, shelter, and entertainment, it will be never forgotten by the individual learner.

Furthermore surveys bring learners closer to realities of life enabling them to personally gather information based on their own exploration and experiences about the life in their environment. This too is a permanent gain making the individual realistic in this statements or decisions.

The schedule through which data for surveys is collected and the hurdles that come in the way, yield insights which other situations cannot impart.

Furthermore the learner also learns about the importance of little bits of information when he reaches a solution where for want of a small piece of information he feels disabled in reaching conclusions.

Surveys in fact become enjoyable when the learner has an eye on the end result and hopes to collect information for substantiating an existing tenet or for disproving it. In this process, exceptions always attract his attention and these prove the rule.

Surveys should not be undertaken as a formality but should be purposeful and the purpose when firstly understood by the learners whet their motivation by igniting their interest in them.

28

Participatory/Group Learning

28.1 Introduction

Participatory learning is an innovation mothered by necessity. Eventhough an outcome of compulsions to practice, it has started paying valuable dividends by way of:

- speeding up the process of collection of educational information as compared to individualised endeavours.
- consolidation and internalisation of self-acquired learning as compared to teacher dispensed information.
- reduction of teacher's workload and more particularly, his speaking load.

These gains are not just encouraging but enticing and tempting to be pursued.

28.2 The Genesis of Participatory Learning

In 'Participatory Learning' it is not just that each learner pursues his course of action for acquiring the gains of learning. It is the group or team that pursues learning as a joint venture by sharing responsibility, replicating the concept of 'division of labour'.

28.3 Prerequisites of the Approach of Participatory Learning

A well equipped School Library/Laboratory

28.4 The Process of Participatory Learning

The process of participatory learning consists of the following flexible and adaptable steps:

- ➢ Announcement of the theme/topic to the class by the teacher.
- ➢ Taking the class to the library to browse through the books on the subject and identify those that deal with the given topic.
- ➢ Dividing the class into viable groups.
- ➢ Distributing the books to the groups.

- Loud reading of the concerned theme from the books by learners in their respective groups by taking reading turns. This could be done in the course of any decided span of time and at any place the group may decide, with each member of the group taking his/her own notes.
- Return of the groups to the class in the next scheduled class period when the teacher may, in consultation with the learners, draw-up on the black/white board, an outline of the sub-themes of the main theme and throws them up for a discussion.
- Taking up each such theme for a detailed discussion one by one, with learners contributing on the basis of whatever books they consulted. Different points of view or approaches could thus emerge.
- Simultaneous development of black/white board summary by the teacher.
- Concluding observation by the team/group leaders and the teacher.

Participatory Learning has infact become the need of the hour particularly because knowledge is growing every fast and becoming redundant faster. An individual cannot all by himself explore the many sources that contain knowledge. Therefore, a division of labour is a valuable innovative approach. If a number of learners set out to collect information about a particular theme in a planned manner, almost everybody will be discovering something different. The compilation of this knowledge and its presentation to the group is enriching to one and all of them. Every member of the group will also thus derive a unique satisfaction for contributing to the common pool of knowledge. This will become a meaningful exercise to everybody, because of the eagerness that will automatically get generated in each one. There will thus be a beginning of both **competition for advancement and cooperation for strength.**

Participatory or team learning will not thus be restricted to only library research but could take the form of *surveys, projects, exploration, experimentation etc.* It will offer examples of situations where *learners will learn without being taught* even though the teacher will remain a planner and a guide in these activities. Even the teachers would stand to learn from these initiatives of the learners and he would always be looking forward to what new the learners may discover through their strides.

It needs to be specifically pointed out here that when there is a *teacher learner interaction* in the course of a teaching learning session, the concentration level of the learners is minimal. When this becomes a *learner-learner interaction* the level of this concentration improves and when it is the interaction of the learner with himself (as in self learning and self-directed learning episodes) the concentration is at its highest level.

28.5 Conclusion

Thus the aims stand more than realised with children learning much more than what they could ever have dreamt of, while pursuing learning individually. All the learners can take pride in contributing to the theme in his own way. The process leads to abiding learning, and the learners do not usually forget what they learn. The teacher too saves time and labour.

The approach is simple, easy, effective and economical. It is also an encouraging proposition aligned to the standard of the class. Institutions would however need to have a good library. The method could be usefully used from class VII/VIII onwards.

29

Action Research

29.1 The Concept

Action research is in fact a problem solving strategy in the teaching process. Whenever and wherever a hard spot is identified, that situation could become the starting point of Action Research. The problem that arises has first to be analysed for getting to its source. Steps for overcoming it are then designed. The action is instant and so it disallows any snow-balling of the confusion or lack of clarity that may have emerged. Action research is not any theoretical construct but a practical approach specifically designed for the specific situation. The approach therefore is a *hand maid of the teacher*, who exercises full freedom and flexibility in designing and implementing a strategy specific to the situation for making teaching amenable to learning.

29.2 Designing of Steps

The teacher being the master of the situation designs the exercise as per his own thinking in the hope of solving the problem through it. In the process he often breaks down a complex situation into smaller sub-situations and helps pupils move on step by step for overcoming them, wherein the success they realise at each step gives them the confidence for realising success in the subsequent steps. This also leads to a better consolidation of learning in the pupils. This approach for realising the goal is termed as Action Research Hypotheses.

Both the strategy and the targeted goals can change midway at the discretion of the teacher on the basis of the need for change experienced by him. Action Research thus admits immense flexibility and adaptability.

Success in a particular situation in action research does not go to enunciate a principle or a theory or a generalisation, particularly because it is based on situation specific ingenuity of the teacher. This characteristic differentiates it from basic or fundamental research as in Action Research the teacher and in some measure the learners become the sole judges of the effectiveness of the approach in realising the anticipated success.

29.3 Operation of Action Research

Action research, is an informal methodology and satisfaction of the teacher and the learners is the measure of success which does not offer any quantitative enunciation.

The outcomes of Action Research are also not normally presented formally as the findings result in self-assuring experiences, which may encourage other teachers to devise their own approaches for solving the problems they may face from time to time.

Unlike fundamental research where the findings are normally used subsequently by others, in action research there is no such time gap and the teacher is both the designer of the approach and its follower. Thus he is both the producer and the consumer of the research. He also thus translates his knowledge of theories into practice.

Action Research admits a very wide operational scope. It can be used in any teaching, learning or testing situation and at any step or juncture. It can also serve as a useful tool of management of different operations for making them effective.

Action Research bears a striking similarity with *micro teaching*. In fact the diagnoses of shortfalls is the starting point of both. In the former the purpose is transmission of ideas to others (pupils), in the latter it is for self-improvement. Improvement however is the common goal.

Though an invariably successful strategy it often turns out to be time consuming but the time spent becomes an investment because internalisation of learning, leads to faster learning of subsequent steps. The time saved at later stages thus compensates for the extra time spent now.

Though the conceptual terminology of Action Research introduced by *Stephen Corey* sounds new there is nothing new about it, as teachers have all along been using it for transmitting knowledge to the pupils. It is in fact common sense which is not uncommon in its utilisation. Corey, however, gave a formal shape to this informal approach.

SECTION V
ICT in Instructional Designing

30

ICT in Instructional Designing and Curriculum Implementation

30.1 Introduction

Since the second half of the 20th century the global society has been witnessing unprecedented changes at unprecedented speed.

We have witnessed transitions

- From the Data Age to the Information Age
- From the Information Age to the Knowledge Age
- From the Knowledge Age to the Competency Age

Multi-media and technology have been mainly responsible for these changes where the computer has been the most versatile of the technological devices for fostering them.

The changes, however, have not just remained confined to science and technology but have permeated into almost every area of significance in our lives and the environment.

Among other things, the attributes of speed and accuracy have motivated the workers in different fields to use computers in their day-to-day work. Computers can be seen to have entered for wider applications in the fields of:

- Business and Industry
- Trade and Commerce
- Offices and Banks
- Scientific and Economic Research
- Communication
- Warehousing
- Architecture
- Engineering
- Meteorology
- Museology
- Medicine
- Education and
- so on

Computers are welcome to the functionaries in different fields because they are satisfying the newer needs of these specialisations.

We are thus increasingly witnessing examples of:

- Computers Aided Design
- Computer Aided Manufacture
- Computer Aided Innovations

The leaders in different areas of specialisation have particularly got interested in multimedia because of its wide applications and utility for:

- animation
- graphics
- video
- digitally recorded sound
- movement

which offer a much richer and a more efficient means of conveying ideas and information.

The above listing of computer utilities is by itself adequate for even motivating even the lay man about the unique and versatile gadget called the computer for:

- enlarging the catchment area of the sources of extracting knowledge
- energising the process of its acquisition
- enhancing the human treasure of heritage of knowledge

30.2 Evolution of Computers

It is desirable to know a little more about the evolution of this versatile invention.

The history of computers is just about seven decades old and hence quite recent. It was in 1944 that the first functional computer *Mark I* was developed at Harvard. Closely following on the heels of this human achievement, the University of Pennsylvania produced another similar machine called ENIK.

The use of computers was injected into education at the University of Illinois through a project called *"Programmed Logic for Automatic Teaching Operations (PLATO)"*.

As a follow-up the system for using several thousand terminals by different users was then evolved at the Universities of Urbana and Chicago (the author saw the first computer in 1958 as a student at the University of Chicago. It was a huge machine assembled in the basement of the Education Faculty Building.)

Originally computers were used only for research and programmes used to be written in the machine language FORTAN. It was only in 1963 that 'Jon Kemney' and 'Thomas Jurtz' at Dartmouth developed an easy to use language called BASIC. This marked the beginning of wider uses of computer in different fields including teaching and learning.

The most significant support to the *computer education programme* came from the National Science Foundation of USA in 1960.

In Seventies with the miniaturisation and economisation of computer hardware, personal computers (PCs) got invented. This tremendously increased their access and availability to the common man giving a giant-push to their use.

The two tables that follow summarise the Evolution of Computer Assisted Learning (CAL) Programmes and the evolution of related hardware, present a birds' eye view to the readers.

EVOLUTION OF COMPUTER ASSISTED LEARNING PROGRAMMES (CAL) IN EARLY YEARS

Year	*Contributors*	*Contribution*	*Supporting Agency*
Late 1950s	Patrick Supples (Grandfather of Computer Assisted Learning), Stanford University	First Teaching Machine for Teaching Binary Arithmetic	IBM
1960	Kemeney and Kurtz	Basic	University of Illinois
1968	Bitzer	Programmed Logic for Automatic Teaching Operations (Plato)	University of Illinois
		Courses for Elementary Students in Maths, Eng., Biology, Chemistry and Accounting (Introduction of graphics and sound-teaching)	
1972	Bunderson and Mitre	Micro-computer International Framework Dictated the Computer	Bungham Young University
1980	Papert	Logo project (Specific Learning Approach enunciated)	
1963	Patrik Supples	Instructional System (IBM 1300)	Institute of Mathematics Studies and Social Sciences

EVOLUTION OF COMPUTER ASSISTED LEARNING RELATED HARDWARE

Year	*Developmental Item*	*Contributor/Supporter*
1924	Multiple Choice Response Scoring Machine	Sydney Pressey
1939	Electronic Digital Computer (EDC)	Vincent Atanasofi Cliford Barry
1944	First Operational Computer (MARK-5)	Harvard University
1946	Electronic Numerical Integrator and Calculator (ENIC)	US Deptt. of Defence, Pennsylvania University
1959	Computer for Schools (Teaching of Binary Arithmetic in Elementary Schools)	IBM (1600)
1960	Large Frame Computer	
1980s	Colour Television added to a computer	Victor Bunderson Dexter Fletcher National Science Foundation

30.3 COMPUTER AIDED INSTRUCTION

Education too has not lagged behind in the use of technology including computers for exploring the possibilities of the new development.

Selly Brown developed settings for enabling students to apply their knowledge. *Wallace Feurzeig* developed situations for problem solving in Algebra. *Eugene Stanley* worked on shortening the lead time.

With the above and other developments three following basic uses of computer in education have by now got crystallised.

- providing educational input to students
- leading students for higher performance
- assessing the gains from education

The fundamental corner-stones of a Computer Aided Educational Programme could be diagrammatically presented as in Fig. 30.1.

The three corner-stones of an instructional programme viz. the computer, the programme and the learner have a two-way relationship among themselves and each one of them has a two-way relationship with the curriculum. They are these interactive relationship that impart life to Computer Aided Instruction (CAI).

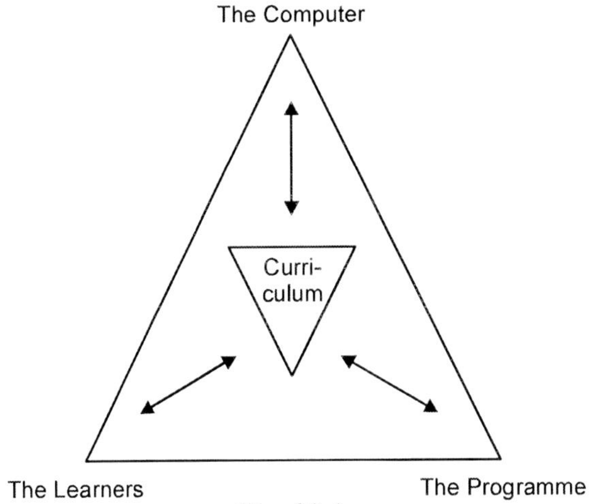

Fig. 30.1

30.4 Strategies of CAI

There are basically two strategies of CAI:

- Instructional System Design (ISD) – This is the commonly used approach in vogue for quite sometime. It consists of (a) the statement of objectives, (b) the development of course content software, (c) designing the instructional process and methodology (through the teaching machine computer) (d) designing evaluation instruments.
- Hypermedial Design Model (HDM) – This focusses on the targets that a student sets for himself and the approach he plans for collecting the needed information for the realisation of the goals.

30.5 Purposes Served of by CAI

While the goals of teacher conducted instruction and those of CAI do in many ways coincide with those of education as such some of the main of those related to CAI are as under:

- To complement and supplement the traditional methods of instruction.
- To motivate students for self-learning.
- To actively engage students in the learning process.
- To energise the learning process.
- To deliver the content of the courses through the computers.
- To enrich learning through computer applications.
- To energise the learning process by distancing learners from memorisation and motivating them to critical thinking as also leading learners from one way to interactive learning.
- To diversify the learning process through video conferencing.
- To increase personal productivity of learners through enhanced speed improved accuracy and higher efficiency.

30.6 Components of CAI

The components of Computer Aided Instruction mainly get divided into the following parts:

- Expected Outcomes
  - Objectives and their specifications in terms of what a learner will be able to do to demonstrate to us that he has achieved the particular objective.
- Content Outline
  - Topics and sub-topics (sequence and graded)
  - Visual impacts and effects
  - Diagrams
  - Illustrations
- Support Material
  - Infrastructure
  - Aids
  - Sound effects
- Operational Strategy
  - Instructions for teachers and learners
- Self-Evaluation Exercises
- Objective-based developmental questions
- Balanced end-of-the-topic-tests

Hardware

PIV Processor
256 MB DDR RAM
50 MB HARD-DISK for programme and Data Base
Internet connection

Software

Operating System: Windows XP or above version
PHP, MYSQL, Apache
Apache Server
PHP Scripting Language Server Side
Internet Browser
MYSQ Data Base

30.7 Salient Attributes of CAI

- Personalised Approach
  - Programmes pitched at learners
    - level of previous knowledge and
    - assimilation ability

- Motivational enticements to learners through
  - devices
  - animations
  - illustrations
- Variety
  - variety of inputs from a variety of sources and settings
  - catering to different settings – home, social and economic background
  - availability of alternative routes/approaches
- Self-needed speed
  - self-controlled adjustable learning speed
  - computer moves at learner desired pace
- Attention catching, impact making and excitement generating content
  - diagram
  - graphics
  - pictures
  - examples
  - sound effects
  - movements, etc.

30.8 Programmed Instruction

Programmed instruction contains the seeds of Computer Aided Instruction. It was developed by *B.F. Skinner.*

Approaches to Programmed Instruction

Skinners' Stimulus Response Model (Leniar or Extrinsic model)

This approach consisted of

- Breaking-up of content into smaller parts
- Determining a logical graded sequence
- Requiring students to respond to specially framed questions in "fill-in-the blank" situations by composing their own answers.
- Hinting, prompting and suggesting for evoking the correct response.
- Subjecting learners to confirmatory questioning.
- Correct Answers the end
- Behaviour analysis

The content covered through the approach is small.

Norman Crowder's Multi-track Model

Almost at the same time as Skinner Norman Crowder, working with the armed forces was pursuing the idea of machine-based approach to instruction. While Skinners' *approach was psychological, Crowder's was a communication or a transactional approach.*

The main characteristics of Crowder's programme were:

- Focus on communication between the user and the programme.
- Each 'frame' contained more text than the average learner frame.
- Optional frames were presented for responses (mostly corrective)
- Transfer of the learner to the earlier frame, in case of a mistake, after informing the learner.
- Use of remediation on difficult themes on the basis of the diagnosis.

Developing Instructional Designs and Material for Designing Instruction

The following broadly sequential steps are followed in developing and implementing programmed instruction programmes.

- Need Assessment
  - Previous knowledge of learners
  - The ability level of learners for learning and assimilation
- Listing of Terminal Behaviour Outcomes
- Listing of topics and sub-topics and arranging them in a logical sequential order for presentation.
- Choosing the approach (Skinner/Crowder)
- Assessing and conforming achievement level in respect of measurable, knowledge, attitudes and skills.

30.9 The Garbs of CAI

Computer Aided Instruction assumes many forms based on the purposes, desired to be served. These are briefly enunciated below:

- *Education about identified predetermined themes* – This involves building on the instructional doses based on the students' previous knowledge and his capacity for educational intakes. This involves graded presentations of the concerned subject matter, punctuated by questioning for recapitulation and cross-questioning for consolidation.
- *Drill or practice* – The time allocated and devoted for the above mentioned teaching-learning activities is no doubt adequate for gaining an acquaintance with the basic paradigms of the themes but not enough for the internalisation of the concerned knowledge. Drill and practice are follow-up steps consisting of a variety of situations requiring the student to invoke his abilities for application of knowledge in life situations, involving critical thinking, analysis and interpretation of information for drawing conclusions. The outcomes provide valuable evidences about the insight gained and foresight acquired about the concerned subject area by the learner.

Diagnosis and Reinforcement (D&R)

Interim ongoing evaluation which is built into the total teaching-learning process, as an integral part, is meant for identifying strengths, shortfalls in learning. This should never be treated as the end but the beginning for designing remedial/enrichment material for addressing the identified shortfalls in the attained level of achievement/proficiency for further improving them.

Higher Abilities Programmes

While the exercises related to benchmarking get concluded with reinforcement inputs there are also some special programmes in specific areas, which take students attainments to higher intellectual levels. These are advanced level enrichment programmes for those with whetted interests and aptitudes for studying these specific areas. The programmes do not just require the learners to tackle issues related to the subject concerned, but move its relationship with other subjects and application in life situations. Similarly the integration of different themes in the subject itself is focussed upon. The programmes invariably offer pleasure and satisfaction to those who pursue them. Such programmes also include tough and complicated testing exercises the solution of which offers them a unique sense of achievement and a feeling of fulfilment. This type of programmes though originally conceived are not generally witnessed being pressed into service in usual practice.

Simulation Exercises

In these exercises exhaustive instructions are provided to the learner to proceed with the problems posed. The situations are basically macro-level ones and both real and hypothetical. The learner is offered the freedom to manipulate and choose the parameters of the problems presented to work on. The learner is also required to visualise the implications of the choices s/he makes and to make his own decisions about the path he logically thinks more viable and useful to treed. The creativity of the learner is thus really at test.

Micro Computer-based Programmes

The learner is expected to explore the versatility of the computer. The learner is presented with a life-problem with multiple subject dimensions. He is expected to be an explorer, adventurer and a discoverer in using the internet and the www for finding a solution. He thus collects the relevant information required for the case, compiles it systematically and logically, classifies it for enhancing its interpretability and draws his own conclusions, which he is capable of fully defending on all counts. These programmes too are rare.

Computer Games

Computer games were originally concerned as instruments of offering learning incidentally and effortlessly particularly because of the sounds and graphics they used. Puzzles and quizzes and Mind Teasers were visualised as important parts of computer games. They consist of exercises that require deep thinking, identification of cues from complicated data for solving the problem; attempting of alternative approaches for reaching the correct one; analysis, synthesis and evaluation of data and arriving at conclusions for establishing a principle etc. etc.

While there were some old programmes of this type serving the desired purposes these have somehow now got degenerated into entertainment programmes with some suspense, excitement and humour. They are being used by young students normally around 5-15 years of age. In the form in which they exist now they can hardly be called educational programmes by any definition. Children normally waste their time on these without learning anything significant. They are proving to be diversions that drain away valuable time.

30.10 Dividends of CAI

CAI has come to be increasingly used because of some of its undeniable strengths.

- It improves the chances of an individuals' employability as the use of computers has become the fundamental feature of the work-culture.
- It raises the level of effectiveness of an individual on the job by ensuring accuracy and increasing the speed of work.
- It is economical both in terms of basic infrastructure and running cost.
- It systematically overcomes the problem of large numbers and scattered location of students because of its extensive outreach in situations like those of distance education and large classes.
- It stimulates interest, motivates self-learning, sustains attention and sharpens capabilities.
- It offers global connectivity and improves access.

The applications of computers have come to be widely used in education for—

- The realisation of the objective of the teachers and learners.
- The safe storage and instant retrieval of information.
- The development of teaching-learning materials and programmes.
- The energisation of the process of education through interactive teaching and learning.
- The optimisation of the outcomes of learning by addressing learning gaps.
- Economisation in educational infrastructure.
- The individualisation of learning (self-teaching)
- The internalisation and consolidation of learning on the part of learners.
- The enlargement of the catchment area of educational inputs—books, bulletins, newspapers, audio and video material, pictures, graphics, internet, www.

SECTION VI
Some Ancillary Teaching-Learning Facets/Situations

31

Assignments and Work at Home

31.1 Assignments for Consolidation of Learning Exercises

Assignments constitute that part of the instructional activity which are aimed at consolidating previous learning and for laying the foundation for future learning in an effective manner. Assignments helps in the planning and organisation of ideas when both the teacher and the pupils prepare for the next step. It is a co-operative experience in which the teacher is a sympathetic director or guide and pupils willing participants.

The assignment method is also based upon the principles of *learning by doing*. It provides opportunities to pupils to work independently in the class or laboratory or home and in the course of study by themselves. Learners are thereby helped to develop the habit of extra study. They learn how to consult references and collect data and information.

The assignment method is an economical one because pupils in a class could even be given different assignments, depending upon their interests and abilities. Each learner too can work at his own speed. The weak learners do not stand in the way of bright pupils. Learners can refer their difficult *experiences* to the teacher who is in a position to give individual guidance.

31.2 Characteristics of Assignments

The success of the assignment method depends upon how well the assignment is developed/drawn, and how well-equipped the library and laboratory are for assignments to be allotted to individual learners. Some problems encountered in using the assignment method in the institutions, are a heavy curriculum which cannot be finished within the limited time available. Dearth of books and references, non-availability of literature on all topics and the tendency for some learners to copy from others are some of the main problems faced.

Assignments should be challenging to enthuse learners and to motivate them to explore and experiment. The problem of copying by the weak pupils can be eliminated and overcome by asking oral questions and at times requiring them to write short answers in the class itself to know whether or not a particular concept or principle has been understood.

Assignments as a technique of teaching, are yet to be recognised in education. The significance of the assignment method is based on the premise that the desire for self-learning is more important than that of learning through teaching. It is learners' attitude towards learning that matters, and not the courses of instruction, however well organised they may be. In the words of *Douglass and Hubert*, "The assignment represents one of the most important phases of teaching". If good assignments are prescribed, learners can and will study independently with success; but with poor or routine assignments they will fail to profit.

Assignments rouse learners interest, stimulate their thinking, whet their motivation, encourage initiative, clear-up misunderstandings, develop insight and boost morale. They help learners to plan and outline the work to be undertaken in the future with new and wider avenues and to discover facts and phenomenon through their personal efforts. Assignments thus supplement class-room teaching. They provide the teacher with an opportunity to augment learning through extra study. Assignments are of two types:

1. Home assignments
2. School assignments

Home assignments include writing of answers to questions or undertaking of tasks assigned by the teacher. School assignments could take the form of performing experiments in the laboratory and answering questions put forth by the teacher in the class. According to *Yoakam*, assignments may be of the old type or the new type. Those assignments which have been long in use, such as prescribing the number of pages, paragraphs, topics, themes, exercises, questions and experiments are of the old type. In contrast the new type of assignments include the project activity and problem solving. The new type ones are the outcome of the shift of focus *from teacher-directed study to self-directed learning.*

A good assignment must be related to the topics of the prescribed curriculum. It should be brief, clear in purpose and flexible. It should aim at realising the goals, prescribed in such a way that it stimulates reflective thinking and gives freedom to learners to discover facts for themselves, appealing to the curiosity of the learners, as also thought-provoking and challenging and aligned to the age, intelligence and abilities of learners.

31.3 Steps in Assignments

The *first step* is to analyse the prescribed course and allot suitable assignments possible to be completed within the time at disposal. With the calendar and course requirements, the teacher should find out the total number of assignments which could be undertaken by the learners within the working days in a year by a particular class. The *next* step is to list the assignments and lay down the objectives for each assignment, desirably with the co-operation of the learners and guide them through the following stages :

1. *Reference to previous experience*—If for example, the previous lesson was 'planning the house', references should be given from the previous lesson, to motivate and prepare the learners for doing worthwhile assignments. The assignment could relate to a study of different designs observed by them at home or in the institutions. While giving such references for the assignments, the teacher should see that the books suggested are within the comprehension ability of the pupils.
2. *Discussion*—The teacher can organise a discussion on any suitable topic. Various proposals for the execution of the assignments could be then suggested by learners. The teacher should guide the discussion indicating the time allotted for completing various parts of an assignment.
3. *Explanations and clearing difficulties*—Any doubts and difficulties regarding content and process of the assignment will be cleared by the teacher.
4. *Distribution of tasks*—Suggested activities like collection of pictures, making models, writing essays will be distributed to the learners either individually or in groups. When assignments are part of class work, the teacher will offer on-the-spot guidance.
5. *Starting the activity*—Learners take up the assignment as a new project.
6. *Evaluation*—Assignments should then be evaluated jointly by the teacher and learners for positive results and for offering further motivation through diagnosis and remediation.

31.4 Work at Home

Work at home is independent work which the learners do at home, to supplement the instruction received at school, away from the atmosphere of the class room, in the midst of home surroundings. As a practical teaching device, work at home is a step towards self-education. It enables the learner to use his own acquired knowledge, resources and work without external help and supervision.

Work at home facilitates formation of habits, of independent effort, self-study and work habits and above all operational autonomy. It accelerates the advance of learners in their studies and gives opportunity to teachers for securing more effective co-operation from parents in the education of their children.

In order that work at home may be effective, it should be graded. The nature and amount of home work must be determined by the capacity of the learners and allowing time for leisure-time activities. Work at home should never be considered as a punishment. All the subjects in the curriculum must get due share of home work.

32

Organisation of Exhibitions

32.1 Introduction

Exhibitions are unique aids to teaching. Exhibitions involve the display of a variety of two or three-dimensional objects for communicating different ideas and pieces of information to the observer. The impact of an exhibition has immense educational value.

As they are the learners who participate in preparing the exhibits, setting them up and explaining to the visitors, they not only learn new concepts but also consolidate their learning. Interesting exhibits also motivate pupils to undertake further explorations and obtain new information.

32.2 Basic Principles of Organising Exhibitions

- Have an overall theme for each particular exhibition. The exhibits should necessarily have an educational value, should always have a message to convey which may be possible to be immediately perceived without the need for its being told through speech or written word. The message should be crisp and clear and have an appeal. It should effectively convey the central idea and project the unity of the displays.
- Locate the exhibit centrally at an easily accessible place for being observed.
- The settings of the display should not be crowded. They should be demarcated by using bright colours and strong broad lines.
- Use movement if possible.
- Follow artistic principles—proportion, balance, colour, shape, rhythm.
- Some exhibits have to be just seen, others understood. What has to be read should be placed at the appropriate eye distance.
- Label the exhibits properly. Labels should be possible to be read from a distance. Labels should normally be of uniform size pattern and style.
- Display only latest up-to-date material, old, soiled and dust settled items should not be displayed.
- Give optimum dramatic effect—setting lighting etc.

- Have the exhibits of all children displayed. Parents will be interested in seeing the exhibits prepared by their children. Judicious use of colour and illumination help capture the attention of the viewers.
- Use the principles of advertising even in an educational exhibition as the objective of all advertisements is to sell ideas.
- Survey the place allocated and the material and accessories available in advance. A map of the place be prepared and location of objects decided.
- Train learners to explain exhibits. They should be level-headed, respectful and intelligent for giving pinpointed appealing answers to questions asked. Answers to anticipated questions be prepared in advance.
- Use a variety of display techniques for reaching ideas to many people to save time of the viewers, for appropriately targeting the viewers and to make them think.

32.3 Characteristics of Exhibits

- Exhibits should involve and attempt to capture as many senses for appreciation as possible—visual, audio, tactile etc.
- Colour imparts attraction to the exhibits and should be judiciously used particularly because colours also convey different meanings.

Yellow	–	prosperity
Red	–	danger
Brown	–	monotony
Green	–	production
Grey	–	submission
Orange	–	cheer
Black	–	sorrow

- Motion in exhibits is a great attraction but all cannot have that. Soft background instrumental music adds interest to an exhibition.
- Provide for at least some opportunity to the viewers to touch, turn, press operate, open as that can sustain their interest in the exhibits.
- None can compel a person to look at an exhibit except the exhibit itself.

As mentioned earlier, harmony, balance, artistically designed settings are crucial for making an appeal.

Exhibitions need not always be an elaborate or a ceremonial affair. There could even be exhibitions put up by different classes to share with the learners of other classes. For example, the conclusion of a project the class concerned may present the process and outcomes of the same.

Such events could also trigger a healthy competition among classes for sharing with others what they may have accomplished and which they may consider is worth sharing.

The classes or groups of learners of representations of different Houses of the school could even produce a wall magazine periodically spurring creativity and innovation among learners.

33

Educational Field Trips and Excursions

33.1 Introduction

Field Trips and Excursions enable on-the-spot study of different things/facets of the environment by putting the school on the wheels. Children are enabled to come face to face with realities. Field Trips and Excursions, offer such experiences which though necessary for learning cannot be brought into the classroom. They give meaning to classroom learning through personal observations and experience.

33.2 Purpose of Organising Field Trips

Field-trips and Excursions serve a variety of educationally fruitful purposes. They enable the pupils:

- a change from the routine activities.
- to gain first hand experience about facts and phenomenon they study and investigate.
- to critically observe and scrutinise things for arriving at personally made conclusions which are never forgotten by them.
- to obtain clarifications about different concepts and processes.
- to launch on self-directed educational activities.
- to broaden and change attitudes in desirable directions.
- to discover areas of interest other than the existing ones.

Educational trips assume three main forms:

- *Field trips* are taken to places of the neighbourhood like a post office, farm/factory, construction sites.
- *Excursions* to places where people live or work. They are outside the institutions but not very far from it. They may take a day or half a day. They may include visits to a bakery, a poultry farm, water purification plant, a nearby factory or a manufacturing unit like a sugar factory, a power generation plant, a museum, a zoo, a monument and so on.
- *Study Tours* are normally of longer durations and cover wider or distant areas. They may also involve long journeys.

33.3 Organisational Steps

There are some common essential steps for organising educational trips excursions/tours:

- *Identification of a trip.* This is done for different learner groups in consultation with teachers as per their curricular needs. The purpose of the trip is also simultaneously defined and impressed upon the learners before commencement.
- *Planning* : Advance planning is a pre-requisite for a successful trip. This involves:
  - detailing of objectives of the trip in the context of its relationship with the curriculum.
  - listing of places to be visited and of details of items to be observed.
  - drawing-up of an itinerary with dates and timings with expert help.
  - contacting the authorities for obtaining permission to visit the proposed sites.
  - obtaining the permission of the parents.
  - arranging necessary finances.
  - making arrangements and reservations for travel transport and accommodation.
  - delegation of responsibilities to the learners during the trip.
  - collecting technical information about places to be visited.
  - collecting necessary material/equipment etc.
  - preparing a 'medical help kit'.
  - prescribing do's and don's to the learners.
  - holding a stock-taking meeting every evening.
  - supplementing learning with-sight seeing to make the trip interesting.
  - advising learners to carry essential items.
  - asking learners to carry note books for on-the-spot observations mobiles for keeping in touch with families.

33.4 Post-Trip Exercises

On return after the trip, some other often overlooked items of action are:

- writing thank you letters to all those who were helpful.
- reporting to other classes about the trip.
- writing poems, stories for the bulletin boards about the trip.
- convening meeting, for acquainting others about the highlights of the trip.

Field Trips and excursions could be used for several other useful purposes. Surveys of different kinds for collecting first hand information is one such potential use. In fact, when an individual himself collects informations and draws his own conclusions, this learning becomes abiding. The survey or also imparts valuable insights about different things in the process of collecting, compiling analyzing and interpreting information. No text book or any other enrichment material can offer, this kind of enlightenment. The learner thus constructs his own set of tenets which yield him a sense of achievement.

SECTION VII

34

Instructional Aids and Support Material

34.1 The Genesis of Instructional Material and Aids

The singular target of the teacher is to communicate ideas to the pupils in a manner that they are able to assimilate them. Towards this end, he makes a mental picture of the ideas and transforms this mental picture into words. Such a communication often suffers from limitations, at both the ends. Sometimes this linguistic transmission of their mental picture is not as effective as it should be. While the teacher may feel that he has been successful, he may really not have been so. The result is that the pupils are not able to comprehend the communicated ideas properly and may miss the points made.

The situation can be resolved if the teacher does not solely depend on oral communication and supplements it with other media of communication. These other media are commonly referred to as *Audio-Visual Aids*.

34.2 Utilisation of all Senses for Learning Arise

Senses constitute the main link between man and the environment—physical, mental (intellectual) and moral. Vibrations of assimilation get stimulated through experiences and perceptions from the senses.

Senses as in-take routes receive the information from the environment and transmit them to the learners individually. These channels could be through touch, taste, smell, hearing and sight and all of them influence the mind.

The aids that impress upon the mind through the sense of hearing are referred to as 'audio-aids', while those which impress through sense of sight as 'Visual Aids'. The aids which impress upon the mind through both sight and hearing are known as Audio-Visual Aids. These aids transmit their respective images either directly or indirectly, pictorially/graphically or symbolically. All these support materials called teaching aids, help learners not just in learning but more so in assimilating what they learn easily and abidingly as well.

34.3 Purpose of Instructional Aids

Audio visual aids serve a variety of purposes. They:

- reinforce and consolidate teaching and learning.
- accelerate the teaching-learning process.
- help pupils assimilate learning easily and effectively.
- evoke and maintain pupil interest.
- reduce the teachers' work load particularly their speaking load.
- help in transforming abstract concepts into concrete realities.
- promote the interplay of different senses in the acquisition of learning
- impart joy to learning.

34.4 Types of Teaching Aids

Educational aids and support materials assume a variety of forms.

Audio Aids like:

- Radio
- Recordings

Visual Aids:

- Graphic Aids
- Pictorial material
- Diagrams
- Maps
- Charts
- Sketches
- Display Boards
- Flannelograph
- Bulletin Boards
- Three-dimensional models
- Working models
- Internet

Audio-Visual Aids:

- Television
- CD ROMs
- Projective Aids—Films, Film-strips, Video films
- Video
- Internet

The main purpose of the Teaching Aids is to supplement information for facilitating the comprehension of ideas, concepts' facts, etc. They save space and the labour of long explanations.

34.5 Situations for the Use of Instructional Aids

Use of these aids at appropriate junctures is as important as their quality. Their relevance to the content is equally important and they should always be accompanied by appropriate explanations, so that they are able to serve their purpose.

Normally, When we talk of teaching aids, we think about the material which may already be available for reinforcing the process of teaching. There is the other type of material also which is instantly produced by the teacher, by way of an example or a diagram for satisfying an instant emergent need of clarifying a confusion or of communicating an idea in the course of teaching. Such aids are instantly produced by the teachers when their learners encounter some hard spots in learning. The teacher, in such situations thinks of an example which may resolve the difficulty of the learners. He may even draw a diagram to explain the concept for bringing it home to the learners.

These illustration through instantly produced often prove to be more powerful than the ones developed in advance in response to anticipated needs of the teacher in the course of a particular lesson.

While teachers continuously develop such material, no record is normally kept of them. It will be very useful for the teachers make it a point to document them. They can constitute an important part of remedial programmes.

35

Edgar Dale's Cone of Experience

Dr. Edgar Dale has classified and arranged audio-visual aids in a pictorial form, called the 'Cone of Experience'.

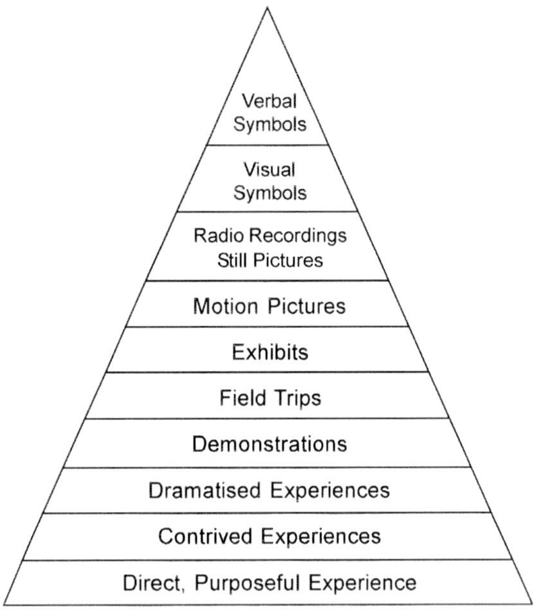

Diagram 35.1: Edgar Dale's Cone of Experience

The cone is by itself a visual aid which helps to explain the gradation and inter-relationships of various types of audio-visual materials and illustrates their 'positions' in the learning continuum. *At the bottom of the cone, Dr. Dale has placed the most concrete and direct experiences and at the top the most abstract ones. Heading from the bottom these experiences are*:

1. *Direct, purposeful experiences:* These are realities as we experience them first hand—going to the bazaar, preparing a meal, repairing a piece of furniture, giving a party at school for mothers etc.

2. *Contrived experiences:* A contrived experience differs from the original in size, or in complexity, or in both. We use a working model in order to make learners understand easily the real/original visualisation of the model, e.g. a model of a loom to show how cloth is made, models of childrens' toys, models of the human body, etc.

3. *Dramatised experiences:* Dramatic experiences help to get closer to realities that are not easily accessable or available at first hand. For example, acting the role of a Head Master/Principal.

4. *Demonstrations:* A demonstration is a visualised explanation of an important fact, or idea, or process.

5. *Field trips:* Excursions or field trips are taken to see life situations and how other people do things. Learners might be taken to a house that is being built to see the construction.

6. *Exhibits:* There are two general types of exhibits, the 'ready-made' and the 'home-made'. Exhibits planned and prepared by learners with the help of the teacher, are to be preferred. Preparing exhibits, such as different types of models or the equipment to use in caring for a sick person.

7. *Video pictures*: Video pictures can reconstruct periods with dramatic intensity and realism. They help understanding of other peoples' lands, ideas materials and events.

8. *Recording-radio and still pictures:* All of these are less direct than the audio visual experiences previously discussed.

9. *Visual symbols:* These include items like blackboard and chalk, flat maps, diagrams, charts, models etc.

10. *Verbal symbols:* These symbols bear no physical resemblance to the objects or ideas which they represent. The term iron does not look like an iron or feel like an iron for pressing clothes like an iron. But it is a term we use that has more or less common meaning for all of us. Although they are abstractions, we use these verbal symbols like *An iron man* with every other audio-visual material on the cone.

An old Chinese proverb says:

If I see, I remember
If I do, I know.

The most effective communication is a combination of seeing, hearing and doing. When visual aids are used along with demonstration they make a deep impact.

SECTION VIII
Evaluating Learning Outcomes

36

The Meaning of Educational Evaluation

"Evaluation is a process of collecting, analysing and interpreting evidences for judging the value and worth of the degree of goodness of an entity, being evaluated for making different types of decisions".

—R.H. Dave

Definitions of concepts involved do need to be explained for being understood and appreciated. Attempting this in regard to the above definition it could be safely concluded that—

1. Evaluation is a process and not an event.
2. Being a process it has but to be continuous – built into the total teaching-learning process.
3. It is based on concrete evidences and not in any bias imbued conjectures or opinion.
4. It involves the collection of information and details of evidences of growth which can be said to be the outcomes of the educational inputs from different quarters (sources).
5. Quite naturally these evidences, collected over the entire process of education, wherein they will be built into the teaching-learning process as an internal part, will cover different facets of personality cognitive affective and psycho-motor.
6. Such a collection of such evidences would necessarily call for the use of a variety of techniques and tools of evaluation beyond the traditional ones to be presssed into service.
7. The evidences collected are then subjected to a process of critical analyses for making logical and purposeful interpretations.
8. The interpretation will relate to the degree and kind of growth engineered through the various inputs of the educational process.
9. These interpretations become the basis of decisions about the attainments and proficiencies of the individuals concerned.
10. The decisions are used for a variety of purposes for judging the levels of attainments, abilities and potentials.

The above is the genesis of evaluation in education.

36.1 Examinations and Evaluation

The meaning and concept of evaluation are hoped to become clearer through its analytical comparison with the more commonly known term examinations which is attempted below.

Aspect	*Examinations*	*Evaluation*
Purpose	Assessment of the attained levels of achievement and proficiency	Further improvement of the attained levels of achievement and proficiency
Coverage of Personality	Mainly scholastic areas of personality	Both scholastic and co-scholastic areas of personality (personal and social qualities, interests, attitudes, values, outdoor activities)
Techniques of Evaluation	Mainly written, oral and practical examinations	Observation in addition to written, oral and practical examination.
Tools of Evaluation	Mainly questions and question papers	A variety of tools like inventories, checklists, rating, scales, observation-schedules, besides question and question papers.
Periodicity	Mainly terminal events	A continuous process built into the total teaching-learning process as an integral part.
Status of the Student	An incognito roll number	An individual with strengths and weaknesses

36.2 An operational explanation of Evaluation

Evaluation

- does not just identify gaps in learning but attempts to address them.
- tries to cover the total personality of learners in their scholastic and co-scholastic manifestations and does not draw conclusions about the attainments and proficiencies of an individual on segmentary information just on the basis of academic achievements.
- incorporates diagnosis and remediation/enrichment and thus tries to further improve the level of growth and thus advocates assessment for learning rather than only assessment of learning.

- covers both institution based evaluation and external examinations incorporating both formative and summative evaluation with separate/ undependent certification.
- implies education-based examinations replacing the old concept of examination-based education.
- Paves the way for holistic development through holistic education and holistic evaluation.
- focusses attention not just on "learning" but on "learning-to-learn" finally culminating in "self-directed learning".
- attempts to transform education from being "content-based" to becoming "process-based" to learnability, employability etc.

37

Purpose of Evaluation

37.1 Some Important Purposes of Educational Evaluation

E.J. Furst lists some important purposes of educational evaluation as under:

- judging the effectiveness of learning
- tasting assumptions and practices
- classifying objectives
- selecting and appraising objectives
- planning instructional programmes
- motivating learners
- guidance of learners
- certification of candidates
- selection of candidates
- in-service development of workers

These purposes remain undeniably valid even after nearly half a century of their enunciation, both in letter and spirit. However, when applied to the current testing scene they have functionally got shrink to

- Bench-marking and certification of the level of attainments of an individual used as an eligibility criteria for a variety of future academic and professional pursuits. This is reflected through the certification of candidates for degrees, diplomas, certificates etc.

37.2 Selection Tests

Selection tests are now widely in use mainly for

- admission to courses of higher/professional education
- recruitment for jobs
- promotion and on-the-job in institutions

In these instances though they are called aptitude tests but in actual practice are just achievement tests.

The phenomenon has come into place because aptitude tests are difficult to construct and expertise for it is not easily available. Secondly because the number of candidate aspirants are many times more than the actual positions available and the tests in vogue also turn out to be *elimination* rather than *selection* tests.

It needs to be noted that while the bench-marking achievement tests are based on '*content*' the selection tests are based on "*proficiencies*".

The selection tests, by and large, have come to have the following components:

1. General awareness
2. Linguistic ability
3. Quantitative ability
4. Subject matter competence
5. General mental ability (verbal and non-verbal)

This broad framework with some adaptations and varying weightages to different aspects is used in most situations.

The tests consist of multiple choice variety of items. The number of test items normally being more than what the candidates can possibly attempt in the given time, they just become *speed tests* rather than being *power tests*, eventhough they ought to be power tests, except in some special situations.

Furthermore, apart from the mistakes and shortfalls in the basic principles of constructing multiple choice test items, they often ask for *insignificant microscopic details*. This no doubt raises the difficulty level of the questions but imparts little predictive validity to the test.

The greatest shortcoming of these tests in most cases is that the test items test mainly memorisation (recall and reproduction of information).

The other higher abilities of understanding application of acquired knowledge in unfamiliar situations, analysis and interpretation of information, synthesis and drawing of inferences, based on given information and overall evaluation of situations are not attempted to be tested. This is because the prescribed *syllabus* mostly gives only topics to be covered and no indication about the *abilities* to be tested and the weightages to the two.

These shortfalls pass off undetected and unquestioned particularly because the establishments needing to fill vacancies do not have specialists in testing/ measurement/evaluation to man the operations related to testing and the decisions are taken administratively. A glaring example of this is the delayed announcement of the date of the tests and then expecting the tests to be prepared as a turnkey job. This makes test construction and its uploading a fire fighting exercise where many essential requirements like vetting of tests have often to be sidelined causing mistakes to creep into the tests.

Sometimes the agencies require five alternatives in a multiple choice test, which is a long discarded practice. Another more grave cause is that the business of test construction is often outsourced on the basis of tenders where the establishments are obliged to select the cheapest and not the most efficient agency with experience and expertise in testing. In this game of sorts many unqualified agencies have come into play. Many unemployed people too have found employment in this manner taking testing as a business and not as a field of specialised functioning.

Furthermore, the employers seldom undertake any *job analysis* of the positions required to be filled in and easy generalised solutions are attempted to be pressed into service for solving specialised problems.

In evaluation situations designs for tests are but necessary, in any case.

This is being discussed in subsequent sections.

37.3 Class Promotions in Institutions

Both these are internal matters of the institutions and the employing establishments but the tests in the two situations however display quite a lot of similarity.

Promotion from One Class to Another in Institutions

These have some basic characteristics. They are based on "norms" set by the institutions for example in schools, they may be say the attainment of 30% marks in each subject of study, at the university level they may be 40% and in professional institutions they may be 50%.

Promotions from class to class should ideally be based on assessments done throughout the year. In higher education it is usually based on the level of attainment mainly on the academic/scholastic front. At the school level, it normally covers both the scholastic and the co-scholastic areas of personality.

The concept of Comprehensive and Continuous Evaluation (CCE) which is *institution-based* in school situations broadly covers—

- Health status like height, weight, chest expansion, eye-sight, hearing etc. (which can be assessed by the teacher)
- Personal and social qualities like regularity, punctuality, habits of cleanliness, discipline, diligence, sense of responsibility, emotional stability, cooperation, civic consciousness, spirit of social service (for whichever evidences are available).
- Interests in the literary, artistic, scientific and cultural and social service areas (selected by the learner to be pursued)
- Attitudes towards studies, institutional programmes, public property as also towards societal issues.
- Values like dignity of labour, honesty, courage, courtesy, tolerance, forgiveness, team-spirit (for whichever evidences are available).
- Outdoor activities like games, sports, gymnastics, scouting, NCC, swimming, gardening, adventure activities, first aid (in whichever area a learner participates).

Besides

- Academic achievement where beside evaluation through questions, question papers, laboratory experiments, projects, assignments, surveys and case studies also becomes subjects of evaluation. The outcomes of learning are also evaluated not just in terms of marks but also in terms of symbolic grades through rating scales (usually five point) observation schedules, inventories, check-list, etc.

Being comprehensive covering both scholastic and co-scholastic aspects as enunciated above such evaluation has but to be continuous, spread over the total teaching, learning process as an integral part.

While in the co-scholastic areas, the outcomes of evaluation may not be aggregated, in the scholastic/academic areas they normally are aggregated and used for purposes of class promotions as presented through the following hypothetical diagrammatic representation. The diagram presumes that an academic session starts in July and ends in April.

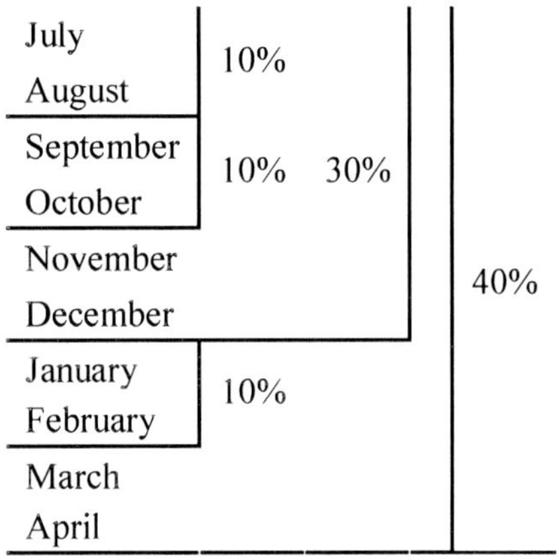

Test Time	*Weightage*	*Syllabus Covered*
Aug end	10%	Jul & Aug
Oct end	10%	Sep & Oct
Dec end	30%	July to Dec
Feb end	10%	Jan & Feb
April end	40%	Jul to Apr

The tests carrying 10% weightage are supposed to focus exclusively focus on the topics covered, within the time span concerned. The tests carrying 30% and 40% weightage, will in addition also focus on linkages between the topics of the concerned span without repetition.

At the terminal stages, *two different independent supplementary certificates*, one issued by the institution and another by the external examining and certifying agency are proposed. This is meant particularly for overcoming the malpractices which are likely to creap-in. The institutional certificate will be issued on a format prescribed by the examining agency. The Certificate of

External Examination will carry a foot note that the certificate issued by the institution may also be studied for judging the total personality of the learner.

37.4 Promotion in Jobs

There are two types of situations in vogue. In one case an individual moves to another job. In the other case the individual is given a new designation and a higher scale of pay but continues to do almost the same job in a supervisory capacity.

In both these cases, it is entirely an internal matter. In smaller establishments it is more of a subjective decision. In large scale establishments elaborate criteria, rules and procedures are used for imparting greater objectivity and transparency to the process.

Ideally, these promotions ought to be based on:

- The workers' self-evaluation report.
- The supervisor's report of individuals performance on the job covering both technical abilities and personal attributes.
- The peer evaluation report about things like cordiality, team spirit etc.

In large-scale establishments, there are detailed proformas and procedures available for periodical performance evaluation.

Promotion tests both formal and informal are used in both job promotions and class promotions. In both cases observation turns out to be an important technique of evaluation.

In promotion on jobs the evaluation should be done regularly/periodically and a record maintained to be aggregated instead of an individual evaluated on the basis of the last impression to avoid subjectivity. It is desirable that an external expert is also involved in deriving the final ratings. To be objective and transparent the methodology for quantifying qualitative information in terms of a numerical index like the PREP Index ought to be used.

38

Evaluation of Attainments in Abilities and Proficiencies

Techniques and tools of evaluation are dependent on the areas and attributes intended to be evaluated. In the scholastic areas, for example, the techniques of written, oral and practical examinations can be used while in the co-scholastic and functional/operational areas observation will be a more suitable technique.

Before proceeding further, the concept of "techniques" and "tools" of evaluation does need to be clarified. While "written examinations" are a technique the question paper/test is a tool. While "observation" is a technique, "observation schedule" is a tool.

The concept of "Evaluation Criteria" which is the conduit between techniques and tools also needs to be explained for ensuring clarity about the components of the process of evaluation. Suppose "Outdoor Activity" are the area and "games" the specific aspect desired to be focussed upon for purposes of evaluation, the "Evaluative Criteria" on which the proficiencies will need to be evaluated could be:

(a) performance.
(b) discipline on the field
(c) team spirit
(d) sporting spirit

In this context basing judgments about the level of attainments in a global overall manner could carry an element of bias. It is, therefore, that evaluation is done of each of the above four facets, for deriving the overall conclusion about the attainment level.

Suppose on a five point scale the ratings on the above four aspects of 'games and sports' are as under

Performance	4
Discipline	3
Team spirit	2
Sporting Spirit	2
	12

As there are four facets which have been evaluated and the total marks on all the four are twelve, the overall numerical score for games and sports will be $12 \div 4 = 3$

Such continuously awarded indices could be totalled up for obtaining an over all index.

In *written examinations*, the evaluative criteria could be:

(a) coverage of objectives
(b) coverage of areas of content
(c) effective coverage of the forms of questions

In *practical examinations*, they could be:

(a) process of performance and
(b) product of performance

In *oral examinations* they could be:

(a) accuracy of perception about the dimensions of the question
(b) marshalling of facts for answering the question
(c) accuracy and logical sequence of facts presented
(d) conviction about answers
(e) ability to face cross questions etc.

It is in correspondence with the evaluative criteria that evaluation tools are evolved.

This summarised introduction appears to be adequate for dealing with some of the main techniques in some detail.

39

Preparing of Objective-based Questions of Different Forms

In any comprehensive programme of educational reform, improvement of examinations and the improvement in the quality of the question papers is a foregone conclusion. Individual questions would, therefore, have to be framed in such way that when put together in the form of a question paper, they fulfill the prerequisites of good measuring instruments. We may make use of essay type, short-answer type, very short answer type and objective type questions or some combination of them but they should all conform to and satisfy the basic characteristics of a good question of the given form. This is discussed below :

39.1 Characteristics of Good Questions

Objective-Based

A good question should be framed on a predetermined objective and it should to able to test the concerned ability effectively. Questions may sometimes test more than one objective. They may also sometimes test one or more specifications of a particular objective on which that question is based. *In case a question attempts to test more than one objective, it is designated as one testing the highest objective in the hierarchy which it aims to test.*

Content-Specific

The content or subject matter on which a question is based is closely related to the objective being tested. The framer of the question, has, therefore, to take into account the topic or the sub-topic he is going to prepare a question on. He should also ensure that a question samples exactly the same area of content, which is desired to be tested through it.

Form of Questions

Essay type, short-answer type, very short answer type and objective-type questions are the main forms of questions in use. In a question, the form depends considerably on the *kind of ability as well as the nature of the content desired to be tested.* Some forms are more suitable than others for testing certain abilities. Essay-type questions for example, are more suitable for testing abilities like organisation of thoughts, analysis, interpretation etc. through written expression. Therefore, a judicious mix of the appropriate question forms will have to be attempted, while setting questions which may finally be woven into a question paper. A decision about this has to be made while preparing the design for the question paper itself.

Wording of Questions

To bring about objectivity in evaluation, there is need for using clear, precise and unambiguous language while framing questions. Use of unfamiliar and difficult terminology may be avoided so that the comprehension of the question itself may not become a problem for the learners by and which may even influence their difficulty level. A question should be so worded that by-and-large, all learners as also examiners may make the same meaning out of it, about the scope and length of the expected answer. Here special care is to be taken *to avoid the use of stock, phrases like describe, elucidate, discuss or write short notes on, write an account of, write a report on, what do you know, etc.* What is expected to be written by the learners has to be explained to them in unabiguous terms, while wording the questions themselves.

Structuring the Situation

In writing different questions, selection of an appropriate situation is an important step in the framing of questions. Textbook situations could be alright for testing knowledge. Other situations discussed in the class may be suitable for testing knowledge or understanding. But to test application of knowledge, some unfamiliar situations real or hypothetical will need to be identified or even concoted. Although in such cases situations are likely to go beyond the textbook yet they should be in keeping with the ability levels of learners and related to the content studied by them. It will be advisable if the teacher collects such situations and keeps a record of these so that they may be available to him as and when needed.

Estimated Difficulty Level

While writing a question the framer of the questions should be conscious of the estimated difficulty level of the question in relation to the ability of pupils for whom the question is meant. The difficulty level of a question usually depends upon the complexity of the mental processes involved (objectives) in responding to it, the area of the content desired to be tested and the time available which can be spent for answering it. The difficulty level of a particular question can be estimated fairly well in advance by an experienced teacher. Actual difficulty index, can however be statistically calculated only after the question has been really tried out and its responses analysed. Established procedures are available for analysing responses of multiple choice type of question and calculating the difficulty level. However, an experienced teacher can easily estimate the difficulty level in approximately in broad terms. Such decisions helps in deciding the distribution of questions of varying estimated difficulty while preparing question papers.

Discrimination Value

It is also not possible to estimate the discriminating value of a question unless it is tried out. Nevertheless when some novel situations are involved and common place questions are avoided, the questions definitely go a long way in discriminating the bright learners from the weak ones. *Questions at either extremes of the difficulty continuum are poor discriminators, while those in the middle range are found to be more effective in this respect.*

Delimiting the Scope of the Answer

The question framer or paper setter should in respect of free response questions ensure that while constructing a question s/he gives due thought to the expected answer. S/he is also required to develop an outline of the expected answer alongwith the marks (value point) to be devoted to each part of the expected answer, as part of the marking scheme. This is desirable to be done at the same time as the preparation of the question. This would reveal the weaknesses (if any) in the wording of the question itself. It should be specific and precise in language so that the scope and length of the expected answer stands clearly delimited and defined. This would evoke the expected answer. In case the test constructor discovers that the question as worded is not likely to yield the expected answer he would change its wording.

Key/Marking Scheme

In case of objective-type questions, the key must be prepared alongwith the questions. In case of long answer, short answer and very short answer questions, outlines of expected answers and the marking scheme has to be prepared. Weightage in terms of marks to each value-point or aspect of the expected answer has also be indicated.

A question framer or paper setter, while constructing each question, should be conscious of the various dimensions of questions discussed above as also the other considerations and rules for framing different forms of questions.

The keys and the masking schems should be prepared at the same time as the questions are framed.

39.2 Forms of Objective-Based Questions

Objective-based questions are questions designed to test definite objectives/abilities of teaching and testing. They could assume different forms, of which objective type questions are one. The other three varieties being Essay Type (Long Answer Type), Short Answer Type and Very Short Answer Type. All the forms (types) of questions are used for testing, some objective/ability/ competency/proficiency beside some designated content. Thus *all objective type questions are objective-based, though all objective-based questions are not objective type questions.* Questions could broadly be classified into different forms/types as under:

Classification of Question Forms

- Fixed response questions
  - Objective Type
    - True False Type
    - Matching Type
    - Fill-in-the blank Type
    - Multiple Choice Type
      - Only Correct Answer Type
      - Only Wrong Answer Type
      - Best Answer Type
      - Mixed Type
  - Very Short Answer Type
- Free response questions
  - Short Answer Type
  - Essay Type or Long Answer Type

It is intended here to discuss different forms of questions in terms of their characteristics, their strong and week points and the rules governing their preparation.

It has already been mentioned that depending upon the objective (ability) and the content area (subject matter) we can select the most suitable form of the question (essay type, short answer, very short answer or objective type).

The most commonly used tools of evaluation in the written tests are the questions which are generally of two types – the free response type and the fixed responses type. The long answer/essay type questions which are basically free response questions have been in use for quite some time. They used to be the sole variety of questions in traditional question papers. Now with the realisation of the shortcomings of these questions (as proved through research studies both in India and abroad) and their adverse effects on the accuracy, dependability and objectivity of examination results, short answer questions which also fall under this category are also being increasingly used. Fixed response questions (Very Short Answer types and Objective type) are those where the answer is fixed and any deviation from the expected answer is taken as incorrect. In free response questions as compared to this situation the examinee exercises freedom to manipulate his answer in his own language.

The long answer or free response type questions are still being used but in limited numbers, only for testing those abilities which other forms of tests cannot effectively test.

Operational descriptions of questions of different forms are attempted below:

(i) Objective Type (*Multiple Choice* with four alternatives).

(ii) *Very Short Answer (VSA)* questions usually carrying one or two marks and requiring an answer in one word, one phrase or at the most one sentence or involving one or two steps of mathematical calculation. They should need about a minute to answer.

(iii) *Short Answer Questions (SA)* carrying two to four marks which require answers in about 25 to 50 words or involve four to six steps of mathematical calculation. Each of these questions usually require 3 to 5 minutes to answer.

(iv) *Long Answer or Essay Type Questions (LA/ET)* which require answers between 100 to 400 words or upto a maximum of ten steps of mathematical calculation. These may carry 5 to 15 marks.

(v) In languages the composition questions require the learners to discuss certain themes using their own vocabulary, usage, syntax with originality and in their own style. These questions would also need to be given a rough time limit based on the expected length of the answer. Therefore, the length of the answer will also be required to be approximately indicated preferably in terms of words and not lines or pages as part of the wording of the question itself in the question paper. In case a question paper carries 100 marks and 100 minutes are given as the time limit, then 50 seconds could be given for answering a question of one mark (leaving 10 seconds for revision). The length of the expected answer could also then be determined on the basis of the age group for which the question is meant in view of the marks devoted to a question.

39.3 Preparing Long Answer or Essay Type Questions

These questions are considered to be easy to prepare and administer in the traditional scene. They also offer quite a lot of freedom to the examinees who can use their own language and style of writing. These questions require examinees to choose the language, select the facts, organise the ideas for presenting a response to the question asked in the way they choose.

These questions provide examinees an opportunity *to analyse, synthesise, re-organise, integrate, synthesise and evaluate situations, as also to investigate, interpret them for drawing conclusions for justifying or negating a particular stand.*

They also have the potential of testing the originality and creativity of the particular examinee. Thus they can most effectively test those abilities and mental processes which are not possible to be tested through any other form of questions.

Shortcomings

Despite the positive points, the long answer or essay type questions are also imbued with some very serious shortcomings. While they provide freedom to the examinee, they also provide freedom to the examiner to go by his whims. Thus they breed subjectivity in scoring. Quite often they are criticised and quite rightly so, for introducing a substantial element of unreliability in scoring.

Besides, there is also another serious shortcoming and that is that because they require long answers, they also need longer time to answer and because they need a long answering time, only a few of such type of questions can be asked in a given time. Again because only be few questions can find a place in a question paper, they are able to test only a small part of the prescribed syllabus. The use of such questions, in question papers, more often than not, leads to selective study and selective teaching, which in turn endangers the validity (or accuracy) and reliability (or dependability) of the result, because of restricted and poor sampling of the content.

In this background, therefore, while long answer questions are incorporated in the question papers, their number and the quantum of marks devoted to them are deliberately restricted to the barest minimum.

In spite of these shortcomings the long answer type questions continue to be used in examinations, because as already mentioned *they can test those abilities which no other form of question can effectively evaluate* e.g., the capacity to weigh ideas, to argue in favour or against a proposition, to establish relationships, to critically analyse situations, to judge the implications of a given phenomenon and so on. These questions also promote self-study with insight.

Some Guiding Principles for Preparing Long Answer Questions

Preparation of good essay type or long answer questions is by no means an easy task. Some tips for preparing this type of questions are spelt out below:

- Long Answer or Essay Type questions because of their limitations, should be set to test only those instructional objectives (abilities), which are not possible to be tested by other forms of questions.
- Essay questions should be prepared for specifically testing the mental processes or learning outcomes implied by the objectives in view.
- These questions ought to be so worded that the scope and approximate length of the expected answer is clear to the learners.
- Maturation level of the examinees must be taken into consideration while constructing an essay/long answer type question. Length and nature of expected answer will differ from class to class. For example, questions requiring discussion, interpretation, summarisation or evaluation may be asked in higher classes, whereas those testing abilities like listing, describing, selecting etc. may be considered suitable for lower classes.

- Outline answers of each question with value points (the allocation of marks) to different parts of the expected answer also needs to be specified as part of the marking scheme. This should be done at the same time as drafting the questions themselves. After framing each the question the test constructor, revert back to the language of the question and check that it would evoke the expected answer from the examinees. In case it does not do so, changes may be introduced in the wording of the question in question, so that it may be ensured to yield the expected answer.
- The use of directional words or phrases like the following need to be systematically avoided:

	Or
Elucidate	Relate
Exemplify	Evaluate
Criticise	Weigh
Discuss	Examine
Justify	Write an essay on..
	Write short notes on ....
	Write a report on ....
	What do you think of......................................
	What do you know about ....

The purpose of these words or directions is not clearly understood by learners and also sometimes by examiners. What the learner is expected to write in the answer, should therefore be clearly and unambiguously stated instead of using these unintelligible directional words and phrases.

- This will also contain the tendency of the learners to write all that they know about that topic, instead of responding to the requirements of the questions.
- The question ought to be worded in such a manner that each question presents a definite problem. Though the learner should be provided freedom to choose the language and style, this should be exercised within the dimensions and parameters which may be indicated by the wording of the questions.
- The marks that each question carries should not be indicated against them as a whole (e.g. 10). They should be clearly distributed among the various parts of the expected answer or various expected abilities attempted to be tested and indicated as say (2 + 4 + 4).
- The questions should not be repeated vertatim from among those asked in previous examinations or lifted from those given/listed at the end of the chapters of the books/work-books.

- The questions set may not just be direct questions, answers to which may be found directly in the books and could be lifted as such from a particular portion of a book and memorised. The questions should also invariably present situations or problems which *call for thinking* rather than just recall and reproduction of memorised information.

Scoring of Long Answer Questions

Essay/Long answer type questions in the traditional set-up are prepared quickly but they take a much longer time to answer. Furthermore though easy to prepare, they are difficult to answer, mark and evaluate.

A detailed marking scheme, giving outline answers and value points in terms of marks for different aspects or facts of the expected answer (desired to be taken into consideration for purposes of evaluation) have to be prepared alongwith the framing of questions and adhered to in letter and spirit while evaluating answers.

The aspects of an answer required to be evaluated should be made known to the learners through the wording of the questions in the question paper itself e.g. there may be situations where spelling mistakes, may be taken into account for deducting marks and others where the opposite may be true.

Correction of a sample of scripts by at the time of Co-ordination Meetings and the modification of the marking scheme prepared by the paper setter, wherever considered necessary, needs to be meticulously done for finalising it. This would iron out ambiguities regarding the interpretation of the wording of a question and thus ensure objectivity.

As far as possible scoring of essay/long answer type questions should be done on an *analytical* basis. *Impressionistic* scoring may be done only in cases where it is absolutely unavoidable.

However, the directions in the question paper may clearly indicate to the learners, the major points of emphasis in the scoring pattern. They could even be built into the language of the questions themselves or form part of the general directions. Furthermore, if a *diagram* or an *illustration* is required to be given by the learners as part of the answer, it should be clearly mentioned in the question and not left by the paper setter to the initiative of the learner or the imagination of the evaluator.

In the marking scheme, which may be finalised for the evaluation of scripts, the aspects and the sub-aspects or the steps of the process of the expected answer be clearly spelt out. Each of these may be given a definite weightage e.g. in a given situation, and wherever applicable its analysis, interpretation and drawing of inferences may be allocated separate weightages. Similarly, if spellings, language style, coherence, and unity of presentation deserve to be given independent weightages these also should be made known to the learners. *In short the learners should know what is expected of them, what will enable them gain marks and what will make them to lose them.*

In Mathematics the steps of calculation and weightages to them be clearly indicated in the marking schemes.

39.4 Preparing Short Answer Type of Questions

Short answer questions present a compromise between the long answer and objective type questions. They enjoy the advantages of both the types of questions.

While the long answer questions suffer from lack of objectively and reliability, the short answer questions are technically better off in regard to these criteria.

On the other hand while the objective type questions are largely unable to test abilities like expression, organisation and synthesisation of ideas, the short answer questions possess, at least in a limited measure, the capability of testing these abilities.

As these questions enjoy the advantages of both essay and objective type questions, without their disadvantages, to some extent, the short answer questions have come to be increasingly used in examinations.

A rule of thumb used in many examinations is the provision of a weightage of 50% marks in a question paper to short answer questions with the remaining 50% distributed between the long answer and the very short answer/objective type of questions.

Short answer questions too have always to be carefully structured in wording, so as to require specific and to the point answers. They should not be vague in their wording and should not encourage or admit vague and global answers. This is what differentiates them from the traditional, open-ended *short note questions* indicating themes without enunciating the dimensions of the given themes expected to be tackled by the examinees, like "Write short notes on democracy", where a learner does not know as to how long or how short the short note has got to be on such a topic like democracy, on which even books can be written. The intent of such a questions could be more than satisfied if we break-up the questions and structure it as under to give it an edge of specificity, "Define democracy. Give two merits of Indian democracy and two demerits of Indian democracy."

The construction of short answer questions also requires lesser level of competence in preparation as compared to the objective type questions.

As the limits in regard to length/dimensions of short answer type questions could vary quite a bit, they cannot be precisely defined. Still some rough and ready explanation of their physical dimensions is attempted here.

Short Answer Questions normally require:

- A 30 to 50 word answer
- an answer with upto 6 steps of mathematical calculations

They usually have 2 to 4 credit points and they approximately need 3 to 5 minutes for answering them.

Thus there can be many short answer questions in a question paper covering a larger proportion of the syllabus, than what few long answer questions can possibly accomplish. With this increase in the length of the test they tend to provide a more reliable/dependable estimate of an individual learner's proficiency and potential.

The following examples of short answer question could illustrate the above points be worded as under :

History : Give two evidences to substantiate that Clive was the real founder of the British Empire in India.

English : Write a paragraph in about 40-50 words on trees. You could use some of the following words:

Beauty	Utility
Pleasure	Forest
Branches	Shade
Twigs	Fruits
Birds	Logs

A long answer question could also sometimes be converted into short answer questions with great advantage as illustrated through the following example.

Usual Form of Long Answer Question

Give a brief account of various theories of organic evolution. (Essay-type question)

Modified Form (Short-Answer Questions)

(i) Name the various theories of organic evolution.

(ii) Which theory better explains the mechanism of organic evolution? Give two reasons.

(iii) Write two fundamental principles on which the theory of Lamarck is based.

(iv) How does d'Vries' theory differ from that of Weismann's.

Such questions can be profitably used in both external and internal examinations. They also ensure better reliability, because such questions are more definite and specific and can be scored more objectively. They also cover a larger segment of the syllabus as we can have a number of such questions in place of a single long answer type question. Therefore, they draw upon a wider range of learners achievements than the usual long answer question do. They also ensure adequate sampling of content and thereby help improve the validity of the question paper.

It is, therefore, desirable that we should encourage the use of such questions in our examinations to improve their validity and reliability and objectivity.

39.5 Preparing Very Short Answer Type Questions

Very short answer type of questions have been discovered as a possible substitute to objective type questions. While they can be assessed as objectively as objective type questions, they do not require as many conditions or rules to be satisfied in construction as the objective type questions do.

Very short answer type questions require an answer in one word, one phrase or at the most one sentence. They have *just one or two testing points and* thus ensure almost the same level of *objectively* in scoring, as exists in the objective type of questions. Normally they are assigned just one or two marks and need about a minute to answer.

In view of the small answering time and low mark weightage, many such questions can be set in a question paper by using a very small quantum of marks. They can also therefore be spread over a larger chunk of the prescribed syllabus thus improving upon the *reliability* of a question paper.

Sometimes when the forms of questions are classified as *Selection type* and *Supply type questions*, the very short answer type of questions are classified among the 'supply type questions' because unlike most of the objective type questions, the answer has to be supplied by the learner and not just selected from out of the given ones.

Very Short Answer type questions could assume a number of forms. Some examples of these related to English are given below :

Fill-in-the-blank type:

I am not satisfied .... your answer

Completion Type:

I was so worried. ....

Analogy type:

Soyabean: Protein :: Rice:

Location type:

Show the location of Sydney on the outline map of the world

Transformation type:

Questions on

Reported speech
Voices
Synthesis
Transformation of Sentences

Usage type:

Use the following words/phrases in your own sentences :

Break/Break-up
Look/Look-after

Question type:

What is a mole?

39.6 Preparing Objective Type (Multiple Choice) Questions

Objective-based and objective type tests are often confused with each other. It, therefore, needs to be stated again that when a question is framed with deliberate attention to the objective (ability) which we want to specifically assess it is an *objective-based question.*

But when a question is designed to provide a measure of learner's achievement in an objective rather than a subjective manner, we call it an objective type question.

There are various forms of objective type tests. Two alternative questions, which are commonly known as *true/false* or yes/no type is the oldest of the objective type of questions in use. *Fill-in-the-blank type* questions are the other commonly used variety of questions. *Matching type* items have two or more columns. In a two-column matching question for example, we can give principles on one side and the illustrations-based on those principles on the other. The learner is required to write the matching number of the principle involved against the related illustration or example given. Among these the *master-list type* of questions consists of two parts. One is the list of closely related terms, concepts etc. which form the alternative and are called the master-list. Then it is followed by another often a longer list consisting of a number of statements pertaining to the master-list and the learner is required to relate each statement with the corresponding one, of the master-list for identifying the right response. *Multiple Choice Items* are those in which a statement or question is followed by normally four alternatives out of which the learner is to select the correct one.

The form of objective type tests commonly used for examination purposes is the multiple choice type of question. It consists of a *stem* which may be in *the question form or in the form of an incomplete statement* followed by a number of words, pharases or statements which answer the question or complete the statement. The learners' task is to select from the given alternatives, the one which correctly gives the answer. The effectiveness of the item should depend on how well the item has been framed, to test the desired objective. The following points may be kept in view while structuring a good multiple choice test item.

Suggestions for Writing Multiple Choice Test Items (questions)

A multiple choice type item, as already mentioned comprises a '*Stem*' in the form of a statement or a question followed by usually four *alternative* choices or distractors. The whole item when constructed must make complete sense and be accurate in respect of language and information.

The following are some suggestions for framing such items:

1. It should be ensured that there is only one choice/alternative which is correct or the best. Alternatives which are overlapping with one another should be avoided. The response should be agreed upon as the best or the most suitable one from among the plausible ones given, by competent critics.

2. The stem of the item should be comprehensive enough to contain the central problem by including in it as much of the item as possible. The alternatives should not contain anything which could have been put in the stem.
3. The pupil should not be required to copy the correct response but only mark or write the serial number of the alternative to answer the question.
4. The use of the text-book language should be avoided. The rote learner should be mislead by using familiar or stereotyped phrases as distracters.
5. The stem and all the alternatives should be made as succinct and consistent as possible.
6. It should be explored if a better item can be obtained by turning round a partly formulated question into an answer and the answer into the question.
7. All the choices provided ought to be sufficiently plausible to be selected by a fair proportion of the examinees. Both correct and incorrect choices, should be homogeneous in their mode of linguistic expression, physical length and other external characteristics. The distracters should represent errors commonly made by the learners, who are to be tested.
8. Each choice (alternative) should be studied for any possible irrelevant clues. For doing this the following steps are suggested.
   (a) The correct response should not be consistently longer or consistently shorter in length than the incorrect ones.
   (b) All choices should be grammatically correct and consistent with the stem. The use of singular and plural number, or tenses etc. should not be allowed to serve as clues.
   (c) The choices may be arranged in a logical order, if one exists; otherwise they should be arranged in the alphabetical order.
   (d) The position of the correct answer in the series ought to be chosen entirely at random. The first and last places should be used as often as any of the intermediate places.
   (e) No part of the stem should follow the distracters.
   (f) All the above or none of the above should not be used as distractors.

To conclude it may be said that while the multiple choice type of questions are used in examinations, other form of *objective type questions could be effectively used as teaching devices* for initiating discussions in class. Such discussions could greatly help in consolidating ideas. These objective type questions, other than the multiple choice questions however can surely be used upto class two even in examination situations as well.

The multiple choice type of questions are particularly used in examinations because, there are a variety of statistical measures available for calculating their characteristics/qualities like the Difficulty and Discrimination indices. Various types of sophisticated statistical analysis approaches have also been evolved.

40

Written Examinations — Preparation of Balanced Question Papers

40.1 The Backdrop

There are various *techniques* of testing like Written Examinations, Oral Examinations, Practical Examinations, Observation. Each of these techniques uses different tools of 'testing'. For example we use observation schedules, check-lists, inventories, rating scales and question papers as *tools* of evaluation in different techniques as per need. Among these the question papers and tests are the most commonly used of the tools.

While tests and question papers are the basic tools of evaluation in written examinations, they are also used for other techniques.

As public/external examinations are the most common types of examinations used and since they are predominantly written examinations, question papers have become the most important of the tools of testing the situation needs to be studied in greater detail.

The traditional form of question papers used to suffer from a variety of flaws which have been attempted to be overcome as a part of the Movement of Examination Reform Programme of the NCERT, where in the author played a crucial note. These reforms, however, have been by and large confined to the education sector. Now testing is also being widely used for purposes of selection, promotion recruitment etc. in trade and commerce, business and industry, science and technology with evaluation as a scientific approach having also diversified into project evaluation, programme evaluation etc.

Examination Reform at the school stage has been influenced by the latest developments in the science of evaluation which have revolutionised education in respect of its concept, content and process. Earlier it was thought that anybody who knows a subject can teach it, anybody who can teach can also test. These notions no more hold ground with the evolution of the Science of Pedagogy and the Technology of Evaluation. In fact both pedagogy and evaluation have germs of science and art.

Without getting way-laid into the wider realms of pedagogy and evaluation let us revert to the central theme of Setting Balanced Question Papers/Full Tests.

40.2 Shortcomings of Traditional Question Papers and their Remediation

Some of the main shortcomings that had come to infest the traditional written examinations particularly because of the pattern of question papers are:

- Over-emphasis on memorisation
- Subjectivity
- Poor Content Coverage and
- Some administrative shortfalls

Let us now take up these one by one and analyse the nature of each shortfall its implications on teaching and testing and the measures for overcoming them.

Over-Emphasis on Memorisation

The questions contained in the traditional question papers used to be mainly focussed on content where the examinees were supposed to *memorise and reproduce information*.

Since we tended to *teach what was tested rather than tested what we taught*, the development of higher abilities like understanding, application analysis, synthesis, critical thinking, evaluation were almost completely overlooked. Education so imparted, turned children into parrots and mechanical beings rather than creative individuals not just in examinations but also often in their future lives. While this served the needs of the foreign rulers for developing lower and middle level workforce, for running a colonial administration, they have turned out to be utterly inadequate for the emerging demands of independent India.

It has been because of this that the *ability* dimension has been added to the *content* facet in testing. In addition to the sub-division of the content (topics and sub-topics), objectives (abilities/competencies) too have been identified in respect of each subject and these have been further sub-divided into *specifications*. For example the objective of comprehension/understanding has been divided into its constituent components (specifications) like discrimination, classification, comparison and contrast, identification of relationships, giving examples, detecting and correcting errors, giving examples etc. These ability sub-divisions have thus now become integral and focal components of testing devices (questions) besides content. The phenomenon has encouraged educational institutions to try to develop the higher mental abilities also, besides memorisation—recognition, recall and reproduction—which in the good old days used to be almost the sole ability tested because of the main focus on the memorisation of content.

Furthermore, in the traditional scheme of things the focus was predominantly on the mental facets. The reformed system also attempts to cover the *total personality consisting of the abilities of the head (intellectual cognitive abilities), of the heart (attitudinal affective abilities) and those of the hands (actional psycho-motor abilities)*. Taxonomies of these objectives too now stand developed as discussed earlier in the chapter on objectives. Evaluation of different cognitive, affective and psycho-motor abilities is being taken up as a part of *Comprehensive and Continuous School-based Evaluation.*

Testing in written examinations through question papers, however, mainly covers the Cognitive area and only partly the Psycho-motor and the Affective areas of personality. In developing balanced question papers, objectives desired to be tested in the concerned subject are listed and weightages allocated to each of them (in terms of marks) on the basis of the relevance and importance of a particular objective in the subject in question. For example in subjects like Geography and Biology a substantial chunk of marks would be devoted to 'skills', in subjects like Physics and Chemistry to Application of Knowledge, in History to Knowledge and so on.

The next step is to construct questions equivalent to the allocated weightages allocated to content and objectives. In this process the choice of the form of question will be an important criteria, for example, for testing the ability of expression, a long answer/essay type question and not an objective type question has to be chosen to be constructed. Furthermore each form of question has to follow some rules which have already been discussed separately in the chapter on preparing questions of different forms.

All these measures help overcome the over-emphasis on memorisation by systematically including questions testing higher abilities in the question papers in due proportion.

The steps will also help improve the *validity* of the question papers.

Subjectivity

Traditionally subjectively too has been a great shortcoming of the written examinations. It operates mainly at three levels. *Subjectivity of the question paper setter* used to operate in a wild manner particularly because the question paper setters enjoyed complete unrestricted freedom to pick up or drop any item from the syllabus for setting question papers and nobody could question their authority. *The questions were basically factual and the directive words like 'elucidate', 'illustrate', 'elaborate' were indiscriminately used.* Invariably there was a short note question giving themes like 'Democracy' on which books could be written.

This unlimited freedom stands checked now because the paper setter is now given a '*Design*' (Format appended) of the question paper to be set and clear instructions given about the language of the questions, their unambiguous/specific wording indicating the precise scope and length of the expected answer. The paper setter is also now required to develop a *marking scheme* indicating the parts and outline of the expected answer and the marks to be allocated to each part. This curbs the paper setter's vagaries and helps him correct many mistakes in the questions on their own.

While the format of the design is appended to the chapter, it is pertinent to mention here its main parts which are:

- Weightage to objectives

- Weightage to major areas of content
- Weightage to different forms of questions
- Scheme of sections
- Pattern of options

In addition to this the paper setter is also required to prepare a '*Blueprint*' (Format enclosed) for setting the question papers. This indicates the precise placement of each question in respect of objective and topic attempted to be tested by it, the form in which it is to be framed, and the marks it is supposed to carry. These requirements make him check the comparability/compatibility of the design of a question paper with its blueprint, and of the blueprint with the questions, and of the questions with the marking scheme. The question paper setter besides preparing the blueprint, the questions, the marking scheme is also required to prepare a *question-wise analysis* (format appended) which is yet another confirmatory device for him to conform to the paradigms of each question he has prepared. This table of question-wise analysis incorporates the following details *about each question or part thereof.*

1. Objective and specification tested
2. Content Area (topic & sub-topic) covered/tested
3. Form of the question
4. Marks carried by the question
5. Estimated difficulty level (easy/average/difficult)
6. Estimated time for answering

Subjectivity of the Examinee

This too is a common phenomenon and occurs mainly because of the vague wording of the questions where the learner himself has to interpret about what he has to write. In response to the questions in the traditional question papers anything and everything could be written. Learners therefore chose to write all that they knew about that topic rather than answering the question as such.

With restrictions on the language of the questions which has now to be precise and pinpointed, exactly spelling out the scope and length of the expected answer, the examinee now precisely knows what is expected of him to write and what the parts of the answer have to be, how long the answer has to be and what marks each part of the answer would carry. In the new question papers the marks carried by different questions are not given in the margin as say 10 in all, but the marks to parts of the expected answer as well like (2 + 4 + 4).

Subjectively of the Examiner

This too has been a common phenomenon and one which stands scientifically proved. The technical term ' Stand Error of Measurement' owes its origin in to it.

Edwin Harper's study 'Hundred Marking Ten' in 1967 done at Allahabad proved that marking variations operate within a range of 5% and 8% and in more than 50% of the cases, they are likely to be more than 5%.

The NCERT study of 1998 where 20 examiner evaluated the same 10 History answer scripts of Class XII of CBSE, did not have any different story to tell. The scripts and the examiners were both randomly selected. The examiners evaluated these photostated scripts when they were actually evaluating the actual answer scripts of the same subject, of the same examination, using the same marking scheme, which they were expected to follow in evaluating these photostated scripts.

The marks awarded out of 100 by the most lenient and the most strict of the *twenty examiners* to the same ten scripts were as under:

Script No. / Examiner	1	2	3	4	5	6	7	8	9	10	Mean
Marks Awarded by the Most Lenient Examiner	50	66	23	35	37	74	54	53	39	37	46.8
Marks Awarded by the Most Strict Examiner	21	28	02	10	14	43	23	19	05	07	17.2
Difference Between the Two	29	38	31	25	23	31	31	34	34	30	29.6

The position could only be worse twenty years back. Though things have no doubt improved with double checking a lot still needs to be done.

A concrete measure taken by the *Council for the Indian School Certificate Examination (CISCE)* is that though a marking scheme already stands developed by the paper setter, each Deputy Head Examiner is required to evaluate 20 or so scripts himself. This is followed by a discussion in the course of the *Coordination Meetings,* only after which the marking scheme to be used is finalised. Another suggestion could be for the Boards and Universities to make it compulsory for all affiliated institutions to dispute teachers for purposes of evaluation for continuation of tneir affiliation to the Board. This is because the good institutions do not send their teachers for evaluation. The non-availability of examiners in adequate numbers also forces the Boards and Universities give more scripts for evaluation to each examiner than what should ordinarily be given for doing justice.

There should also be a provision for appointing some *additional hands at the evaluation centres*, who may *only check that the totals are correct, that all parts of answers have been evaluated, that marks to all parts of answers have been individually awarded and that the marks have been correctly posted on the cover page of the script and also on the mark sheet.* They should also check that the member of *supplementary sheets* indicated are all there. The Deputy Head Examiners in-charge of evaluation centres should also actually check the sample of scripts they are supposed to check and not just initial them as a formality. He and the checker should ensure that the marking scheme is being followed for evaluation in letter and spirit so that the errors of measurement can be minimised.

With the above measures the *objectivity* the testing instrument (the question paper) will become possible to be ensured to a large extent.

Inadequate Content Coverage

When no 'Designs' and 'Blueprints' were used the situation was alarming. It among other things led to *poor content coverage prompting selective study and selective teaching.* The provision of *options* further aggravates the problem. Suppose there are 20 topics in the syllabus, 16 are covered by the question paper and a learner can attempt full 100 mark questions if he attempts questions on 12 topics and he can pass if he gives correct answers to questions on say topics. In this case

20 Topics	imply	100%	Full coverage of content
16 Topics in the question paper	imply	80%	Apparent coverage of content
12 Topics which can yield full marks	imply	60%	Actual coverage of content
5 Topics for passing the examination	imply	20%	Real coverage for passing

In this commonly witnessed situation, a learner can easily omit 40% of the syllabus and yet aspire to get the highest possible marks. One needs to study just 20% of the course content to pass. Is the situation not shocking?

This is not all about options, which do lead to selective study and selective teaching. They also make examinations a farce.

The traditional question papers normally used to have about 8 questions or so and the instructions used to be "All questions carry equal marks attempt any five". These *overall options* meant that any question could be substituted for any other. The presumptions that the situation made were that:

- if an examinee knew one topic it was taken that he knew any other.
- all questions tested the same ability and same content.
- all questions needed the same answering time.
- all questions were pitched at the same estimated level of difficulty.
- all of which could not stand any of the above tests.

In addition, in such a situation, different learners attempted different sets of questions – in effect, different question papers. If A got 40 marks, B got 50 and the C got 60 it *could not be said* that C is first, B is second, and A is third because all the three of them have not been subjected to the same tests. The situation is similar to the one when a learner X does 1.83 m. long jump, Y does 1.22 m. high jump and Z 2.44 m. high pole vault, where one cannot say who is first, who is second and who is third.

Options could, therefore, be provided if the questions given as options.

- cover/test the same content/topic
- test the same objective/ability
- are of the same form

- are pitched at the same estimated level of difficulty
- take the same approximate time for answering
- carry the same marks

Satisfying all these conditions at the same time is not just difficult but near impossible for ensuring equivalence among options.

Satisfying all these conditions at the same time is not just difficult but near impossible for ensuring equivalence among options.

There are *Overall options* like all questions carry equal marks, attempt any five, *Internal option* within questions like write short notes on any three of the given five and *Alternate options* of *the this or this* type.

A rule of thumb in this regard if options have to be offered is

Objective Type Very Short Answer Type Short Answer Type	No options
Long Answer Type	Alternate internal equivalent options

It, therefore, appears necessary that major areas of content may be identified and each given an appropriate weightage (marks) out of the total marks for the question paper for preparing questions equal to these weightages which could be determined on the basis of :

- the importance of the particular area in the subject
- the difficulty level of the area
- the time needed for covering the theme in teaching and learning

These weightages would stand indicated in the '*Design*' prepared by the examining agency and should be appropriately reflected in the grid of the '*Blueprint*' prepared by the question paper setters. Questions could then be framed on that basis. This is a technical exercise and cannot be done by anyone and everyone without training in the concept and techniques of evaluation with particular reference to setting of question papers, which should be arranged to be organised and become essential eligibility criteria for being appointed as question paper setters.

11.2.4 *Administrative Inadequacies*

Question paper setters, and moderators/vetters have but to be trained in the Concept and Techniques of Evaluation with particular reference to the Technology of Setting Question Papers to execute the technical job assigned to them.

Detailed instructions should also be prepared and issued to the question paper setters, besides of course the design.

Three question papers based on the same design should be prepared at the same time. This should be a team task with the team of three consisting of *a content expert*, a *pedagogue and a practising teacher*. All the three should be given the same design for preparing their own blueprints and question papers marking schemes and question-wise analysis on them. The three of them should then come together to discuss and finalise the three question papers, their respective marking schemes and question-wise analysis of their papers. The *content expert* would be able to check the accuracy of content of the questions, the *pedagogue* the technique of framing questions and the *practising teacher* the appropriateness of standard of the questions. The three sets of such question papers and related material be then packed and sealed separately. One of these question papers may be picked up for the annual examination, the other for the supplementary examination and the third may be kept for a possible emergency. The three papers based on the same design will be *parallel at the level of the design and hence substitutable*.

Another administrative measure relates to the situation where a significant portion of the question paper/test may be consisting of objective type and very short answer type questions with some questions of the other forms (short answer and long-answer type) as well. In this situation if the section with objective type and very short answer type questions remains with the examinees' for longer than necessary there could be a likelihood that they may try to check their answers with their neighbours. It is, therefore, desirable that the question paper be divided into two sectional booklets, section one with objective type (Multiple Choice) and very short answer type questions and the other section may have short answer and long answer questions. Both the sections may be administered together but the one with objective type and very short answer type questions be collected earlier at the end of the prescribed *tight time limit*. In case it is an *on-line test* this section should not be available for the candidates to see beyond the stipulated him.

Adequate publicity about this strategy will also be necessary for a general acquaintance about the merits of the proposal.

40.3 Steps of the Action Plan

In respect of each question paper test the following action points related to different sequential steps will need to be taken:

1. Preparation of a *Design* (Policy statement about the paradigms of the question paper) to be prepared by the examining agency/institutions.
2. Preparation of a Blueprint based on the Design to be prepared by the question paper setter. Format to be supplied by the examining agency alongwith instructions. This presumes that the question papersetter/ test constructor will be trained in the concept and techniques of evaluation with particular reference to the preparation of balanced tests/question paper.
3. Transfer of blueprint details on to the item sheets with one question to the written on each answer sheet with the details about objectives,

specifications, topic, sub-topic, form, marks, expected, answering time and estimated difficulty level in respect of each question filled in. The key for the multiple choice questions and marking scheme with expected outline answers and marks to different parts of the expected answer written on the back side of the item sheet in case of question requiring description answers. Adequate number of item sheets to be provided by the examining agency alongwith instructions.

4. Papers for writing the consolidated question paper and consolidated marking scheme to be also provided to the paper setter.
5. Format/Proforma for the preparation of question-wise analysis be also supplied to the paper setter alongwith the instructions.

40.4 FORMAT OF A DESIGN OF A QUESTION PAPER/TEST

Subject : Physics
Unit/paper : Refracton Dispersion and Lense
Time : 40 minutes
Marks : 25 Marks

Weightage to Objectives:

Objective	K/KE	U/CO	A/EX	S/AP	Total
Percentage of marks	40	40	15	10	100
Marks	10	10	3	2	25

Weightage to Forms of Questions:

Forms of Questions	E/LA	SA	VSA	O	Total
No. of Questions	1	5	9	6	16
Marks Allotted	5	10	4	6	25
Estimated Time	10	15	6	9	90

Weightage to Major Content Areas:

	Units/Sub-Units	*Marks*
1.	Refraction	9
2.	Dispersion	4
3.	Lenses	12
	....	....

Scheme of Sections : Nil ....

Pattern of options : No option ....

Estimated difficulty level: Difficult : .... % marks.
Average : .... % marks.
Easy : .... % marks.

Abbreviations : K (Knowledge), U (Understanding), A (Application), S (Skill)
KE (Knowledge of Elements of Language), CO (Comprehension), EX (Expression), APP (Appreciation)
E (Essay or Long Answer Type), SA (Short Answer Type), VSA (Very Short Answer Type), O (Objective Type – Multiple Choice)

SAMPLE MINI TEST IN PHYSICS

UNIT: REFRACTION, DISPERSION AND LENSES

Time: 40 Minutes M.M.: 25

Objectives	*Elements of Language*				*Comprehension*				*Expression*				*Appreciation*		*Total*
Forms of Questions	*Knowledge*				*Understanding*				*Application*				*Skill*		
Units/ Sub-Units	*LA*	*SA*	*VSA*	*MCQ*	*LA*	*SA*	*VSA*	*MCQ*	*LA*	*SA*	*VSA*	*MCQ*	*LA*	*SA*	
Refraction		(11) 2(1)	(7) 1(1)	(1,2) 2(2)		(13) 2(1)	(8) 1(1)	(3) 1(1)							9(7)
Dispersion		(12) 2(1)				(14) 2(1)									4(2)
Lenses	(16) 3(1)*						(9,10) 2(2)	(4,5) 2(2)		(15) 2(1)		(6) 1(1)	2(–)*		12(7)
Totals															

Note: Figures within brackets indicate the number of questions and figures outside the brackets indicate marks.

* Denote instances where a question tests more than one ability (objective) and gives the division of marks of the particular question among the different objects tested by it.

* Entries within circles indicate the serial numbers of question in the test.

Summary:		*No.*	*Marks*	
	Essay (E)	1	5	Scheme of Options: NIL
	Short Answer (SA)	5	10	
	Very Short Answer (VSA)	4	4	Scheme of Options: NIL
	Objective (O)	6	6	

TEST ON REFRACTION, DISPERSION AND LENSES

CLASS X

Time: 40 Minutes M.M.: 25

General Instructions

(a) All questions are compulsory.
(b) Each question from 1 to 9 carries one mark. Marks for the remaining questions are shown in the right-hand margin.
(c) In each of the questions from 1 to 6 there are five answers marked (a), (b), (c), (d) and (e). Only one of these answers is correct or best. The letter indicating the correct or best answer should be written in bold letters against the Question Number in the answer book. In respect of the rest of the questions also answers be written in your answer book with the serial number of the question.

1. Refractive index can be determined by the formula (with usual notations):

A. $\frac{i}{r}$ B. $\frac{\sin i}{\sin r}$ C. $\frac{\sin i}{\sin e}$ D. $\frac{r}{i}$ E. $\frac{\sin r}{\sin i}$

2.

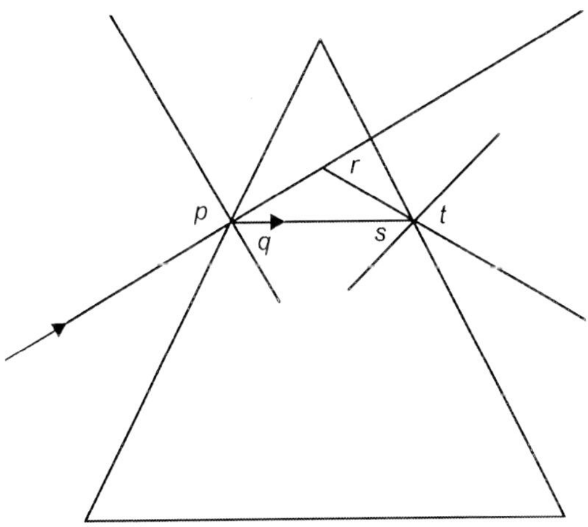

Fig. 1

In the above figure, the angle of deviation is:

A. p
B. q
C. r
D. s
E. t

3.

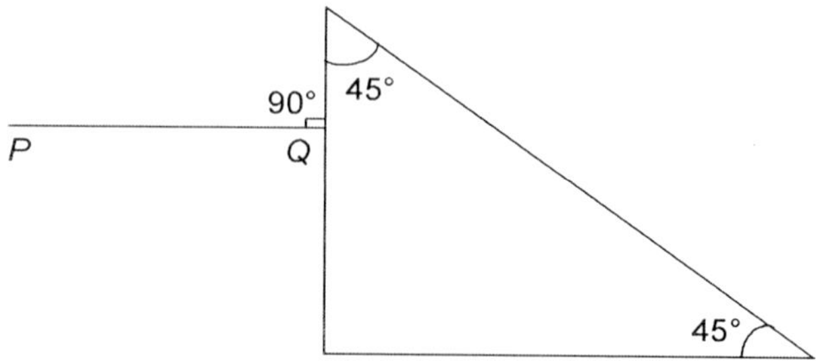

Fig. 2

In the above diagram, PQ shows the path of a ray of light. A prism intercepts it. Then there will be:

A. reflection only.
B. refraction only.
C. total internal reflection only.
D. reflection and total internal reflection.
E. refraction and total internal reflection.

4. The optical instrument that gives the idea of depth along with that of length and breadth of pictures is called:

A. microscope.
B. stereoscope.
C. telescope.
D. spectroscope.
E. periscope.

5. An object 2.5 cms. high is kept at a distance of 15 cms. from a convex lens of focal length 30 cms. If the size of the image is 5 cms. the distance between the object and its image is:

A. 60.0 cms.
B. 45.0 cms.
C. 30.0 cms.
D. 15.0 cms.
E. 10.0 cms.

6. You have a simple microscope and you want to make a magic lantern. The additional materials required are:

A. a concave mirror and a convex mirror.
B. a concave lens and a convex mirror.
C. a concave mirror and a convex lens.
D. a concave lens and a convex mirror.
E. a plane mirror and a convex lens.

7.

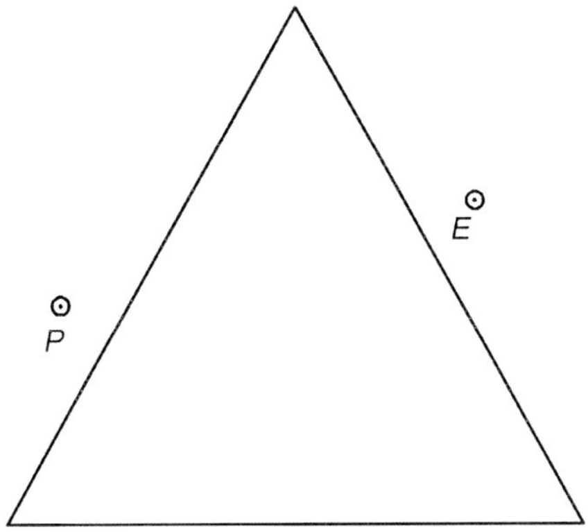

Fig. 3

An observer placing his eye at E and seeing through the prism tries to touch the pin P. Explain why he is not successful.

8.

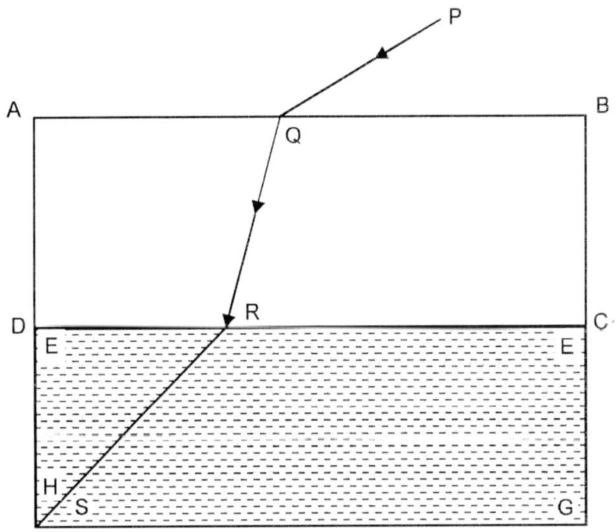

Fig. 4

In the above diagram, PQRS is the path of a ray of light passing through a glass slab ABCD. If a rectangular vessel EFGH of very thin glass containing water is kept alongside as shown in the figure, what change, in the direction of RS, will take place in water?

9. You are given two lenses mounted on stands-one is a convex lens and the other a concave. How will you know without touching them as to which one is a convex lens?

10. Find out two errors in the following diagram of an image 'AB' of the object AB formed by a convex lens.

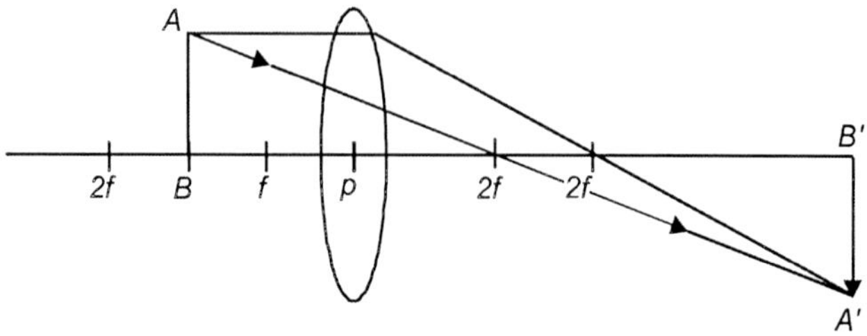

Fig. 5

11. State the laws of refraction excluding the sine law.
12. Give two points of distinction between the images formed by a concave lens and a convex lens when an object is placed between f and $2f$.
13. State the principle underlying the formation of a rainbow. Name the colour of the uppermost arc of the primary rainbow. In which direction do we see the rainbows in the evening?
14. Why does a pin look coloured when viewed through a prism in some positions?
15. When a book is kept at a distance of 5 cms. from a convex lens, the letters from the book appear five times enlarged. Find the focal length of the lens.
16. Draw a neat labelled diagram of a compound microscope. Show how this instrument considerably magnifies a small object.

SCORING KEY

Q. No.	1	2	3	4	5	6
Key	C	C	C	B	D	C

Q. No.		*Value Points*	*Marks for each point*	*Total Marks*
7.		Due to refraction	1	1
8.		Bends toward normal drawn at point R.	1	1
9.		By taking the image of a distant object on a screen	1	1
10.	(a)	The ray passing through $2f$ should pass through 'f'.	½	
	(b)	The ray passing through f should pass through p.	½	1

(Contd.)

Q. No.		*Value Points*	*Marks for each point*	*Total Marks*
11.	(a)	First law	1	
	(b)	Second law	1	2
12.	(a)	In a concave lens, the image is virtual, erect, and diminished 1+ ⊙.	1	
	(b)	In a convex lens the image is real, inverted and magnified. × ⊙.	1	2
13.	(a)	Dispersion or total internal reflection	1	
	(b)	Red	½	
	(c)	East	½	
14.	(a)	Due to dispersion	1	
	(b)	Only some rays enter our eyes	1	2
15.	(a)	$\frac{I}{0} > 0 \quad] \quad \frac{I}{0} > 5$ $] \quad V = 5 \times 5 = 25$ cms	1	
	(b)	$\frac{I}{f} > \frac{I}{v} . \frac{I}{u} > \frac{I}{25} . \frac{I}{5} \;] \; f = 6.25\, cms.$	1	2
16.	(a)	Correct labelled diagram	2	
	(b)	Position of the object with reference to the object lens	½	
	(c)	Formation of the image by object lens.	1	
	(d)	Position of the first image with reference to the eye lens.	½	
	(c)	Formation of the final image	1	5

QUESTION-WISE ANALYSIS

S. No.	*Objective+*	*Specification*	*Topic*	*Form*	*Marks*	*Est. Time*	*Est. Diff. Level*
1.	K	Recalls	Refraction	O	1	1 m.	C
2.	K	Recognises	Refraction	O	1	1 m.	B
3.	A	Predicts	Refraction	O	1	1 m.	B
4.	U	Selects	Lenses	O	1	1 m.	B
5.	U	Identifies relationship	Lenses	O	1	1 m.	B
6.	A	Suggests modification	Lenses	O	1	1 m.	B
7.	U	Sees cause	Refraction	VSA	1	1 m.	B
8.	A	Predicts	Refraction	VSA	1	1 m.	A
9.	U	Selects	Lenses	VSA	1	1 m.	B
10.	U	Locates errors	Lenses	VSA	1	1 m.	B

(Contd.)

S. No.	*Objective+*	*Specification*	*Topic*	*Form*	*Marks*	*Est. Time*	*Est. Diff. Level*
11.	K	Recalls	Refraction	S	2	3 m.	C
12.	U	Sees dissimilarity	Refraction	S	2	3 m.	B
13.	K	Recalls	Dispersion	S	2	3 m.	B
14.	U	Sees cause	Dispersion	S	2	3 m.	B
15.	A	Predicts	Lenses	S	2	3 m.	A
16.	K and Skill	Recalls and Draws	Lenses	E	5	15 m.	B

* A = Difficult   B = Average   and C = Easy
+K = Knowledge   U = Understanding   A = Application   S = Skill

41

Oral and Practical Examinations

Oral and Practical Examinations have somehow not received their due place in educational programmes. These aspects are therefore being discussed here.

41.1 Oral Tests

While oral examinations are almost a continuous and an ongoing exercise in institution-based evaluation, they usually take the form of a supplementary test in external examinations. They usually supplement the practical tests in some Science, Home Science, Crafts etc. Questions in oral tests as parts of external examinations are in a way confirmatory tests. These probing questions and cross questions attempt to dig out the degree of real assimilation of learning where a learner cannot easily dodge.

In the institutional (class-room) situation, oral tests usually serve a very valuable diagnostic purpose for the teacher to ascertain the hard spots as well as the strong points in the learning of a learner. These enable the teachers to develop remedial programmes for the weak and enrichment programmes for the bright learners. They also enable teachers to get an understanding of the level of success that they may have themselves attained in teaching his learners and where he needs to invest alternative inputs or more intensive inputs or where he needs to change the strategy for better realisation of his goals.

In institutional situations oral examinations assume a very special importance particularly in language subjects where there are important aspects of learning which are beyond any other form of examinations to evaluate. In this context, content for oral examinations is provided by:

- day-to-day life experiences
- immediate environment
- current affairs and
- hobbies and interests
- subject of study

Situations can be offered through:

- Conversations

- Short speeches and
- Question Answers

The competencies which need to be inculcated and assessed are:

- Pronunciation
- Grammatical accuracy
- Vocabulary and usage
- Ideational content and its organisation
- Manners and Etiquette
- Fluency
- Delivery
- Effect

The main tools of evaluation are:

- Check-lists
- Rating Scales

It will, therefore, be incorrect to try to test the same things through oral examinations as we do with written examinations. Oral examinations can test many things which written examinations cannot.

In view of the above it will be incorrect to ask learners the same or similar question that are asked through say written examinations for eliciting information.

41.2 Conducting Science Practical Examinations

It is in the realm of practical skills in some subjects that written tests are not usable and hence practical tests should essentially be supplemented to measure the acquired practical skills, although other objectives such as knowledge, understanding or application need not be entirely overlooked. For this purpose *practical skill was mainly conceived as a combination of two components*:

(a) the process of performance, and
(b) the product of performance.

They were further sub-divided in respect of each aspect subject to delimit their scope.

Process of Performance

To demonstrate the skills related to process of performance, the learner:

- selects appropriate apparatus tools etc.
- checks apparatus, tools, regarding their working condition.
- detects error and limitations in the fitting of apparatus.
- rectifies errors if possible, under laboratory situations.
- cleans apparatus, tools etc.
- sets up apparatus, tools etc.

- sketches the arrangement of apparatus, (if necessary, at the very outset).
- prepares and follows a systematic and sequential plan of action for taking observations and prepares proformas for the same.
- states the principle formula (explaining the symbols, etc., useful in the experiment).
- manipulates apparatus, tools, etc., while performing the experiment.
- measures quantities and accurately reads instruments, apparatus, etc.
- takes precautions in handling instruments, substances etc.
- makes accurate observations of parts, specimens, processes, etc.
- records observations and makes calculations where necessary.
- verifies observations.
- performs experiments with reasonable speed.
- performs experiments with reasonable accuracy.
- performs experiments with neatness taking necessary precautions.
- adapts himself to somewhat new and different apparatus in setting novel experiments.
- explains orally the procedures, principles, etc. involved in the experiments.

Product of Performance

To demonstrate the *abilities related to 'product of performance' the learner*:

- summarises observations.
- calculates and finalises the results.
- interprets data and draws conclusions.
- records experimental procedure and conclusions.
- dismantles and cleans the apparatus after the experiment.
- arranges the apparatus, substances, etc., and stores them at their appropriate places at the end of the work.

Sessional Practical Work

Some of the skills that may be appraised from this aspect of practical work are:

- drawing of diagrams and sketches from observed facts.
- collection of specimens like ores, minerals, crystals etc.
- display of material collected.
- improvisation of simple apparatus.
- construction of models.

41.3 Development of a New Pattern

For the purpose of improving the validity and reliability, the practical examinations are to be modified in the following respects:

- *Increasing the Number of Exercises*: Instead of giving a few long exercises, a number of short exercises may be introduced, e.g., in Physics one major comprehensive experiment may be retained and the other replaced by four or five short experiments. The maximum marks and the time, however, may be kept the same.

- *Making the Exercises Objective-based*: Exercises may be set to test predetermined specific aspects of skill (or understanding) as laid down in the objective and as defined as part of the process and the product of performance. This is likely improve the *validity* of the practical examination.
- *Improve the Sampling of Abilities and Content*: Increase in the number or exercises which enables the test to cover many different abilities as specified under the specifications of the skill objective and also to cover a variety of content areas. This helps in improving the coverage and consequently tends to improve reliability and validity.
- *Improving Scoring Procedures*: Developing detailed marking schemes giving minute analytical details of assessment of performance not only for major and short exercises but also for sessional work and viva. Detailed instructions for the use of examiners and candidates for this purpose be also developed. This helps in improving objectivity of scoring and controlling inter-rater reliability by minimising the variability in scoring by examiners emerging from extraneous factors like personal likes and dislikes.
- *Improving and Reporting and Interpreting Procedures*: Detailed proformas end instructions may be developed for the use of examiners. When these reports would be properly used by institutions, they will be able to improve science teaching in many respects.

Experimental Try-outs

The above ideas were experimentally tried out and it is desirable to present the outcomes for developing faith and confidence in them. Four examiners in each of the subjects of Physics, Chemistry and Biology, who were involved in the development of the new pattern, tried out these procedures, three times in actual situations specially arranged for this purpose. In the first try-out 10 candidates and in the second and third try-outs 15 to 20 candidates were involved in all the three subjects. In all the try-outs the four examiners made observations simultaneously and marked independently. The experience of earlier try-out was always invariably used to improve the exercises and to refine the scoring procedures of the subsequent try-outs. The results of assessments were then studied and correlations found. The findings in the try-outs of *Biology* are given here as an illustration. In other subjects also findings were similar.

Comparative Study of Three Sets of Examiner Inter-correlation, in Biology Practical Examination in Three Try-Outs where A, B, C and D are examiners

Averaged across questions

Examiner/Try-out	*AB*	*AC*	*AD*	*BC*	*BD*	*CD*	*N*
I.	.78	.65	.67	.83	.74	.68	12
II.	.94	.95	.95	.92	.94	.93	15
III.	1.00	1.00	1.00	.99	.99	.99	15

Based on total test scores

Examiner/Try-out	*AB*	*AC*	*AD*	*BC*	*BD*	*CD*	*N*
I.	.78	.65	.67	.83	.74	.68	12
II.	.94	.95	.95	.92	.94	.93	15
III.	1.00	1.00	1.00	.99	.99	.99	15

Based on ranking of difficulty indices of questions

Examiner/Try-out	*AB*	*AC*	*AD*	*BC*	*BD*	*CD*	*N*
I.	.89	.88	.59	.78	.82	.63	12
II.	.87	.45	.84	.55	.90	.45	15
III.	.97	.99	.98	.98	.98	.97	15

Significance levels of Rhos:

When N = 9 : .05 = .600; .01 = .783
When N = 12 : .05 =.506; .01 = .712 and
When N = 15 : .05 =.439; .01 = .623

In this subject (Biology) during the first try-out three out of six examiner inter-correlations are not significant at the .01 level but are significant at the .05 level. The agreement among the examiners in try-out II is at or above .92. All the inter-correlations substantially increased in try-out II. Again in try-out III, the examiner inter-correlations averaged across the questions reached unity in 3 out of 6 cases, and in the rest they were at .99. Thus the inter-examiner agreement in Biology practical tests reached almost the optimum level as a result of intensive training, practice and development of well-designed scoring procedures.

41.4 Implementation of the Scheme

Preparation

Encouraged by the above findings, it was decided to launch the reform programme on a large scale. Brochures were then developed by the Examination Reform Division of NCERT in each subject entitled 'Improved

Pattern of Practical Examination', through the examiners who participated in the try-outs, and circulated to schools. New examiners were also trained in the new pattern of practical examination in the three science subjects. They were given training in the theory of conducting the examinations through four-day workshops organised for the purpose. They acquired practical experience in conducting the new type of practical tests in actual examinations, which were specially arranged at various places as a part of the training programme.

Implementation

With these and other preparatory steps carefully and systematically executed, the-Boards of School Education introduced the new pattern in the Higher Secondary Examinations of 1968. Its impact on school practices has been found to be quite encouraging according to the follow-up studies the outcomes of which are outlined below:

Some Problems

During implementation some problems were faced which were already anticipated.

Lack of Adequately Equipped Laboratories

Many schools do not have good laboratories. For want of such laboratories, it becomes difficult to conduct the practical examinations effectively. This also proves to be a serious handicap in traditional pattern of examination also.

Some laboratories do not also have trained laboratory assistants. Services of trained assistants are essential.

Number of Candidates Per Examiner

This pattern envisages close observation of ongoing pupil performance during the period of examination. One examiner cannot obviously cope up with 40 candidates at a time as is, the practice, in vogue. Perhaps, 20 may be a manageable number.

Trained Examiners

Not only in the initial stages but even afterwards, it will have to be ensured that practical examiners are acquainted with the new pattern, as also the spirit and technique of the new pattern of examination, before being entrusted with the job.

Implications

For the efficacy of this new examination pattern, cooperation from different agenda will also be needed. Some implications of the scheme for such agencies are indicated below:

State Departments of Education and Boards of School Education

(a) School laboratories will have to be better equipped.
(b) Syllabus of practical work in science subjects may be detailed.

(c) Flexible time-table will have to be permitted.
(d) Better inspection and guidance programme will have to be developed.
(e) Only qualified and trained examiners will have to be selected.
(f) Examiners' reports will have to be scrutinised and the findings reported to schools for action.

Schools

(a) Greater initiative on the part of individual, teachers and pupils will be needed.
(b) Rigidity of time-tables will have to be reduced.
(c) The evaluation data should be used for remediation and improvement.

Teachers

(a) Variety of practical activities will have to be designed and organised to develop specific skills among pupils and to discourage the tendency of mechanical repetition of standard experiments.
(b) Initiative on the part of pupils will be required to be encouraged.

Practical work in science subjects is aimed at the realisation of some specific purposes, which cannot be otherwise achieved successfully through other means. Practical examinations, therefore, have to be so planned that they measure the degree of success achieved by practical work, as a contribution towards the multi-faceted development of learners' innate capacities and subsequent achievements. The new pattern suggested here aims at this. It defines the outcomes of the process and the product of performance, stresses the need for developing valid and reliable tools of measurement and builds-in ways of evaluating the results of measurement. It also envisages sound feed-back procedure for utilising the results of evaluation in improving school practices. It is hoped that given a fair trial this pattern will work as a catalytic agent in making science education a dynamic process and a creative activity in our educational institutions.

It may be mentioned that the scheme as developed through this experiment as outlined above has attracted the attention of science teachers and experts and is of great help in their effort at making evaluation of practical work as an integral part of science teaching and they have been increasingly using the above approach.

42

Grading Learner's Performance

42.1 Emergence of the IDEA of Grading in India

A discussion about grades has but to start from the concept of marks, as a shift from which, they are taken to be more desirable departure.

Marks and grades are both approaches for identifying/determining presenting/declaring the judged level of attainment or competency or potential of an individual in a particular activity/area.

Apart from this similarity both the concepts have marked differences.

'Marks' are points on the spread of a distribution while *'Grades' indicate the slots or ranges* within which the proficiency level of an individual is judged to lie in respect of a given quality or ability.

When we use 'Marks' as indices of the level of performance, we normally use a 101 point scale (0-100). In using 'Grades' we use a much smaller scale say a nine or a five or a three-point one. In the situation, where marks are used the likelihood of mis-classification of the levels of competencies of individuals, or of their potential is also therefore much greater than when we use a much smaller number of grades.

In awarding 'grades' as compared to marks we are also much more confident about the accuracy of our decisions. The swinging in decisions which often generate chance elements, also naturally get crossed over. It is because of this that *approximations* in terms of 'grades' are considered as more valid and reliable than 'marks' which proclaim *precision*. One cannot just vouchsafe that an individuals' mathematical or linguistic ability is exactly say 57% and nothing more or less or that the honesty of an individual is say precisely 68%. One can only be general and not specific in such assessments.

There are, of course, human attributes that lie beyond the range of any technique or tool of evaluation to assess. *Grading therefore is an honest confession of our inability to assess human qualities with precision.*

42.2 Why Grading?

To just say that the National Policy on Education NPE 1986/92 has recommended the replacement of marks with grades is not enough for convincing others to advocate and practice it. One has to go into the reasons that have led to this recommendation. In fact there are variations in the clientele taking the same examination in different years. Teachers always say that a particular year's batch of learners is better or not so good as that of the previous year. Clear evidences of this were found when learners pursuing a 10+2 pattern went to colleges as compared to the previous batches who had been educated in the 8+3 pattern.

Apart from the variations in the clientele taking the same examination, there are also always marked variations in the *ranges of marks* obtained by the learners in different subjects due to the *mark yielding nature of the subject* (e.g. English 30-80 marks out of 100 and Mathematics 0-100). Furthermore the standard of question papers in the same subject also vary from year to year. This goes against the sacrosanct use of the same cut off scores (33%, 45%, 60%), year after year in all subjects for classifying learners into different categories on the basis of their attainment level.

42.3 Grading and Concept of Pass and Fail and Award of Divisions

In view of the above logic the perpetual use of a 33% level of attainment for clearing the examination in each subject, also does not stand the logic.

The concept of pass and fail and of the award of 'Divisions' is alien to the concept of grading, as grades are awarded subject-wise without aggregation.

Grade Point Average

When the practice of awarding grades in place of marks is adopted grade-point averages could be calculated if it is necessary for granting *admissions* or for awarding *scholarships*. Even raw scores could be used, if necessary in such instances. In such a situation the numerical values (5, 4, 3, 2, 1 etc.) of the obtained symbolic grades (A, B, C, D, E etc.) in all subjects is added up and divided by the number of subjects graded.

Suppose the symbolic grades and their corresponding numerical value on a nine-point scale is as under. It needs to be observed that letter/symbolic grades could assume different forms.

Symbolic Grade	I	H	G	F	E	D	C	B	A
	E	DE	D	CD	C	BC	B	AB	A
	E	D_2	D_1	C_2	C_1	B_2	B_1	A_2	A_1
Numerical Value of Grades	1	2	3	4	5	6	7	8	9

Also suppose that there are six subjects and the symbolic/letter grades on a nine-point scale obtained by a learner in the six subjects are as under:

Subject	*No. 1*	*No. 2*	*No. 3*	*No. 4*	*No. 5*	*No. 6*
Obtained Symbolic Grade	B	C	A	D	C	B
Numerical Value of Grade	8	7	9	6	7	8

$$\text{GPA} = \frac{\text{Sum of the numerical value of the letter grades in all subjects}}{\text{Number of subjects graded}}$$

$$= \frac{8+7+9+6+7+8}{6} = \quad = 7.5$$

A GPA will be able to give a value upto two decimal points which should satisfy the usual needs.

In special cases as per need some additional weightages could be provided to one or more subjects. The procedure of calculating GPA with cognisance to the weightages will, however, remain the same.

42.4 Methods of Awarding Grades

There are various approaches of awarding grades which deserve to be explained for the choice of the one to be adopted in a particular situation.

Diagrammatically these approaches can be presented as under:

GRADING

- Direct Grading
- Indirect Grading
  - Absolute Grading
  - Relative Grading

Deciding about the Scale to Follow

In each of the above situations, it is desirable to first decide upon the scale to follow.

The scales normally used have middle points as in a three-point or a five-point or a nine-point scale.

A Three-Point Scale

C B A

A Five-Point Scale

E D C B A

A Nine-Point Scale

I H G F E D C B A

With the increase in the number of points in a scale the discrimination becomes finer. While choosing the scale one has therefore to take a decision on the basis of the fineness of discrimination desired.

Direct Grading

In direct grading *each piece of performance or a part thereof, is required to be individually graded.* Grading is done on the basis of the criteria evolved by the evaluators or on the basis of those forwarded to them by the examining agency (University or Board). Usually letter or symbolic grades (A B C D ...) are used in Direct Grading.

After the award of Direct Letter Grades the numerical value of each grade (as per the scale selected) is often tabulated and added up. This sum of the numerical values of obtained grades is then divided with the number of questions or parts evaluated in an answer script, for the calculation of GPAs. This total is again converted into a letter grade for obtaining an overall index of performance of the learner in that particular question paper in terms of a symbolic grade.

Use of Rating Scales

Rating scales are the main tools of evaluation for assessing co-scholastic aspects of pupil growth. Five point rating scales are recommended to be used. In such a rating scale (A, B, C, D, & E). A rating of "E" which is supposed to correspond to failure is not proposed to be used at all and the learners may be classified into only four categories (ranges of competencies).

In some cases, e.g., in Personal and Social Qualities only one Rating scale will be required to be used as illustrated below in respect of 'Discipline'.

RATING SCALE FOR DISCIPLINE

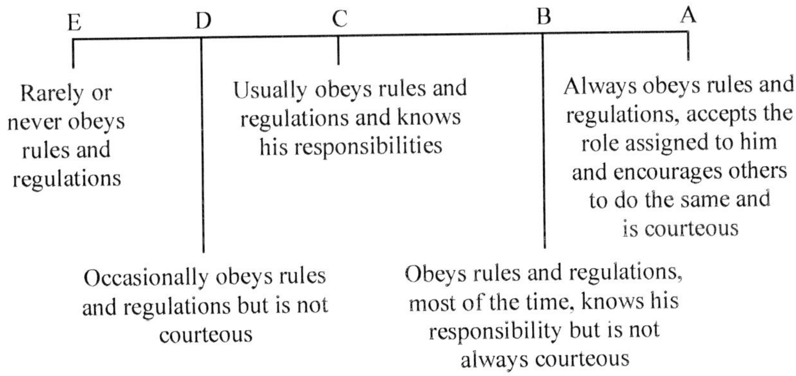

In some other cases as in activities related to interests and other co-curricular activities, there may be more than one evaluative criteria on which it may need to be evaluated for example in 'Dramatics' they may be:

- Make up
- Acting
- Dialogues
- Emotional Appeal

In such cases rating scales would need to be developed for each evaluative criteria and for arriving at the composite overall grade in respect of the activity to be recorded in the certificate the following procedure could be used :

Numerical Value of Different Symbolic Grades	*Symbolic Grades Obtained by a Student on the four Evaluative Criteria*		*Numerical Grades Corresponding to the Symbolic Grades obtained by a Student*	*Derivation of a Symbolic overall Grade*
A = 5	Make-up	B	4	4 + 4 + 5 + 4 = 17
B = 4	Acting	B	4	17 + 4
C = 3	Dialogues	A	5	= 4.25
D = 2	Emotional Appeal	B	4	= B
E = 1				

GRADE RANGES

E	D	C	B	A
0.6↔1.5	1.6↔2.5	2.6↔	3.6↔4.5	4.6↔5.5

As 4.25 falls within the grade range of grade B, the final symbolic grade for recording in the certificate is B.

With a view to ensuring uniformity in the standards of assessment, the rating scales may be developed centrally by the examining agencies and supplied to the teachers.

This by itself is a tedious process and it is difficult to check and make needed corrections. The current practice of awarding marks on the otherhand is itself infested with mistakes of totalling calculation etc. In the event of the introduction of Direct Grading such mistakes are bound to multiply and checking the accuracy of the calculations, will be a near impossible exercise. The problem will be unwieldy and unmanageable particularly in large-scale examinations as in Boards and Universities.

It is because of this that Direct Grading cannot be recommended or adopted in large-scale public examinations and particularly so when the number of questions in the question papers are many.

Direct Grading is also devoid of transparency and is infested with the chance elements and subjectivity which could severely undermine the credibility of examinations.

In institutional situations of in-house evaluation, however direct grading could be used subject to the condition that:

- the number of items to be evaluated are few.
- the number of learners whose performance is to be evaluated too are few and manageable.
- the grades awarded have to stay as such without the need for making necessary calculations for obtaining a GPA and again converting the same into grades.
- comparisons are not required to be made.

Situations like project work which have an independent identity could admit direct grading. However, if it is a part of a subject with a particular weightage for it out of the total marks of a subject the problem would become difficult.

A similar problem would also arise in respect of question papers where questions may carry different marks.

Indirect Grading

Indirect grading is *grading through marks*. In this practice the usual procedure of awarding marks to the units of performance continues. This being something to which the evaluators and teachers are already used, this is not likely to create any problem.

Indirect Grading can assume two forms:

- Absolute Grading and
- Relative Grading

Absolute Grading

Absolute grading is the one where the boundary scores for different grades stand *decided in advance of the examination.*

In fact the practice of declaring learners as pass or fail and of awarding divisions and distinctions is a familiar example of Absolute Grading as illustrated below:

75% and above marks	Distinction
60% to less than 75% marks	First Division
45% to less than 60% marks	Second Division
33% to less than 45% marks	Third Division
Below 33% marks	Failure

As mentioned earlier the indicators of overall levels of performance will not be comparable because of reasons for which the replacement of marks by grades has been recommended.

Such decisions about boundary scores for different grades will invariably be *ad hoc and arbitrary because they would be decided in advance of the examinations and normally for all subjects alike, particularly because the same score in different subjects is not equivalent and comparable*. In fact the recommendation of the NPE for the replacement of marks with grades is a reaction against the practice of absolute grading using sacrosanct cut of scores for all subjects and all examinations uniformly.

The procedure takes raw marks on their face value irrespective of the errors of measurement due to chance element and subjectivity.

Even though the procedure has a diagnostic value and the learners can make efforts for achieving the highest grades, the system of absolute grading cannot be technically recommended or accepted for adoption as it has evident shortfalls whose remediation was indeed called for, while suggesting the replacement of marks by grades. Any cut-off boundary scores for grades, decided in advance of the examination, does not take into account the actual performance of the learners in a particular subject of a particular examination which is likely to vastly.

An example of Absolute Grading on a nine-point scale is given below:

Symbolic/ Letter Grade	*Numerical Value of the Grade*	*Range of Marks*	*Description*
A	9	90% and above	Outstanding
B	8	80% to less than 90%	Excellent
C	7	70% to less than 80%	Very Good
D	6	60% to less than 70%	Good
E	5	50% to less than 60%	Above Average
F	4	40% to less than 50%	Average
G	3	30% to less than 40%	Below Average
H	2	20% to less than 30%	Marginal
I	1	Below 20%	Unsatisfactory

Evidently, in such a scheme of things, there may be no top grades in some subjects and more of them in some others implying thereby that only some subjects can breed talented learners and not others.

Relative Grading

Relative Grading is another approach of Indirect Grading but is quite a contrast to its sibling of Absolute Grading.

Unlike Absolute Grading where grade ranges are decided in advance of the examinations and applied to all subjects, for all years, *the boundary scores in Relative Grading are determined,*

- after the examination has already been held.
- on the basis of the range and distribution of the obtained scores.
- for every subject at each examination separately

In relative grading, therefore, grade ranges could keep on changing for each subject, in each examination, of each year, as they are based on the range and pattern of distribution of obtained scores.

Decided in this manner, *Relative Grades, successfully overcome problems of the variations in the mark yielding nature of different subjects, variations in the standards of question papers of different years and differences in the groups of examinees taking the examination in different years.*

Relative Grading is based on the premise that whenever any population of learners is subjected to a particular test for testing any attribute/s ability or abilities through any mode—written, oral or practical—using any tool and their scores plotted on a graph, the true level of achievement in this graph would take the form of a symmetrical bell—shaped Normal Probability Curve.

In actual practice, however, there are *errors of measurement* which lead to differences in the 'true' and the 'perceived' levels of attainments and the obtained curve is not usually 'normal' but a 'skewed' one. This also happens because we usually work on samples (rather than populations) which are much smaller than the population, which would have yielded a normal curve of distribution. The obtained curves, therefore, are unvariably found to be skewed positively or negatively. These obtained curves are negatively skewed if a larger number examinees obtain higher marks and are *positively skewed* when a larger number of candidates obtain lower scores.

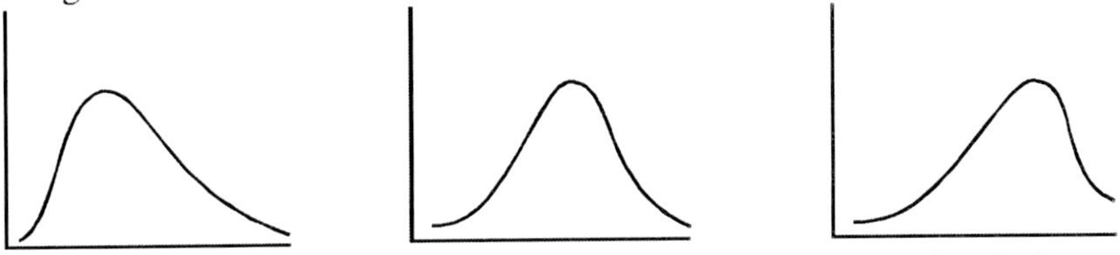

Positively Skewed Curve | Normal Probability Curve | Negatively Skewed Curve

If then the obtained curve were to be converted into a normal curve it would allow us to scientifically categorise the candidates on the basis of the obtained curve, into grades. It is *because the obtained curve is infected with a number of shortfalls (errors of measurement) explained earlier which account for differences between the perceived and the true attainments of candidates, the element of skewness is ignored for practical purposes of awarding grades and taken as if it is a normal one.*

In regard to the choice of a scale for categorising (classifying) learners attainments or potentials, our choice in large-scale public examinations falls on the *Stanine Scale*. This term is a contraction of 'standard nine'. It is a scale evolved by the Air Force in World War II for categorising professional levels of proficiency of its workforce on different abilities on a nine point scale (into nine grades). The scale has come to be widely used in educational and many other situations.

In using this scale the entire distribution of obtained scores is divided into nine parts 1 to 9 with a mean of 5 and a Standard Deviation of approximately 2 units. The Stanine scale, clusters and clubs together the two tail categories at either end of the distribution for bringing the categories to the convenient number of nine instead of eleven. The measure does not make any significant difference because the number of learners whose performance falls in the two tail-end categories is insignificantly small.

The percentage-wise distribution of learners falling in each of the nine grades in a Stanine Scale follows a symmetrical pattern representative of a normal curve and from either the top or bottom it is

4% 7% 12% 17% 20% 17% 12% 7% 4%

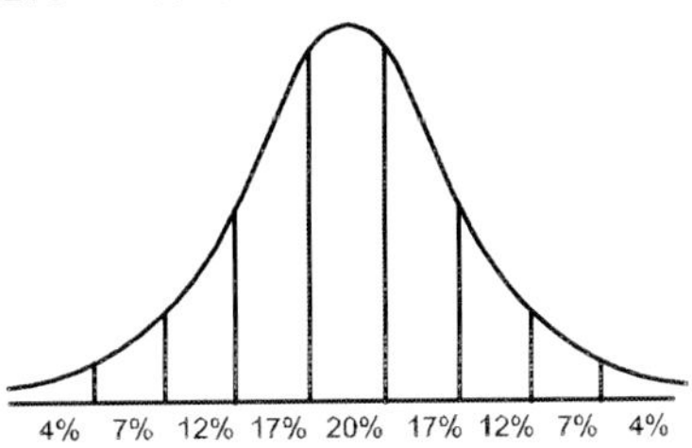

Symmetrical Curve
(Normal Probability Curve)

These percentages represent the approximate rounded off *area of the curve covered by a particular grade* if the curve is sub-divided by vertical lines drawn from the demarcating points for grades, on the base line representing the total distribution. These points on the base line are situated at a distance of ½ a Standard Deviation from one another in a stanine scale.

These are proportions (rounded off to the nearest whole value) which would be formed in the corresponding ½ σ intervals in a normal distribution. The area relationship under the normal curve would show that 9.9 per cent of the area lies between the Median and a point, one quarter of a standard deviation away. Hence 2 × 9.9 = 19.8 per cent or 20 per cent lies in the Median interval.

The percentage to be assigned to grade D is similarly determined from the tables. The area from the mean to three quarters of a standard deviation above the mean contains 27.3 per cent of the area under the normal curve. Subtracting 9.9 per cent from this it is found that 17 per cent of the scores above the Median lie in this slot. The other percentages, are determined similarity.

In the case of a Stanine scale the grade-wise distribution will be as under:

Grade-wise Distribution in a Stanine Scale

Symbolic or Letter Grade	*Interval*			*No. of Cases*	*Numerical Grade Value*
A	1.75 σ	to	∝	4%	9
B	1.25 σ	to	1.75 σ	7%	8
C	0.75 σ	to	1.25 σ	12%	7
D	0.25 σ	to	0.75 σ	17%	6
E	-0.25 σ	to	0.25 σ	20%	5
F	-0.75 σ	to	-0.25 σ	17%	4
G	-1.25 σ	to	-0.75 σ	12%	3
H	-1.75 σ	to	-1.25 σ	7%	2
I	- ∝	to	-1.75 σ	4%	1

In case however we decide to use a five-point scale, again, in a large population, the measurement scale will have to be divided into five parts where the numerical grade values for the symbolic grades will range from 1 to 5 with a mean of 3 and a standard deviation of approximately one unit. Grade-wise percentage of cases in this situation will be as under:

Grade-wise Distribution in a Five-Point Scale

Symbolic or Letter Grade	*Interval*			*No. of Cases*	*Numerical Grade Value*
A	1.5 σ	to	∝	7%	5
B	0.5 σ	to	1.5 σ	24%	4
C	-0.5 σ	to	1.5 σ	38%	3
D	-1.5 σ	to	-0.5 σ	24%	2
E	-∝	to	-1.5 σ	7%	1

It could be mentioned that even though the Stanine Scale is widely accepted to be used, examining agencies could devise their own scales on the basis of their curves of distribution e.g. one examining agency has decided on the following scale for relative grading.

A + A A –	Top Next Next	2% 6% 12%	20%
B + B B –	Next Next Next	15% 20% 15%	50%
C + C C –	Next Next Next	12% 10% 8%	30%

However, a rule of thumb for determining the percentage of candidates falling in different grades on a nine point scale is to use a table of 4.

Grade	I	H	G	F	E	D	C	B	A
	4%	8%	12%	16%	20%	16%	12%	8%	4%

In respect of a five point scale a table 10 could be used for determining the percentage of candidates falling within each grade

Grade	E	D	C	B	A
% of students	10%	20%	40%	20%	10%

42.5 Grading in Institutional Examinations

The differences between the parameters and Paradigms of External Public Examinations and Institution-based testing are quit well known. The most prominent of these to be underlined in the contest of awarding grades to different levels of learner performance or attainments is that the former work with population and the latter with samples.

With a view to branding and lagging different performance levels different approaches examined for their facility and appropriateness in institutional settings.

Direct grading is considered suitable for lower classes (say upto standard II) this is because the groups to be evaluated are small and comparisons are not required to be made imparative. From class III towards, however, one does start experiencing the need for discrimatory comparisons for purposes of identifying the points of intervention and for determining the nature and quantum of inputs of remedial and enrichment material for enabling the learner to read their optimum level of growth in terms of attainmemnts.

It is at this juncture that we should examine the comparative practicability and applicability of absolute and relative grading in institutional settings. Relative grading presents the level/status of performance of learners/candidates in the ext of total groups based on pecentdes. These groups are presumably small (samples) for justifiably adopting and using a nine point scale for purposes of classifying the candidates possessing different kinds and levels of abilities. We will therefore have to be content with using only a two point scale.

On the other hand Absolute Grading while it does present the attained level of performance of individual learners it unfortunately displays a rectangular distribution which is unnatural and unscientific as distributions always take the shape of curves irrespective of what is being evaluated and the tool used for the purpose.

In actual life situation the curves depecting the levels of performance assume a skewed form either positively or negatively, deluding the ideal vision of symmetrical bell-shaped form.

Furthermore absolute grading is invariably based on adhoc and arbitrary presumption about fixing boundary scores of different grades, in advance of the examination disregarding the realities related to variations in the abilities of candidates taking the test, difficulty level of the particular test and above all the mark yielding nature of different subjects.

It is in view of the above backdrop that the following compromise formule which is neither fully correct scientifically nor completely wrong, is being suggested as a convenient rule of thumb.

As high grades may often edude candidates when a when a full grange of marks (0-100) is used, particularly because of the mark yielding nature of the subjects is different (0-100 in Mathematics and say 30-80 in English) we propose that the actually obtained range of marks be used for deciding grade ranges. Thus if in a particular subject in a particular class at a particular examinations conducted by an educational institution the highest score is 87 and the lowest one is 24, the actual range of obtained marks is 87–24 = 63.

As we have zeroed in on using a five point scale, we will divide this range (63) into five parts. We would then get the width of the range for each grade as 63 ÷ 5 = 12.6. We now take only the whole number of 12 ignoring the .6 figure as the range for each grade. Successively subtracting 12 from the highest score we obtain the operational grade ranges as under:

87–12 = 75	Grade range for grade A = 87 to 75
75 – 12 = 63	Grade range for grade A = 75 to 63
63 – 12 = 51	Grade range for grade A = 63 to 51
51 –12 = 39	Grade range for grade A = 51 to 39
39 – 12 = 27	Grade range for grade A = 39 to below 27

The strong point of this procedure is that.

- it uses only the actual obtained range
- by ignoring the fraction .6 it enables a lesser number of learners get an E-grade

SECTION IX
Curriculum Evaluation

As the entire section on Curriculum Evaluation will deal with the evaluation of the elements of curriculum described earlier in the book, there is bound to be some overlap and repetition of some basic facts and fundamental ideas.

43

Curriculum Evaluation

43.1 Preamble

Curriculum is basically a charter reflecting the vision of education of a community for realizing its aspirations through its progeny. This of course, is the deliberately designed entity which has its own strength and weaknesses. It presents a systematically developed document satisfying the theoretical principles of pedagogy psychology, methodology, technology, subject disciplines and above all the nationally accepted and espoused paradigms of goals, political ideology, economic philosophy, cultural heritage, social ethos etc.

However, the learning inputs from formal institutions are but a part of the total learning gains. A learner learns from a wide variety of informal sources quite incidentally. The learning from these sources is often more abiding than the formal deliberately injected inputs. These could be mentioned as the home, the Immediate Environment, the Peer-group, the Television, the Internet, the www etc.

When we speak about Curriculum Evaluation it is the school or university curriculum that we mean. But somehow Curriculum Evaluation is gradually getting extinct from the pedagogical scene both in theory and in practice. What is often attempted in the name of Curriculum Evaluation is only a peripheral lip-service formality and not a technical operation.

While a number of approaches could be suggested, the most plausible and utilitarian ones for Curriculum Evaluation appear to be:

- Evaluation of Curriculum Components
- Evaluation of (and of) different stages of Curriculum Development and implementation

Both these types of Curriculum Evaluation are proposed to be taken up one by one for being deliberated upon in this section.

43.2 Evaluation of Curriculum Components

Technically, curriculum stands divided into the following components

1. Instructional objectives
2. Content material
3. Support material or Aids to Instruction
4. Instructional Methodology
5. Evaluation of Pupil growth

Evaluation of Instructional Objectives

Instructional objective stand classified into three basic facets:

- Intellectual
- Attitudinal
- Actional

Intellectual objectives are also called objectives of the cognitive domain. Their hierarchy starts from Knowledge (information) moves on to Understanding (comprehension) Application in unfamiliar situations, Analysis, Synthesis and Evaluation. For sake of convenience and practicability the objectives of analysis, synthesis and evaluation are clubbed into application. Thus Knowledge, Understanding and Application become the functional or operational objectives.

In language subjects the working objectives, come to be Knowledge of the Elements of Language, Comprehension (Reading and listening) Expression (Written and Oral) and Appreciation.

Attitudinal objectives relate to the 'heart' just as the intellectual ones relate to the 'head'. Their hierarchy consists of Receiving a gesture, Responding to it, leading to the stage of starting to value it, moving on to its organization, culminating in its absorption as a permanent part of ones personality and behaviours.

In common parlance these cover

- Personal and Social Qualities
- Interests (literary, scientific, artistic, cultural etc.)
- Attitudes towards external phenomenon and entities of the environment (individuals, animals and plants)
- Intercultural and inter-faith values and those enshrined in the country constitution

These in technical terms are called the attributes of the Affective Domain.

Actional Objectives: Their third domain of objectives is the one that relates to physical proficiencies of individuals. Their hierarchy consists the stages of Invitation, Manipulation Precision, Articulation and Naturalisation.

These are called abilities of the psycho-motor domain and are called "SKILLS" possessing the following imperative characteristics:

They

- are do'able
- can be physically observed in operation
- involve the joint operation of the mind and the muscles
- possess three basic characteristic of precaution, precision and proportion
- can be imitated
- are manipulatable
- are controllable at will
- take lesser time to do in subsequent attempts
- lead to better quality of the product when repeated
- do not need any drill or revision for retention and once learnt are learnt for ever like cycling, swimming etc.

Growth/Development in Terms of Objectives: Each teaching-learning situation possesses the potential for producing growth. This growth takes place simultaneously in one or more domains of development. The quantum of growth so produced through each dose of education could and does vary is different domains. The quantum of growth and the domain in which it will get produced, cannot be anticipated or estimated. The teaching learning situation could be within or outside the school, formal or unformed.

Some other characteristics of objectives to be evaluated: Objectives constitute the first area of curriculum to be subjected to evaluation. The characteristics they ought to possess for serving their role in the scheme of education, in fact, become their evaluative criteria. It is in respect of these that each one of them, has to be evaluated. The main facets of these which cannot be ignored are:

- linguistic specificity so that it may not be possible to make out any thing other than what is really intended to be conveyed;
- the wording may indicate both the ability desired to be tested and the subject matter through which it is desired to be realised;
- alignment with the in take capacity of the learners (their maturity level);
- relevance to the subject concerned;
- its achievability with the available or procurable resources;
- its testability with available or constructable tools;
- alignment with the social order economic philosophy, political ideology, cultural heritage and the environmental developments.

Evaluation of Content/Subject Matter and Content Material

Content material is developed for realising the objectives of the three domains set

By and large, content material assumes three main manifestations

- Those used by the learners
- Those need by the teachers
- Those used by both teachers and learners

Content material used by learners are textbooks, work books, laboratory manuals etc.

Content material used by teachers are Teachers Guides, Reference Books etc.

Content material used by both teachers and students are terms like atlases support material in teaching learning and testing, implements and apparatus deployed for teaching and learning besides reference books and material.

The main of these are proposed to be taken up for study. The most important of these are the text books. The evaluative criteria or the facets on which a textbook has to be evaluated are:

- the alignment of the content (facts, terms, concepts, principles etc.) with what has gone before and what has to follow;
- the treatment of the subject, which enables children to grasp the ideas effortlessly;
- the appropriateness of the verbal and pictorial illustrations in enabling the learners to understand complex issues and ideas.
- The ability of the exercises, projects for consolidating learning.

Evaluation of Student Work-books: Student Work-books are designed for consolidation of learning through drill, explorations (in projects), experimentation. The soul of these exercises lies in creativity, necessary to be used in completing them. As the learner is on his own he is also required to demonstrate the outcomes of what he/she has gained through the educational pursuits. The Work-books may also indicate some themes for *projects* and the teacher may supplement some challenging ones to that list. Quite often the learners may be required to prepare a report on what they may have accomplished and in such cases the organizational plan of the report and the language may also become the subjects of evaluation.

Evaluation of Laboratory Manuals: While Work-books may be used by-and-large upto class VIII, Laboratory Manuals have a relevance all through the process particularly after class VIII. Apart from the details about needed apparatus for the experiments cautions and precaution are highlighted. The sequence of different operations particularly in the fixing of apparatus, also find a place in "do's" and "dont's". Many small things which are just glossed over while discussing theory become important, when they are to be practically done while both *product of performance and process of performance* assume importance in practical work in science and other allied technical subjects. It is the process of performance that occupies the centre stage in the laboratory manuals from where the evaluative criteria for them have to be developed.

Evaluation of Teachers guides: While the teachers teach the students they learn from the teachers guides, teachers guides, need to be continuously *reviewed, revised and reinforced.* Teachers guides ought to be a *treasure house of the new material.* The contents of the teacher guides are also continuously reinforced by the teacher himself through what he may be continuously collecting from different sources. Apart from the new developments in content, there are various *unconventional methods of teaching* to be beneficially practiced in the classroom. While the subject matter is continuously growing and there are also simultaneously new approaches and strategies of transaction that are evolving, several of these provide answers to emergent problems like reducing the speaking load of the teacher or his correction load. Apart from these, there are also some unstructional strategies which he may not have used in practice, but which can prove to be great consolidators of learning like the conduct of seminars, symposia, panel discussions, participatory learning etc. How successfully and effectively the teacher conducts his teaching enables us to identify the evaluative criteria on which these approaches have to be evaluated.

The teachers' guides may also contain practical hints, about making an yearly plan, quarterly plan, monthly plan, unit plan and a lesson plans for teaching for each subject of every class.

Practical guidance with examples about the *preparation of objective based questions of different forms* and preparation of balanced *question papers based on 'designs' and 'blueprints'* is to be an important part of this. The teacher guides will also include practical guidance about developing and using *check-lists, observation schedules, rating scales etc.* Complete guidance about evaluating both scholastic and co-scholastic aspects of learner growth is an essential part of the teachers' guide. How far a particular technique and tool of evaluation is effective in judging an individual learner, enables us to identify the evaluative criteria, to select the technique of evaluation and prepare and use the tool of evaluation for the situation.

Evaluation of Support Material Instructional Aids

There is usually no fixed catalogue of such material, which the teacher keeps on changing. They are charts, models, apparatus etc. They enable an understanding of facts and phenomenon. The digestive system or circulatory system are best taught with the help of charts and models. Similarly the human skeleton is best learnt and appreciated with their help. Similarly the working model of a steam engine enables learners to understand the relationship between pressure volume and temperature and the force they create.

Tables, figures and diagrams also present valuable situation for analysis and interpretation offer very useful education. These themselves, alongwith the gainful outcomes that they yield, also become subjects of evaluation. For example tables giving the time of sunrise and sunset of the months of March, June, September and December, can teach about "solstice" and "equinox" better than any oral or written statement.

Similarly a model of the "heart" when explained, helps understand circulation of blood better and so on.

Evaluative criteria of the aids to instruction would mainly be in respect of

- the saving of time in helping understand difficult concepts or phenomenon;
- the degree of thoroughness of understanding of concepts principles etc.

related to the subject matter of the lessons being taught or learned.

Evaluation of the Methodologies of Teaching and Learning Pursued

As there are a large number of methodologies of curriculum transaction both conventional and unconventional and every methodology is not suitable for all situation and for all areas of content, the evaluation of methodologies will be desirable to be attempted on the following counts:

- The appropriate selection of the particular methodology for the particular situation for evaluating a given content and ability;
- the appropriate manipulation of the technical steps of the methodology in question.

The above two points of reference in respect of methodologies have been deliberately mentioned in the very beginning because when visualized in the context of a particular methodology it will be easier to derive evaluative criteria for being used in a particular instance.

Some examples of conventional and Unconventional methodologies of curriculum transaction could be cited as under:

Conventional Methodologies	*Unconventional Methodologies*
Lecture Method	Seminars
Discussion	Symposia
Demonstration	Panel discussions
Observation	Surveys
Experimentation etc. etc.	Participatory learning etc. etc.

The guidelines so emerging will not only help us in evaluating the methodologies but also in selecting them at the initial stages of identifying and designing them.

Evaluation of Techniques, Tools, Procedures and Practices

The fundamental characteristics which any evaluation ought to satisfy are:

- Accuracy – Validity
- Dependability – Reliability
- Justice and – Objectivity
- Practicability – Feasibility

In evaluation also, a judicious selection of the technique of evaluation and the development of the tool of evaluation are the most important aspects of the game.

In regard to *Techniques of Evaluation* a choice has to be made mainly from among

- Written tests
- Oral tests
- Practical tests
- Observation

The technique of written tests is normally used where facts, terms, concepts, principles, trends etc. have to be evaluated; where the mental abilities of discrimination comparison and contrast, classification, identification of relationship, application of knowledge, analysis synthesis and evaluation are proposed to be tested. The tools of evaluation to be designed in such situations are objective-based questions of different forms.

Observation as a technique is selected to be used, where *instances are fleeting* and these changes and formations are not possible to be checked at a future time. The tools in these cases are more often than not based on likely surmises made in advance and incorporated in the form of *observation schedules* through the Rating Scales.

It should be mentioned here that in the instances of the former type evaluation is normally done in *quantitative terms* with a certain degree of presumed precision, while in the latter case (observation) evaluation is almost always an estimate done as approximation. '*Marks*' are thus commonly used in the former case and '*grades*' in the latter.

So far as the tests are concerned their evaluative criteria will be that :

they are "balanced" in respect of

- the weightage to different abilities
- the weightage to different major areas of content
- the weightage to different forms of questions

Apart from these:

- the appropriateness of the distribution of marks over different sections of the content
- the appropriateness of the pattern of options to disallow selective teaching
- the appropriateness of the key and the marking scheme with different parts of the expected answer listed alongwith the allocation of marks to them.

The other tools of evaluation, which may need to be evaluated are—

- Inventories
- Checklists
- Rating Scales (Frequency-based and Degree of Quality based)

The evaluation through inventories normally necessitates the organization of items in clusters based on similarities, if any, among them.

A cluster has all items as essential. An inventory is prepared in advance of an event so that we do not miss an item which is necessary. A check-list is a post-event list which helps us to check that we are carrying all the necessary terms.

On the other hand, a Rating Scale is a valuable evaluation tool, which helps us in bringing about a certain degree of precision in descriptive evaluation.

Normally Rating Scale have a middle point and are therefore usually they are three point, five point or nine point scales. Each point of a scale does deserve to be "defined" or briefly explained with the help of conceptual or symbolic words which signify its being descriptive (outstanding/very good/ good /marginally poor). Alternatively they are indicative of frequency of occurrence (always/mostly/usually/rarely/never). Sometimes a Rating Scale with a larger spread is used while fewer points stand defined as "a five point scale with three points defined".

As stated a rating scale ought to have a middle point as in a three point, five point or a nine point scale. The larger the number of points in a scale the more precise the rating scale is supposed to be

Furthermore, points in a rating scale are more akin to "grades" rather than "marks" and that they are supposed to have a *range and are not points*. (Fig. 43.1)

43.3 Evaluation of Curriculum at Different Stages/Steps of Curriculum Development

There are different stages of Curriculum Development and they are sequential. Each one of these presents a situation for being evaluated both as they start and when they come to a close.

They stages are :

- Curriculum Planning
- Curriculum Development
- Curriculum Implementation
- Curriculum Review
- Curriculum Finalisation

It needs to be mentioned that when each one of these has to be evaluated, (a) objectives (b) subject matter (c)methodology (d) support material and (e) evaluation have but to be taken into consideration collectively

Curriculum Planning

At the school stage in India, we start with a *Vision document* which becomes the basis of the *National Policy on Education* and is the first to be evolved. It is the repository of national aspirations. The vision document is basically

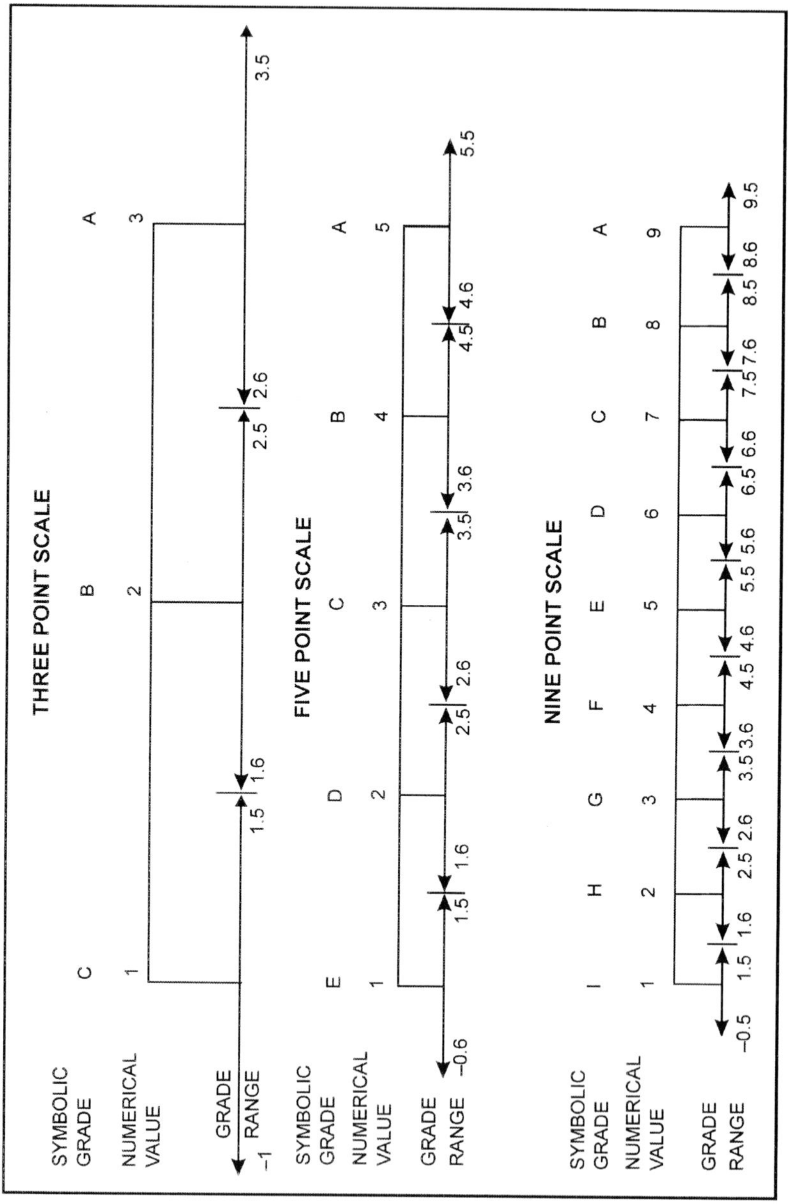

Fig. 43.1: Three, Five and Nine Point Scales Illustrated

imbued with a substantial degree of vagueness in a loosely knit manner.

The National Policy on Education is a structured well defined document indicating a road map and incorporating the directions for our educational endeavours in their totality. It is an outcome of inputs from diverse sectors viz. targets to strive to realize, the subject matter for being pressed into service the management of other diverce inputs, their effectiveness.

All the facets of the National Policy on Education at the point of planning stand screened as they pass through different filters in regard to graded content, manipulated methodology applied psychology, ability-based evaluation and so on.

This could be taken to be the *Curriculum Planning Stage*, where the experience of the contributing experts plays an important role, in imparting unity, coherence and balance to the entire entity. The contribution of the specialists here is not offered individually but collectively and simultaneously in a participatory mode. Thus the map of the building of the curriculum stands sketched on the ground for the construction of building to take place.

The planning stage ensures that all the facets and ingredients of the curriculum have been catered for and given their due place and that the approximations of sectoral and overall time for accommodating each is broadly appropriate.

Curriculum Development

At the Curriculum Development Stage the components of curriculum take a concrete shape as approximations start getting transformed into exactitudes. Objectives no more remain vague but branch off into the three domains as different entities in their own right. This makes everything that follows concrete and well defined. The subject matter gets conceptually and physically crystallised with clear and demarcated boundaries. These boundaries, however, become joining entities rather than separating ones.

The subject matter is divided into grades/classes with due care that it corresponds to the intake capacity of the learners at the concerned age group. It is also attempted to be ensured that what is prescribed for a particular class is the next following, step of the previous class and leads to that of the next one. This will automatically make it more difficult/complex/abstract than the previous one.

This is true of all the prescribed subjects of study which coherently and jointly make up the curriculum for a particular subject of a class.

The outcome of the effort and inputs of the curriculum experts, of the subject matter specialists, of the pedagogues, of the educational psychologists, of the educational technologists and of the educational evaluators, in terms of the body of curriculum along with the environmental influences like those of trade and industry as also of science and technology contribute to the development of the basic document of curriculum the contents of which could infact be treated as technically sound and ready for use even at the cost of repetition it could be said that as a part of the curriculum, the next part will be the learning material. These have to be prepared jointly by the above team for a whole cluster/stage, (Elementary, Secondary and Senior Secondary). The text books are prepared on the basis of the *Principles of Preparation and Evaluation of Text books*. (The NCERT has developed these books for different subjects).

The print material for learners guidance would broadly consist of :

- Main body of subject matter organised into sequential parts.
- Marginal summarised revisionary pithy sentences highlighted italicised etc.
- Main paragraphic or sectional headings
- Written/diagramatic/ pictorial illustrations for clarifying concepts
- Revisionary questions and exercises
- Suggested projects, assignments and exploratory, experimental individual or group work

In regard to the print material, all the above items have to be evaluated through their respective evaluative criteria.

The items to be focused upon are whether and on what degree.

- The content is comprehensive enough to cover the total expected content.
- The language is within the effortless comprehension of the learners.
- The content covered at a particular level is graded in respect of the previous class and the next one.
- The exercises, questions, assignments projects are effective and enriching.
- The time budget is appropriate for the tasks expected to be executed by the learners.

The satisfaction of the above criteria at the desired level, is to be ensured with the inputs of the various teaching-learning processes and subsequently validated through evaluation instruments.

Curriculum Review and Renewal

When curriculum is implemented in a natural setting, it makes a review genuine. We are able to know not just the shortfalls but the precise points where they occur. We are able to know for example about the appropriateness of the sequence of themes, the time required for a particular item, the suitability of consolidation exercises offered by way of projects assignments, explorations and experimentation.

Curriculum review thus becomes a process which permeates the entire process of curriculum implementation. The teachers implementing the curriculum do need some orientation at the beginning to be able to identify and jot down things promptly for purposes of reporting.

The collection and completion of information by itself is not enough this information has to be used in correcting the shortfalls at the right junctures which in fact would be called the Renewal of the Curriculum.

The changes in Curriculum Renewal may not be *big changes* but they are *critical changes* of substance.

The changes accepted for being made are examined by the experts and must meet their approval for the curriculum to be called a 'Finalized Curriculum Ready for Use.'

The trial run of the curriculum is a *verification exercise for checking the presumptions we make at the planning stage and subsequent reinforcement* of the curriculum for making-up the shortfalls that may be discovered

The main items to be critically examined are appropriate difficulty level of the subject matter as that leading from the earlier class to the present one and leading to the next class from the present one.

The appropriateness of the time allocation for theoretical and practical work in school and in work at home, as also for indoor and outdoor activities will be important terms of focus. This is necessary more than ever before because the *curriculum load* and the teachers' perpetual eagerness to further add to it almost inadvertently making good the diagnosed deficiencies through needed reinforcements is the real purpose of this stage/step of curriculum review.

While observation will be the main technique, detailed *observation schedules*, will but have to be designed for different situations. *Evaluation of pupil growth* in different dimensions of different domains of development, will, of course, remain the corner-stones of the diagnostic exercise.

This continuous activity throughout the process will be crucial both as a formative and a summative exercise, for realistic and valid judgments about the quality of the content and process of the curriculum. It may be specially mentioned that our conclusions related to the impact and the outcome will not be possible to be attributed to inputs individually as it will be their joint, collective and coherent contribution. It will therefore be this overall coherent gain which deserves to be taken into account for determining our total dividend from compartmentalised entities as if they never exerted in segregation.

The exercise is in no way mechanical but a creative one. It also requires the investment of deligent effort based on scientific principles by specialists.

Each one of these undertakes a critical examination of the content and process of each step from all desired angles related to his area, identifying the shortfalls and designing and introducing measures for addressing them. All these specialists also then come together and hold detailed discussions about their observations about the suggestions they would like to offer for further improvement. These individual judgements are continuously documented particularly because they have not to remain as individual contributors but

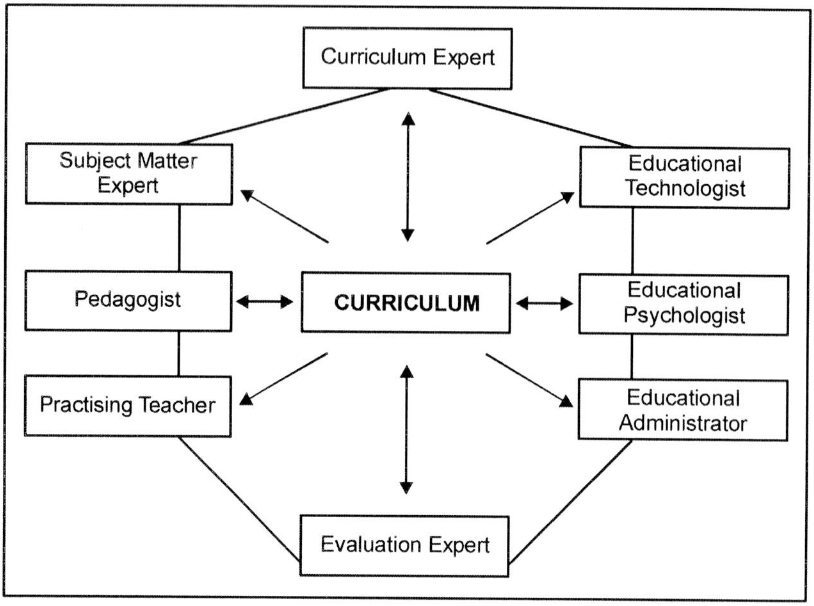

woven into a fabric called the curriculum, wherein the individual contributions lose their identity and the collective outcome of the joint efforts of all of them comes into being as a coherent unit.

The above process also brings to the fore the fundamental idea that curriculum is not syllabus that it is not just content which it is often mistaken to be, to the detriment of its basic concept.

In the course of the trial run instructional methodologies which are most suitable for teaching and testing particular areas of content, or for developing and testing abilities in the three domains too are proposed to be identified for being used. While we are familiar with the conventional teaching strategies like lectures, demonstration, drill, we have now come to realise that the unconventional ones like seminars, symposia, penal discussions are often better approaches particularly for consolidating and internalising learning. This edge that they have over other methodologies would not allow us to sideline then.

Educational Evaluation too occupies an important place in the trial run particularly for selecting the most suitable technique and tool of evaluation. This has repeatedly brought to the fore the need for using observation as a technique of evaluation beside written, oral and practical ones. In turn this necessitates the construction and use of a variety of tools particularly inventors checklists, and more specifically rating scales in the context of the fleeting evidences of the co-scholastic aspects of growth of the affective and the psycho motor domains. As mentioned earlier a five point scale with all the points defined could be safely used. The nine point (Stenine Scale) could be used when the clientele is a population and not a sample as in large scale public examinations, and where comparison too have to be made. A trial run enables the identification of the best applicable techniques, tools and procedures of evaluation.

Usually Evaluation of the elements of Curriculum is qualitative, because when we think of curriculum evaluation our immediate reaction is descriptive. Quantitative evaluation is, in fact, only a derivation from qualitative evaluation. Furthermore, qualitative evaluation, invariable gets stated in generalised terms and is global in nature. The evaluator of qualitative evaluation is by and large quite satisfied with his judgement and confident about its accuracy. This is in fact, impressionistic evaluation which etches it on the mind almost a permanent inscription deep enough to impart an indelible conviction generating marks.

We, however, need to realise that elements of curriculum are rarely evaluated individually. They are evaluated in-clusters

The composition of these clusters, in terms of curricular elements keeps on changing from cluster to cluster. Each comes to wear to own identity in each new situation. It is because of such variation in permutations and combinations that no standard evaluation tools, become possible to be used for purposes of evaluation in a perpetual manner. A new tool specific to the situation/cluster, has therefore to be designed for each particular situation.

This, however, is like a new question paper in the same subject in the half yearly and annual examinations of a particular class.

In qualitative evaluation a Five Point Rating scale with all the points defined are normally considered appropriate. These Rating Scale normally assume two forms—those based on quality of performance and those based on frequency of performance.

Those based on quality of performance where the points of the scale would stand defined as under:

EXAMPLE OF A FIVE POINT RATING SCALE

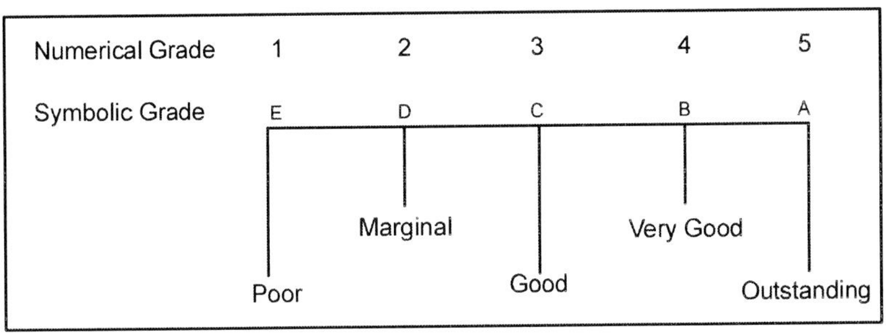

EXAMPLE OF A FIVE POINT RATING SCALE BASED ON FREQUENCY OF PERFORMANCE

Numerical Scale	1	2	3	4	5	Numerical Grades
Symbolic Scale	E	D	C	B	A	Symbolic Grades
	Never	Rarely	Usually	Mostly	Always	

It needs to be appreciated at this point that unlike marks which are points, grades present ranges. For example: the numerical grade—

5 represents a range extending from 4.6 to 5.5
4 represents a range extending from 3.6 to 4.5
3 represents a range extending from 2.6 to 3.5
2 represents a range extending from 1.6 to 2.5
1 represents a range extending from (–) 0.6 to 1.5

Sometimes a piece of performance is evaluated through symbolic grades and the result is required is quantitative terms. In such instances: An assessment that falls within the range of

- 4.6 and 5.5 represents a symbolic grade A
- 3.6 and 4.5 represents a symbolic grade B
- 2.6 and 3.5 represents a symbolic grade C
- 1.6 and 2.5 represents a symbolic grade D
- (-) 0.6 and 1.5 represents a symbolic grade E

43.4 Steps of Procedure of Curriculum Evaluation

Normally, exercises in Curriculum Evaluation or Evaluation of any of its parts or of the steps of the processes of development are qualitative in nature and we have been satisfied with that. But with the waves of objectivity growing, the evaluators have been obliged to think of obtaining some quantitative indices in numerical and symbolic terms about it.

The simplest procedure is enunciated below in terms of some operational steps:

STEP 1: Work out, identify and list the Evaluative Criteria for evaluation for the item to be evaluated. For example for evaluating the text-books some of the evaluative criteria could be;

- Effortless comprehensibility of content.
- Gradation in content—leading the learners from the content of the previous class and as a stepping stone for the next class.
- Appropriateness of illustrations both verbal and non-verbal
- Effective explanation of tables and requiring learners to interpret them to draw their own conclusions.

STEP 2: Establishing clarity about the purpose for which text-book evaluation is to be done.

STEP 3: Selecting the evaluative criteria on the basis of the purpose of evaluation.

STEP 4: Developing five points Rating Scales with all the points defined for each of the identified criteria.

STEP 5: Subjecting each evaluative criteria to evaluation, on the respective five point Rating Scale.

STEP 6: Determining both Symbolic (ABCDE) and Numerical (5, 4, 3, 2, 1) Grades.

STEP 7: Finding out the GPA of the Numerical Grades to obtain an overall index also find a corresponding Symbolic Grade.

In regard to text-books, for example, if different text-books are to be compared for being prescribed, a numerical grade will be enough.

In case, however, the book has to be selected for the library and we only want to use a broad index, a symbolic grade would just serve the purpose.

43.5 Use of Prep Index in Curriculum Evaluation

Quantitative evaluation of qualitative outcomes of education could also be done and by using the concept of PREP INDEX which has been discussed earlier in *chapter eight*. PREP INDEX could be used in any sector for yielding an accurate, dependable and a just measure.

Appendix 1

Some Explanatory Definitions of Curriculum

> The National Council of Educational Research and Training, New Delhi came into existence on September 1, 1961 after a merger of a number of erstwhile educational agencies functioning under the Union Ministry of Education.
>
> To start with the NCERT launched some exploratory projects. Some of these projects related to the collection and completion of some basic information about the status and development in national and international education.
>
> Shri L.P. Kadam, one of the oldest and very enthusiastic members of the faculty, the Department of Elementary Education initiated a project on collecting information about "CURRICULUM" its concept and definitions. The valuable outcomes of this educational adventure were brought out in a mimeographed document in late sixties. The contents give a valuable background and therefore the torn and the brittle pages of the monograph have been resurrected below for the benefit of the future generation of educationists.

Alberty & Alberty. Reorganising the High School Curriculum, The Mac-millan Company, New York.

1. "The nature of the curriculum—defined as the sum total of learner activities which the school sponsors for the purpose of achieving its objectives".

American Association of School Administrators. American School Curriculum, 1953 Year Book. P. 54.

2. "In recent years the curriculum has been most commonly defined as all of the directed learning experiences of children and youth under the influence of the school".

3. "The school's curriculum is the total of those situations which are purposely used to produce favourable learning responses."

Anderson, V.E. Principles and Procedures of Curriculum Improvement, *1956.*

4. Curriculum "is conceived of as the whole of the interacting forces of the total environment provided for pupils by the school and the pupils

experiences in that environment."

5. "The Curriculum is all that goes on in the lives of the children, their parents, and their teachers. The curriculum is made up of everything that surrounds the learner in all his waking hours. In fact, the curriculum has been defined as the environment in motion."

6. "Reading, writing and arithmetic are not the curriculum though they are part of it. Freedom, self-direction and social growth are not the curriculum, but they are part of it. Books, tools, supplies and material are not the curriculum, but they are used by it. School rooms, school buildings and teachers are not the curriculum, neither are homes, churches, stores and parents, yet all these are a part of it."

Association for Supervision and Curriculum Development. Guidance in the Curriculum.

7. "The authors of the year-book conceive of the school curriculum as comprising all of the opportunities for learning which the school provides for children and young people to meet their varying needs. These opportunities relate to much more than the course of study. Just as the selection of text and reference material is part of curriculum planning, so are arrangements for a properly run programme of extra class activities, plans for the choice and display of foods to be served in the cafeteria, and decisions about such things as grading systems, promotion policies, the height of the bubblers and the intramural sports activities. This planning results in a certain range of opportunities available to boys and girls and when these become appropriate for the children or young people. These opportunities from which learning experiences accrue constitute the school curriculum."

Beauchamp, A. George. Planning the Elementary School Curriculum.

8. "For Curriculum to be conceived as the design of a social group for the educational experiences of their children in school. This design should take into account all the demands upon a school programme. Such demands include the needs of the social group, the individual needs of the children, the requirements of custom and the peculiarities of the School as a social institution. Curriculum thus conceived is somewhat different from either the idea that the curriculum represents all the experiences of children under the jurisdiction of the school, or of the curriculum conceived as simply sum of courses of study."

9. "A design of a social group for the educational experiences of their children in school."

Beck, H. Robert; Cook, W. Walter; Kearney. C. Nolan. Curriculum in Modern Elementary School.

10. "The educational experiences that children have in school. This is a broad definition and includes far more than any skills, attitudes or ideas."

11. "We have defined the Curriculum as the sum of the educational experiences that children have in School."

Bossing, Nelson. Principles of Secondary Education, *New York.*

12. "To an older generation the curriculum would simply mean all the subjects studied or offered in school. Popularly the curriculum has been thought of as those compendiums of information and skills which the school has made available for study. *In antiquity our word was derived from the latin word 'curriculum', which mean literally 'a race course'.* It came to mean whatever was offered in the school to be learned. As a result western civilisation has come to think of the school curriculum as a collection of subject matter which the pupil is to study in some order of sequence towards some general goal. Though such goal may be vague or poorly defined."

Modern Concept

13. "The Curriculum consists of experiences the learner has, under the direction of the school."

14. "The curriculum now focuses attention upon what kind of experiences the learner should have, rather than upon the subjects he should study."

Bulletin 560. Principles and Standards for Accrediting Elementary and Secondary Schools, Texas State Board of Education, September, 1961. p. 32

15. Accredited elementary schools are expected to maintain balanced Curriculum offering English language, arts (reading, literature, composition, hand-writing, spelling, mechanics usage and grammar), Science, arithmetic, geography, history and citizenship, art, music, health physical education, and foreign language if desired."

Bush. N. Robert and Allen. W. Dwight. A New Design for High School Education: Assuming a Flexible Schedule.

16. "The planning of curriculum requires the relation of alternatives. Scarce resources-time, facilities, teachers, and learners must be allocated, and all subject offerings compete for these resources."

17. "A model for curriculum planning encourages the consideration of alternatives to traditional course structures, class sizes, use of staff, number and spacing of classes, total time which should be allocated to any one class, or even alternatives to the necessity of a daily schedule.

18. "The entire curriculum can be thought of as an area to be scheduled. The *horizontal dimension* represents the number of learners, the vertical dimension represents the length of time in the schedule module.

Note: (*A schedule module* is that period of time during which the master schedule does not repeat itself: for example in conventional schedules the schedule module is one day.)

Brown, Army Frances. Curriculum Development

19. "All the learning which is planned and guided by the school."

Broady, S. Harry. Needed a Unifying Theory of Education.

20. "Curriculum is more than course content, more than a title in a catalogue, even though it is far less than the total experience of the pupil at school. Curriculum connotes both the content of instruction and the way the materials are organised for instruction."

Carleton, Washburne Thirty Eighth Year Book of the National Society for the Study of Education.

21. "Curriculum is defined broadly enough to include any materials or activities that will affect the learning, development, attitudes, or behaviour of the child."

Caswell. Democracy and the Curriculum. Rugg: Third Year Book of John Deway Society. Edited by Harold.

22. "The design of the curriculum... must be a function of the environment of the child, not just that of the school and the generalised aspects of the culture. It must include *out of school activities as well as in the school activities.* Recreation, health, creative activities, home adjustments, and the like should be taken into account quite as much as problem-solving and work situations in the classroom."

Doll, C. Ronald. "Curriculum Improvement. (Decision making and process)."

23. "All the experiences which are offered to learners under the auspices or direction of the school."

Dotterns, Robert. The Primary School Curriculum, Monographs on Education, UNESCO.

24. "*A syllabus, as the French term* (plan detudes) clearly indicates, affords precise information as to quantity the amount of knowledge to be imparted by the teacher to his pupils in each subject in the course of the school year. A curriculum shows by what kind of educational activities the teacher will fulfil the requirements of the syllabus. The syllabus prescribes the content of the teaching to be given and the curriculum prescribes the method to be used. The curriculum is primarily concerned with method and therefore with education. It is made up of pedagogical directives intended to provide assistance, advice, suggestions and information to assist the teacher in carrying out his task successfully."

25. "A *syllabus*, whether or not it contains suggestions or advice on methods, *is usually binding on the teacher*, who is not free to do more than adopt the content of the syllabus to local geographical and social conditions. A curriculum is more concerned with the education children should receive from the school and it indicates the procedures, methods and activities by which such education is to be provided. In the first case, the main objective is the mastery of facts, and in the second, the acquisition of habits and attitudes which will determine the way children behave and things they do.

Douglass, R. Narl. The High School Curriculum. Ronald Press Company, New York.

26. "The whole of the various courses of study and learning experience conducted by or under the auspices of the school."

27. "All of the school associated learning experiences of any given child."

28. "The systematic arrangements of a number of courses into a unit group for differentiated group of pupils is a type of curriculum, for example, the college preparatory curriculum."

29. *Core-Curriculum*:— "A large block of the curriculum contributing to the objectives of general education and involving materials from two or more subjects and organised around life problems or foci of life interests: may involve or overlap one or more of the other concepts e.g. fusion, integrated curricula, and experience curriculum."

Draper, E.M. "Curriculum Research."

30. The Curriculum is, "often defined today as the total earning experience which pupils have in and out of school under the guidance of the faculty."

Dressell, Paul. The Under-Graduate Curriculum in Higher Education."

The Role of Curriculum

31. It is no longer possible for any individual to come into meaningful contact with all the ideas presently subsumed under the phrase 'liberal arts'. It is equally true that education for any progress can no longer be defined in terms of the completion of some prescribed courses. The body of basic knowledge required in a profession is continuously increasing, and the number of specific items of knowledge, skills and abilities & required for practising the profession is also increasing, Education, then must emphasise the development of a series of experience which will develop in the individual, both the desire and the ability to continue his own education. *Curriculum can no longer be regarded as a fixed set of courses. It must be regarded, rather, as defined by a set of principles, which constitute a means of structuring the association of the teacher and the learner to the end of educating the learner.*

Faunce, C. Roland and Bossing, L. Nelson. Developing the Core Curriculum.

32. "Educational leaders conceive curriculum as composed of the learning experiences which children have in the school. The organisation of the experience curriculum to provide for the *common and special needs of youth* provides the basis for our present conception of core."

33. In modern education the term core has come to be applied to that part of the experience curriculum which is concerned with those types of experiences, thoughts, necessary for all learners in order to develop *certain behaviours, competencies, considered necessary for effective living in our democratic society.*"

34. "The core programme consist of the activities of living necessary for all as worthy members of our social order."

Fitzgerald, A. James and Fitzgerald, G. Patricia. Methods and Curricula in Elementary Education.

35. Subject Matter "a narrower term than curriculum, may be thought of as the substance of such subjects of study as reading, writing, arithmetic, and spelling. It includes facts, ideas, data. It is the materials to be used and the drills to be mastered. It is content presented in textbooks, workbooks, or reference books. More broadly it is the experience of the race, that has been selected for teaching the elementary school child."

36. The Course of Study "is generally thought of as a written, mimeographed or a printed plan to be followed in a year or for the whole elementary school period. It usually contains a statement of objectives, an outline of content, and suggestions for assignments, methods, activities, devices, testing, and evaluation. It frequently present bibliographical references for the benefit of teacher and child."

The course of study is not the curriculum but merely a suggestion for curriculum, activities and procedures, a guide for the teacher to follow in instruction.

37. "The purpose of the curriculum is to provide for the education of children, but *three aspects of education should be unified in a curriculum. They are immediate values, permanent values, eternal values.*"

Fleming, S. Robert (Editor). Curriculum for Today's Boys and Girls.

38. "The totality of the child's experiences for which the school is responsible. This definition would certainly include teaching children to spell correctly and compute accurately. It would also include such areas as room housekeeping and behaviour on the playground. It would certainly include learning to read with understanding. It might include also a ten year old's taking dictation of the first grader's story, or a talk by members of the school council on the perils of running the cafeteria."

39. "The emerging concept of Curriculum for the elementary school considers the child himself, his capacities, his needs, and his interests in relation to selected experience which will foster his growth. Curriculum for today's children in the modern elementary school includes *all school experience, is founded on valid purpose, is developed by sound approaches which demand earlier cogent thinking, and, is designed by sensitive intensive classroom teachers with understanding* of child growth and development of learning theory, and with knowledge and skill in the several areas of curriculum."

Franklin, Bobbit. The Curriculum

40. "As applied to education it is that series of things which children and youth must do and experience by way of developing ability to do the things well that make up the affairs of adult life."

Frazier. Alexander (Editor). New Insights and the Curriculum

41. "The Curriculum organisation is a combination of unified studies on some problems or topic that invites cutting across several areas of knowledge broad fields (like language arts), separate subjects (like mathematics) and non-class activities (like care of the classroom). Within these different segments of the curriculum, teachers provide opportunities for experiences with a wide range of media and their related symbol systems so that the children may gain knowledge of different kinds and from varied sources. Teachers use all sorts of opportunities in different parts of the school day to help children build meanings out of their varied experiences and *to make verbalised connections of many kinds, so that their know/edge is constantly being increased, classified, and systematised."*

George, D. Strayer (Director). Report of the Survey of

42. "Series of guided experiences serve to enrich and make more valuable the experiences that follow."

Good, Cartes. Dictionary of Education.

43. "Curriculum is a body of prescribed educative experiences under school supervision, designed to provide an individual with the best possible training and experience to fit him for the society of which he is a part or to qualify him for a trade or profession."

Goodrich, T.V. and Poisons, A.B. "Frame of Reference for Curriculum Planning." Elementary School Journal, 44.279, Jan. 1944.

44. "All experience, in and out of school, used by the school to attain educational objectives constitute the curriculum."

Gwyan J. Minor. Curriculum Principles and Social Trends. The Mac-millan Company, New York, p. 51.

45. "The curriculum is the means of attaining the aims or philosophy of

education. Being means to the end, and not end in itself, it usually follows and reflects educational trends and changes in philosophy."

46. "The curriculum shows and should continue to show, evidence of conflicting educational theories."

47. "If normal development takes place, the curriculum cannot be the same in each school. It belongs to public, not primarily to the professional educators. School administrators and teachers are not wise enough to determine the curriculum by themselves."

48. "Educators established the purposes of education, then they established the curriculum as the means of attaining the same purposes through the teaching process. Just as methods of teaching cannot be effectively presented to anyone without using the curriculum, so the curriculum cannot be adequately presented without considering teaching methods. The chief methods employed in teaching are therefore presented here, especially as they effect and illustrate the curriculum."

Harold, G. Shane and E.T. M.C. Bwain. Evaluation and the Elementary Curriculum. New York, Holt, Rinehart and Winstonlue, 1958, p. 170.

49. "The psychological Curriculum may be defined as the sum of the experiences the learning skills, habits and attitudes—*that the child has made a part of himself and that govern his behaviour*, as a result of the environment provided by the school."

Harold, Rugg. "American Life and the School Curriculum. Boston Gim & Company.

50. "The Curriculum is really the entire programme of the school's work. It is the essential means of education. It is everything that the learners and their teachers do."

Hollis, L. Caswell and Doak, S. Campbell. Curriculum Development (New York). American Book Company.

51. Definition of the curriculum falls into three general groups: "(1) those that would characterise it as subjects or fields of subject matter, arranged in sequence; (2) As content or subject-matter for instruction; (3) based upon experiences of the learners. In this later, content and subject matter are involved as part of experience, and as part of the curriculum."

52. "All the experiences the children have under the guidance of teachers."

53. "The curriculum consists of all the experiences the learner has under the direction or the school."

Hurley, Beatrice Davis. Curriculum for Elementary School Children.

54. "According to earlier interpretations of curriculum characterised by rigid, fixed content and procedures:— Curriculum was either considered as

the course of study and followed it slavishly; or 'synonymous with the basic textbook; or an outline for teaching separate subjects day by day."

"Today curriculum is considered as comprising of those experiences which children undergo under the guidance of the school."

Jameson, M.C., and Hicks, W.V. Elementary School Curriculum. American Book Co., New York.

55. "All the learning experiences which are planned and sponsored by the school."

Keith, Lowell; Blake, Paul; Tiedt, Sidney. Contemporary Curriculum in the Elementary School. Harper and Row Publishers, New York.

56. Those experiences and activities which are devised by the school for the purpose of modifying the learner's behaviour."

Koosv, Leonard. Junior High School Trends. Harper & Brothers, New York.

57. The term 'Core Curriculum' or sometimes, simply the 'Core', the terminology applied to core type courses includes "general education", "basic education", "basis studies", "social living", and unified studies. With such diverse names, it is to be expected that there would be wide variation in the programmes represented, especially during the period of early growth of the movement, likewise wide variation in the kinds of programmes operating under any single designation.

Krug. A. Edward. 'The Secondary School Curriculum.' Harper and Row, New York.

58. "A curriculum consists of the mean used to achieve or carry out given purposes of schooling. There are many such means that might be used. One who proposes a curriculum must decide what to include and what to leave out. Substantial courses exists on two points: (i) that organised classroom instruction is a necessary part of the curriculum, (ii) that a desirable curriculum includes more than organised classroom instruction alone. On the second point, most people would agree on extra class activities and on counselling services. Some add more controversial items, such as school and community services projects, school related work experiences and school camps."

59. "A curriculum is now being defined—at least by educational theorists concerned with the problem—as all the experiences of the learner that are under the control of the school."

60. "Curriculum becomes the instrumentality by which the school seeks to translate out hopes for education into concrete reality."

61. "The curriculum consists of the means of instruction used by the school to provide opportunities for learner learning experience leading to desired learning outcomes. In most present day discussion and writing, these means of instruction include the classroom studies, the guidance or counselling programme, school and community service projects, school-related work-

experience, school health services, school camps, the school library, and those activities known as "extracurricular" or "extra class."

Leese, Joseph; Frasure, Kenneth and Johnson, Maurit. "The Teacher in Curriculum Making," Harper and Brother, New York.

62. "The curriculum has been defined by specialists in very broad terms. Once thought of as a list of subjects taught in any school; it is now described as all the experiences children have as a result of their attendance in schools. Others more modestly consider the curriculum as all the plans for learning, developed, and organised by those responsible in school." "The term learning experience is used here to denote one which produces change in behaviour, and those which are deliberately designed to do so constitute the Curriculum."

63. "Curriculum is an organised list existing in advance of any face to face relationship between pupil and teacher."

Lee, J. Murray and Lee, D.M. "The Child and his Curriculum." revised edition (New York) Appleton-Century-Crafts.

64. "The Curriculum for each child is the sum total of all his experiences which are in any way affected by the school."

Leeper, R. Robert - Editor - Curriculum Change. (Direction and Process) A-S. C. D. N. E. A. Washington.

GoodLad John. I

65. "The humanistic Curriculum is one which provides a way of life centred upon human interests and values. A humanistic conception sets as its goal the development of each individual's potential, fosters school programmes centered on man; takes teachers and teaching seriously; and values each learner simply because he is a human being."

Mary. John O.P. (Sister) and Mary, Nona. (Sister) O.P. Guiding Growth in Christian Social Living. Vol. I. Washington; D.C. The Catholic University of America Press.

66. "All the guided experience of the child under the direction of the school.... It is guide for directing the child's living in the light of Christian principles, with a detailed plan of the learning activities that are basic to that living."

Mcneil, D. John. Curriculum Administration (Principles and Techniques of Curriculum Development). The Mac-millan Company (New York).

67. "The attainment of instructional objectives derived in response to crucial issues facing society is the integrated responsibility of schools. The cultivation of common outlooks, skills and dispositions necessary for a united culture is consistent with the principles of a 'core curriculum'. It is important to note that the core curriculum does not have correlation as its distinctive

feature. Correlation, the selecting of a number of subjects around a central study, may indeed take place, but the essence of the core is to provide basic grounds and purposes upon which the needs and actions of all members of the community can meet."

68. "The nuclear curriculum in its activity programme requires that teachers select organising centres which are most in accord with the personal educative desires (not mere whims which lead to blind alleges) and the demands made by society upon particular learners. The scheduling of these offerings need not be uniform in frequency and duration."

Mcnerney, T. Chester. 'The Curriculum'. McGraw-Hill Book Company.

Two divergent viewpoints.

69. "Curriculum is that which is taught to a person to educate him."

70. "Curriculum is the environment in which the education takes place."

Core-Curriculum

71. "In a democratic school system the core is the part of the curriculum which provides youth an opportunity to develop an awareness of, and competency in relation to the primary characteristics of a democratic society. It also provides the type of individual and group guidance that enables youth intelligently to select those experiences which help them to maintain and develop their unique interests and abilities. It is always centred upon the common problem of youth but is personalised to provide for the variety of experiences they must use to solve their problems."

Mead, A.R. General Concepts Basic to the Curriculum. "Curriculum Journal".

72. "All the activities of the school-play, games, classwork, activities of all those who have anything to do with the school."

Nolan, C. Kearney and Walter, W. Cook. "Curriculum" Encyclopaedia of Educational Research. Third Edition (Chester W. Hallies ed.) New York, The Macmillan Company.

73. "All the educational experiences that a learner has under the guidance of the school."

Norton, John. K. and Norton, Margaret A. Foundations of Curriculum Building. Boston: Ginn & Co.

74. "The curriculum consists of all the experiences which the child has irrespective of their character or when or where they take place."

National Association of Secondary School Principals.

75. "A Curriculum is systematic group of courses, or other arrangements of subject matter and educational activity, provided by a school of a particular

type-high school, liberal arts college, law school and the like. The Curriculum of a school includes all of the school's organised offerings. The curriculum is a general over all specification of organised learning activity that a school plans to offer its learners. A curriculum is something to be felt and sensed in part, from day to day, so that teachers can make improvements almost dairy, within a general framework of scheduled activity.

National Education Association. The Scholars Look at the School. A Report of Disciplines Seminar, June, 1961. Washington. D.C. National Education Association.

Nuclear end Cortical Organisation of Curriculum:

76. "One part to be called the nuclear curriculum would contain materials from the disciplines, selected to fulfil those objectives of education which are determined primarily by the needs of the developing child and the aims imposed by our culture and society. The second, or cortical, component of the curriculum would be chosen by contrary and complementary principles. It would consist of materials chosen specifically because they are representative of the major disciplines."

Neagley, Ross L. and Evans, V. Dean. Handbook for Effective Curriculum Development.

77. "Curriculum is defined as all of the planned experiences provided by the school to assist pupils in attaining the designated learning outcomes to the best of their abilities."

78. "Subject-Centered Curriculum—under it pupils experiences are organised around each of the separate school subjects or subject areas."

79. "Correlated Curriculum—under this pupils simultaneously study similar topics in each of two or more subjects or subject areas."

Broad Fields or Fused Curriculum.

80. "Under this plan of organisation the content is selected from a number of different but related subjects or subject fields and combined in one broad area."

Ragan, William B. Modern Curriculum. (New York) Holt.

81. "Curriculum comes into existence only in the experiences of children. Teachers, administration and children are always in a process of creating the curriculum."

Ragan, W.B. Modern Elementary Curriculum. Holt, New York.

82. "The learning experiences which are sponsored and guided by the school."

Ralph, W. Tyler. The Core Curriculum. N.E.A. Journal.

83. "The Core-Curriculum is most clearly distinguished from other recent

innovations by fine characteristics. As the term is commonly used, it refers to a course (1) which is devised to serve the needs of all high school learners, (2) which deals with problems involving content from more than 20 one subject, (3) which uses a daily block of time longer than one period, (4) which employs pupil teacher planning, and which provides opportunities for guidance and counselling."

84. "The terms 'Core Curriculum' and 'Common Learning' programme are used interchangeably, and the later term is usually applied to that part of the curriculum which is devised to serve the common needs whether or not the programme has any of the other four characteristics."

Ross, James S. Ground Work of Educational Theory.

85. "Our attitude towards the curriculum has been influenced by a desire to assist children to acquire or develop the habits, skills, interests and sentiments which they will need both for their own well-being and for that of the people among whom they will live."

86. "There can be no doubt that children should be taught those useful things which are really necessary."

Roswell, C. Puckett. Making a High School Schedule of Recitations. New York, Longmans Green and Company.

87. "Curriculum is the selection, organisation and administration of a body of subject matter designed to lead the pupil on some definite life objective."

Ruckner, Ray W. Curriculum Development in the Elementary School. Harper & Brothers, New York.

88. "The Elementary school curriculum is essentially a process of living and learning within a democratic, problem-solving climate for children, each of whom has a unique developmental growth pattern. The curriculum process encompasses the total of all experiences children have under the guidance of the school. Since each child differs from every-child in a host of ways and looks out upon the world from the unique behavioural field the curriculum is different for each child."

Saiyidain, K. G. Introducing the Basic Curriculum.

89. "The curriculum is primarily an aid in the process of adjusting the child to the environment in which he functions from day to day and the wider environment in which he will have to organise his activities later.

Secondary Education Commission, 1956.

90. "Curriculum does not mean only the academic subjects traditionally taught in the school but it includes the totality of experiences that pupil receives through the manifold activities that go on in the school, in the classroom, library, laboratory, workshop playground and in the numerous informal

contacts between teachers and pupils. In this sense, the whole life of the school becomes the curriculum which can touch the life of the learners at all points and help in the evolution of balanced personality." (P. 80.)

91. "The whole life of the school becomes the curriculum which can touch the life of the learners at all points and help in the evolution of balanced personality."

Sharp, George. Curriculum Development As Re-education of the Teacher. New York.

92. "The present view of the curriculum is that it consists of all the educative experiences under the conscious guidance of the school. This conception differs from the older idea of the curriculum as a body of subject matter to be learned. Just as the assigned lesson was the bask unit in the older definition, so an experience is the unit in the new. In the overall, it means a rounded programme of living for every child as opposed to the curriculum as a series of lessons or a collection of courses. Finally in this modern view, the curriculum is not confined to the classroom but flows out into the life of the school and beyond the school itself."

"In short, the curriculum is a series of experiences which are guided in such a way that each child has a rounded programme of living, a conception that is broader and more realistic than that formerly held."

Smith, B.B., Stanley, W.O. and Shores, J.H. Fundamentals of Curriculum Development. Hudson, World Book Co.

93. "A sequence of potential experiences... set up in the school for the purposes of disciplining children and youth in group ways of thinking and acting."

Sowards, G. Welsely and Scobey, M. Margaret. The Changing Curriculum and the Elementary Teacher.

Older Definition

94. "Subject matter presented for study, or the content of instruction, without reference to instructional ways or means, or some subject-matter oriented expressions."

Present Definition

95. "Curriculum consists of all the experiences that children (and youth) have under the guidance and direction of the school. This makes place for classroom experiences, playground experiences and all school experiences in the curriculum. It also suggests much broader concept of conte.t"

96. "The elementary (or secondary) school curriculum consists of those experiences that the school consciously and purposefully provides for children (and youth) in the light of the accepted purpose of the school, using these experiences, also, as the major source of data upon which to base the evaluation of individual and group progress toward these purposes."

Stratemeyer, Mackim, Forkner. Passow. Developing a Curriculum for Modern Living.

97. "The curriculum is currently defined in three ways: the courses and class activities in which children and youth engage: the total range of in class and out of class experiences sponsored by the school; and the total life experiences of learner."

98. "The proposal that indicates the basis for rise selection and organisation of knowledge, concepts, and skills stressed in any given school system is its curriculum design."

Suster, A.H. and Ploghoft, M.E. The Emerging Elementary Curriculum.

99. "The emerging curriculum is a dynamic complex which comes into existence in the opportunities for learning which are created and realised in the many communities and classrooms throughout the nation. The emerging design is variable and complex with the general frame work of unity across the nation."

Thomas, Kirby, 'Class Lectures'. State University of Iowa.

100. "Curriculum is a group of subjects which lead pupils to definite life objectives."

Thomas, L. Hopkin. "Interaction the Democratic Process." Boston: D.C. Heath Co.

101. "In the experience curriculum the curriculum represents all of the activities engaged in by pupils, teachers, supervisors, principals, parents, and others that are in any way affected by study in, and through the school, This means curriculum goes on, both in and outside of school."

Throckmorton, F. Adelon. A Curriculum Guide for the Secondary School of Kansas.

102. "A thoughtful approach to curriculum focuses upon an ideal which is attainable. It seems to identify values that are permanent and concepts embodied in a central core of learning that would serve every normal person in any age that a man can see from here. It strives then to define the unique responsibilities of a school maintained by a democratic people who honestly believe in freedom but are not quite sure just what it is."

Venable, C. Tom. 'Patterns in Secondary School Curriculum'. New York.

103. "Curriculum means all the experiences which take place under the sponsorship of the school. The English course, the publication of the school paper, the football games, the senior prom are all a part of the high school curriculum. It is the learner who does the experiencing. The school provides the environment of the experience; the teacher guides, directs and organises the experience. All aspects of the child's school life-class work, play activities,

special projects, and group life are a part of the child's curriculum."

"The curriculum of today's secondary school rests on three foundation subjects of studies. These are (1) Sociology, (2) Psychology, (3) Philosophy. What is done in the school is the result of the contribution of these subjects to education."

Walter. D. Coeking. Administrative Procedures in Curriculum Making. Teachers Collage contribution to Education, No. 329 (New York) Bureau of Publications, Teachers College, Columbia University.

104. "All activities and instructional work of the school."

Wright, G.S. Core Curriculum Development: Problems and Practices, United States of Education Bulletin, No. 5, 1952 Washington D.C.

105. "Four types of core programmes—

(a) "Each subject retains its identity in the core; that is subjects combined in the core are correlated but not fused."

(b) "Subject lines are broken down." Those included "are fused into a unified whole around a central theme."

(c) "Subjects are brought in only as needed. The Core consists of a number of broad pre-planned problems usually related to a central theme. Problems are based on pre-determined areas of pupil needs, both immediate felt needs and needs as society sees them."

(d) "Subjects are brought in only as needed in (c) above.

There are no pre-determined problem areas to be studied and pupils and teacher are free to select problems upon which they are to work."

References

Adams, G.K., *Measurement and Evaluation in Psychology and Education*, Holt, Rinehart and Winston, New York, 1965.

Aggarwal, R.N. and Vipin Asthana, *Educational Measurement and Evaluation*, Vinod Pustak Mandir, Agra, 1983.

Ahmann, J.S. and Block, M.D., *Measuring and Evaluating Educational Achievement*, Alyn and Bach Inc., Boston, 1975.

Anastasi, A., *Psychological Testing*, London: Macmillan Publishing House, 1968.

Angoff William H., Scales, Norms and Equivalent Scores. In *Educational Measurement*, 2nd Edition Edited by R.L. Thorndike, American Council of Education, Washington DC (1971)

Association of Indian Universities, Scaling Techniques, New Deli, AIU (1985).

Blood, D.F. and W.C. Budd, *Educational Measurement and Evaluation*, N. York, Harper and Row, 1972.

Bloom, B.S., *Taxonomy of Educational Objectives, Handbook 1, Cognitive Domain*, David Mckay Co. Inc., New York, 1956.

Bloom, B.S., Hastings J.T. and Madaus G.F., *Handbook of Formative and Summative Evaluation of Learner Learning*, New York: Mc Garw Hill (1971).

Bose P.K. and Choudhury S.B., Scaling Procedures in Scholastic and Vocational Tests, *Sankhya* (1955) 15. 197.

Carroll, B.J., Partik H.J., *Make your own Language Tests*, U.K. Pergamon Press Ltd., (1985).

COBSE: Report of the Barrow (AET) Committee on Scaling and Grading, New Delhi, (1981).

Cohn, Elchanan, Rossmiller, Richard A., *Research on Effective Schools Implications for Less-Developed Countries*, World Bank, Washington (1987).

Commonwealth Secretariat, Better Schools, Resource Materials for Schools, 7 Module, London (1993).

Cox, D.R. and S.S. Vargass, *A Comparison of Item Selected Techniques for Norm-Referenced and Criterion-Referenced Test*, Pitsburg, Learning, 1966.

Cronbach, I.J., Designing Evaluation of Educational and Social Programmes, San Francisco: Jossey-Bass (1982).

Cronback, L.S., *Essentials of Psychological Testing*, Harper and Row, New York, 1970.

Cuban, Larry, *Managerial Imperative and the Practice of Leadership in Schools*, State University of New York Press, Albany (1988).

Dave R.H., *Review of Research in Educational Evaluation* (1968).

Duffy, Francis M., *Designing High-Performance Schools: A Practical Guide to Organisational Re-engineering*, St. Lucie Press, Florida.

Ebel, R.L. and D.A., *Frisbel Essentials of Educational Measurement*, 3rd ed., Prentice Hall of India Pvt. Ltd., New Delhi, 1979.

Fields, Joseph C., Total Quality for Schools: A Guide for Implementation, ASQC Quality Press, Milwavkee (194).

Freeman, F.S., *Theory and Practice of Psychological Testing*, Holt, Rinehart and Winston, New York, 1965.

Gann, Nigel, *Improving School Governance: How Better Governors Make Better Schools*, Palmer Press, London (1998).

Gassett, H.E., *Statistics in Education and Psychology*, Vakil, Feffer & Simon, Bombay, 1989.

Gronlund, N.E., *Measurement and Evaluation in Teaching*, Macmillan, New York, 1981.

Guilford, J.P. and B. Fruchter, *Fundamental Statistics in Psychology and Education*, New York: McGraw Hill, 1978.

Guilford, J.P., *Fundamental Statistics in Psychology and Education*, New York: McGraw-Hill Book Co., 1956.

Haigh, Gerald, *Managing Classroom Problems in the Primary School*, Paul Chapman, London (1990).

Hallak, Jacques, Managing Schools for Educational Quality and Equity: Finding the Proper Mix to Make it Work, HEP, Paris (1992).

Harding, Peter, *Guide to Governing Schools*, Harper and Row, London (1987).

Harper, A.E., *Preparing Objective Examinations*, Prentice Hall of India Pvt. Ltd., New Delhi, 1990.

James Mary, *Using Assessment for School Improvement*, Heinemann Educational Publishers, Oxford, U.K. 1998.

Kamat A.R. and Deshmukh A.C., Prediction value of Marks at the Preceding Examinations on Forecasting Marks at the Succeeding Examination, Arth Vijan (1961).

Kaplan, R.M. and D.P. Saccuzzo, *Psychological Testing*, Brooks Cole Publishing Co., California, 1993.

Kline Paul, *The Handbook of Psychological Testing*, Routledge, 11, New Petter Lane, London, 1993.

Knight, Brian, Managing School Time, Longman, Essex (1989).

Krathwohl, D.R., *Taxonomy of Educational Objectives, Handbook II, Affective Domain*, David McKay Co., Inc., New York, 1964.

Lele P.T., Patel P.M., Parikh N.P. and Paklar S.G., Empirical Studies in Examinations, Examination Research and Reform Unit, M.S. University Boards (1962).

Levacic, Rosalind, *Total Management of Schools: Analysis and Practice*, Open University Press, Buckingham (1995).

Martura, V.R., *Applying Norm-Referenced and Criterion-Referenced Measurement in Education*, Allyn and Bacon, Boston, 1977.

Mary, James, *Types of Assessment, In Using Assessment for School Improvements*, Oxford, Heinemann Educational Publishers, 1998.

Mauriel, John J., *Strategic Leadership for Schools*, Jossey Bass, San Francisco (1989).

Mehreas, W.A. & Cohmenn, I.J., *Measurement for Educational Evaluation*, Holt Reinhart and Winston, Inc., New York, 1973.

Misra V.S., A Study of Essay Type Test Reliability, Guwahati: Examination Research Unit, Guwahati University (1968).

Morgan Norah and Saxton Juliana, *Teaching Questioning and Learning*, Routledge, London (1991).

NCERT and Board of Secondary Education Rajasthan, Ajmer, Scheme and Manual of Instructions on Comprehensive Internal Assessment (1966).

NCERT and Directorate of School Education, Madras, Scheme of Comprehensive Internal Assessment and Manual of Instructions, Madras (1973).

NCERT Annotated Bibliography on Evaluation and Measurement, New Delhi (1962).

NCERT Developing Question Banks at the Secondary Stage, New Delhi (1977).

NCERT Energising Evaluation Practice (in some selected Universities) 1980.

NCERT Field Work and Laboratory Teachings in Geography in Classes XI-XII — L.S. Bhat and Aslam Mahmood, Oct. 1977.

NCERT Guidelines on Scaling and Grading, New Delhi (1988).

NCERT Improving Examinations, New Delhi (1963).

NCERT Insight into Mathematics: Teacher Guide Classes I-V (Five Vol.), Nov. 1968.

NCERT Instructions to Paper Setters of Boards of Secondary Education, New Delhi (1963).

NCERT Progress of Examination Reform in India (1962).

NCERT Report of the Central Advisory Board of Education Committee on Examinations (1971).

NCERT Research in Educational Evaluation, New Delhi (1961).

NCERT Structure and Functions of Agencies Conducting Public Examinations at the Stage of Secondary Education, New Delhi (1972).

NCERT Studies in Internal Assessment Procedures and Promotion Policies, New Delhi (1963).

NCERT Study of Failures in Secondary Schools, New Delhi (1962).

Newman F.M. et al: Accountability and School Performance, Implications for Restructuring Schools, *Harvard Review* Vol. 67 No. 1 Spring (1997).

NIER An International Comparative Study of School Curriculum, Jan. 1999.

Nikto, A.J., *Educational Tests and Measurement: An Introduction*, Harcount Brace Joyanorich, New York, 1983.

Noll, V.H., Scanel, D.P. and Craig, R.C., *Introduction to Educational Measurement*, Houghton, Mifflin Co., Boston, 1979.

Ogunniyi, M.S., *Educational Measurement and Evaluation*, Longman, London, 1989.

Patton, Michael Quim, *Qualitative Evaluation and Research Methods*, Sage Publications India Pvt. Ltd., New Delhi-110 004.

Popham, W.J., *Criterion-Referenced Measurement*, Prentice Hall of India, New Delhi, 1978.

Pophan, W.J., *Modern Educational Measurement*, Prentice Hall, New York, 1981.

Rao, K. Sudha, *Influence of Continuum Evaluation on Learning*, NCERT, New Delhi, 1986.

Rosow, Jerome M., Zager, Robert, *Allies in Educational Reform: How Teachers, Unions and Administrators Can Join Forces for Better Schools*, Jossey Bass, San Francisco (1989).

Ross, C.C. and Stanley, Julian C., *Measurement in Today's Schools*, Prentice Hall, Inc., New York, 1954.

Sayer, John, *Managing Schools*, Hodder & Stoughton, London (1989).

Schlechty, Phillip C., *Inventing Better Schools: An Action Plan for Educational Reform*, Jossey-Bass, San Francisco.

Schofield, H., *Assessment and Testing: An Introduction*, George Allen and Unwin Ltd., London, 1972.

Simmons, John., (ed). *Better Schools: International Lessons for Reform*, Praeger, New York (1983).

Singh Pritam, Criterion Referenced Testing, NCERT, New Delhi (1982).

Singh Pritam, Evaluating Learners in Elementary Schools, NCERT, New Delhi (1982).

Singh Pritam, Towards Better Question Papers, Novray Publications, New Delhi, (1996)

Srivastava H.S. and Shourie J.P., Instructional Objectives of School Subjects, NCERT, New Delhi (1989).

Srivastava H.S., Khandelwal B.P. and Sharma D.V., *Comprehensive School-Based Evaluation*, S. Chand and Co., New Delhi (1997).

Srivastava H.S., Singh Pritam and Anand V.S., Reforming Examinations, Some Emergent Issue, National Council of Educational Research and Training (NCERT), New Delhi (1978).

Srivastava H.S., Examination Reforms in India, UNESCO (International Bureau of Education), Paris (1979).

Srivastava, H.S. and Menon Kamala, A Handbook of Evaluation in Geography, NCERT, New Delhi (1990).

Srivastava, H.S. and Others, National Study of Scholastic Achievement, NCERT, New Delhi (1997).

Srivastava, H.S. and Qamaruddin, Explanatory Glossary of Technical Terms in Educational Evaluation, NCERT, New Delhi (1991).

Srivastava, H.S., *Challenges in Education Evaluation*, Vikas Publishing House, New Delhi (1999).

Srivastava, H.S., Comprehensive Evaluation in Schools, NCERT, New Delhi (1989).

Srivastava, H.S., *Curriculum and Methods of Teaching*, Shipra Publications, New Delhi (2006).

Srivastava, H.S., *Examination Manual*, S. Chand & Co., New Delhi (2001).

Srivastava, H.S., *Manual for Schools*, S. Chand & Co., New Delhi (Fourth Revised Edition (2013).

Synder, Karolyn J., *Competency Training for Managing Productive Schools*, Harcourt Brace Jovanovich, San Diego (1988).

Taylor H.J. and Taluanga L.N., Grace Marks, A Study of Criteria for the Adjustment of Examination Results, Guwahati: Examination Research Unit, Guwahati University (1963).

Taylor, H.J. and Taluanga L.N., Scaling Tables, Guwahati: Examination Research Unit, Guwahati University (1963).

Thody, Angela, Leadership of Schools: Chief Executives in Education, Cassell, London (1997).

Thorndike, Robert, L. & Kagen, Elizabeth, P., Measurement and Evaluation in Psychology Western-Eastern United, New Delhi, 1979.

Trarers, Robert M.W., *Educational Measurement*, Odyssey Press, New York, 1990.

UGC (ED): Examination Reform in Central Universities, New Delhi, UGC (1969).

UGC Examination Reform: A Plan of Action, New Delhi, 1976.

UGC Principles and Mechanics of Semester System, New Delhi, 1971.

Wood Robert Assessment and Testing: A Survey of Research, Cambridge University Press, Cambridge, U.K. 1991.

Index